FIRST GEAR

FIRST GEAR

A MOTORCYCLE MEMOIR

LORRIE JORGENSEN

INANNA
Memoir Series

Published in Canada by
Inanna Publications and Education Inc.
210 Founders College, York University
4700 Keele Street, Toronto, Ontario M3J 1P3
Telephone: (416) 736-5356 Fax (416) 736-5765
Email: inanna.publications@inanna.ca Website: www.inanna.ca

We gratefully acknowledge the support of the Canada Council for the Arts and
the Ontario Arts Council for our publishing program. We also acknowledge
the financial support of the Government of Canada through the Canada Book
Fund.

Printed and Bound in Canada.

Cover design: Val Fullard

Library and Archives Canada Cataloguing in Publication

Jorgensen, Lorrie, 1959–, author
        First gear : a motorcycle memoir / by Lorrie Jorgensen.

(Inanna memoir series)
Issued in print and electronic formats.
ISBN 978-1-77133-246-0 (paperback). – ISBN 978-1-77133-245-3 (epub). –
ISBN 978-1-77133-248-4 (pdf)

        1. Jorgensen, Lorrie, 1959–. 2. Adult child abuse victims–Canada–
Biography. 3. Adult child sexual abuse victims–Canada–Biography.
4. Multiple sclerosis–Patients–Canada–Biography. 5. Motorcyclists–
Canada–Biography. I. Title.

GV1060.2.J67A3 2015   796.75092   C2015-905007-3
                                            C2015-905008-1

MIX
Paper from
responsible sources
FSC® C004071

for Paula

1.

LENNY SMILED UP AT ME, turned and pulled a chair in beside him from another table. I hesitated and then sat down quickly, suddenly nervous, excited. It was Friday night at the Second Hotel in Swisha and I was home for the weekend from my new job in Ottawa. Bev looked at me from across the cluster of tables, smiled quickly, and then turned back to one of her drinking pals. I'd seen Lenny a few times with Bev, mostly hanging out in the bar she worked at, but this was the first time he'd paid any attention to me. He was in his mid-thirties with long hair, a beard, and he drove a Harley. I was seventeen.

It was the long weekend in August and Kenny Roger's "Lucille" was sharing time with Waylon Jennings recent hit, "Luckenbach, Texas" on the jukebox. I looked around the bar and it felt like a family reunion with my mom Bev, my brothers, John and Craig, each with their own groups of friends, all in for a night of partying and drinking.

My brothers and I were dressed in the teenage uniforms of the day. I wore Howick 5-star, wide-legged pants and a polyester blend blouse with short sleeves that Bev gave me to wear that night. John and Craig wore bell-bottom jeans with jean jackets over patterned shirts. Their hair was freshly washed and blown dry into mullets, proudly trying to imitate the shaggy look and style favoured by their musical idols: Led Zeppelin, Queen, and the Doobie Brothers.

John was going to be nineteen in September. He had just married Donna in June and they were expecting a baby. His father-in-law was a custodian at Mackenzie High School in Deep River and he helped John get a job there. He graduated from high school to work at the same school as a janitor. It didn't last. Neither did the marriage.

It wasn't a surprise. John always struggled with being held to others' expectations. In school he took a year longer than normal to graduate, but he made it through Grade 12 with me doing his homework. He'd either threaten me or bribe me and I'd sit in the basement and listen to Chris DeBurgh sing "Patricia the Stripper," while answering math questions and writing poor, but passable English essays that he'd later re-copy in his scratchy writing.

Craig hadn't been living at home ever since our father Eric had beaten him up and thrown him out. Craig was going to leave anyway because he was afraid Eric would eventually kill him during one of his rages. His willingness to go didn't stop Eric from picking him up by his jacket and throwing him out the side door of our house onto the driveway. The neighbours called the police. Bev hinted that Family Services were involved, but nothing ever came of it.

I followed Craig down our street the afternoon he left, crying and begging him not to leave me. He was beyond listening, intent only on getting away. It was three days before his fifteenth birthday. He was now sixteen and could have moved back in with Bev after Eric left, but he preferred couch surfing with friends and girlfriends. I'd have gladly done his homework if it meant he'd be able to stay and graduate high school. Last week he came to visit me at my new apartment in Ottawa and I found him curled up, sleeping on the front porch.

Craig whiled away most of the night playing pool with his friends at the two tables in the back of the bar. It's where I would have been if I hadn't spent the entire evening sitting beside Lenny drinking beer, smoking, and occasionally dancing when a good tune came up on the box. John spent as much time outside the hotel as in it, mostly with a group of stoners that always seemed to have a joint flared up at the side of the hotel.

I was drunk and happy when Lenny asked me if I wanted to go on a ride with him and his buddy Stan in the morning. They were headed to a swap meet across the border near Buffalo. I looked over at Bev. She nodded, and I said yes.

After last call, we left the Second Hotel and Lenny drove me to my old house in Deep River on his ratted out '63 Harley chopper. He didn't have a second helmet, so he gave me his and he wore an aviator's leather hat and goggles. They made him look like some kind of bearded Snoopy freak. His helmet was loose and smelled of wet leather and stale sweat. What I remember most of the ride was my impression that his headlights didn't work very well. This was punctuated by my yelling into the wind several times over his shoulder, "Can you see ... can you really see?"

It was later that morning, after only a few hours of sleep, that Bev woke me up. "Get up, Lenny's here," she said as she shook me.

"I'm not going." I turned over in bed.

"Oh yes you are. You said you'd go, you're going." Bev replied as she shook me harder.

"No, I'm not."

"Yes, you are."

"Fuck, okay. I'm getting up." My mouth was sticky and dry and felt like I was chewing a swab of cotton. I got out of bed pushing down the sour taste of beery bile, and dressed myself in jeans, desert boots, and a T-shirt. Anxiety pushed through my tiredness bringing with it a slight flitter of fear as I grabbed what other clothes I had brought for the weekend, shoved them into my knapsack, and went downstairs. No amount of blinking or squinting cleared up the grit in my eyes.

Lenny and Bev were sitting on the old brown couch in the living room, drinking coffee and smoking cigarettes. Bev still had her hair up and was wearing a once bright green muumuu with washed out vertical yellow stripes in a zig-zag pattern. She had removed her false eyelashes, but remnants of black liner were smeared below her eyes.

When Lenny stood, the morning light showed me a scruffy-looking, thin guy about six feet tall. His hair was shoulder length, dishwater brown shot through with some grey. It blended in with his beard, which was also long, untrimmed. Worn, grease-stained jeans ended at scuffed rebel biker boots. A faded, brown leather jacket covered a T-shirt that looked like it had been washed so many times without soap it was hard to tell its colour.

"I don't know if I can go," I said. "I don't have a helmet."

"There's my old snowmobile helmet downstairs on the shelf by the washer," Bev replied.

"Well, it's going to be cold," I complained.

"Get your brother's hockey jacket from the front closet."

Minutes later, Lenny and I, with his friend Stan on an Electra Glide, took off to parts unknown to me. I only knew we were going north and then south and we were camping.

Wrapped up in a black, red, and dirty-white Midget "C" hockey jacket, I was sitting on a pillion pad the size of a small pencil case on the back fender of his rigid framed chopper. I'd find out later it was called a bitch pad. My helmet was bright yellow with black stripes bisecting its middle, a beacon marking my travel. A pair of Bev's large plastic sunglasses nearly hid my face, but no matter how hard I rubbed them, they remained greasy with her makeup and sweat. With no backrest for support, I had to cling to Lenny's waist.

During the first night on the road came the unspoken payment for the ride.

***

Every grunt and thrust pushes my head farther into the nylon side of the tent. I press my heels into the soft ground beneath the floor and grip the sleeping bag as tight as I can, but it doesn't help. I match Lenny's grunts with sharp squeaks of my own. He has a really long dick and every thrust he makes drives it into my cervix, making me pull back in pain. I moan loudly, but that only seems to excite him and he goes quicker, thrusting, grunting. It hurts, but I don't know what to do, I'm paralyzed. By the time Lenny finishes, my chin is pressed painfully into my chest, and I don't think he's noticed that he's fucked me across the floor of the tent and we're straining its sides.

***

I ran up nearly 1000 miles riding the back fender of Lenny's Harley that weekend. Going north I spent time drinking and playing pool with a group of bikers at the Sturgeon Falls Hotel. Some guys wanted my company for their own bitch pads until

Lenny said otherwise. After heading south, we got stopped and interrogated twice by the Ontario Provincial Police, detained at customs, coming and going, while the authorities asked questions and searched the bikes. My I.D. was taken from me and I waited in a small, cement-block room wondering what was going to happen to me. There was no response from the U.S. Customs Officer when I told him, "My mom knows I'm here."

Throughout all that, my only real concern was my sore, numb ass and on the second morning I asked Lenny if he'd donate his pillow for me to sit on. I folded it in half, end to end, so it wouldn't get caught up in the back wheel of the bike. The extra softness didn't take care of my cervix, but my butt was a little less tender. Still, when Lenny dropped me off on Monday I was stiff, sore, and chafed. Bev met us in the driveway and offered to pay my bus fare home to Ottawa. I never saw Lenny again.

2.

Thirty-three years later, in July of 2010, I'm riding my own Harley-Davidson, a 2009 Dyna Super Glide Custom, with dual springs and a sheepskin-covered seat for my butt. My ass is still pretty much the same size it was when I went on the weekend tour with Lenny. That's not to say I stayed slim my whole life. I didn't. There were times when I was the fat girl, but my butt didn't really get big, it just disappeared into my back the heavier I got. A couple of years ago it reappeared. I'm grateful.

My machine, Thelma D, is packed and loaded for a road trip through Northern Ontario. I've been travelling for twenty minutes and just passed the western boundary of the city of Ottawa. I'm going to visit my brother Craig and his family in Levack, a small mining town north of Sudbury, by way of Thunder Bay and Lake Superior. An ambitious run and it's my first trip on a motorcycle lasting longer than that weekend long ago when I rode with Lenny and Stan.

I'm riding the paint and I try to loosen my shoulders and relax my legs to see if it's the machine that's making me tremble. It's not. Tremors radiate through me, making my body feel shaky and weak. Tightening my grip doesn't diminish the inner shaking. I'm afraid. I try to swallow my fear, my self-doubt, and insecurities by chanting a mantra of self-help clichés I learned from watching the icons of self-help television and reading bumper stickers. One of my corny favourites is, "Today Is The First Day Of The Rest Of Your Life." I first saw the slogan on a book bag after I moved to Ottawa and thought it was one of the most profound things I'd ever heard. At the time I thought it was wonderful that you could have a new life every day. I've since learned life isn't that simple.

The repetition clears my mind and I start to feel more settled and less frantic from the anxiety of starting out on a journey I haven't written the end for.

Asphalt gets consumed, kilometres roll by, and my breathing gets steadier. The shakes subside and I start to feel stronger, more confident in the saddle. I look around now to take in my flight. Riding a motorcycle, I imagine, is like flying in a glider or parasailing, free and unrestrained, only a little noisier with an internal combustion engine pushing the steel and rubber down the road.

To my left, the centre dashed lines rip by like newspapers coming off a printing press. My boots are inches away from asphalt that races past like the belt on a sander, its abrasiveness always waiting to scrape the best off of you, leaving your body bleeding and broken. That gap is the difference between exhilaration and death. The gravel and stones on the shoulder to my right blend into one another like a continuous carpet of gray felt. Wind pushes against me, rushing past my ears, hissing and seemingly angry at this speed. It can be soothing and caressing at slow speeds and on this hot morning, it's a welcome friend, cooling and refreshing. My heart seems to match the revolutions of the twin engine and is now beating a steady tattoo in my helmet.

Further from the road there are fields of grass with wildflowers. It's impossible to focus on any one feature. The flowers blur together with the pine trees that line the edges of the fields, creating an ongoing mirage and canvas of summer colours. Speeding down the highway, making my own wind, I'm unrestrained, cageless. Feeling the power and heaviness of the big bike between my legs, absorbing the landscape, smelling the exhaust tinted with pine and wildflower puts me on the edge of controlled chaos, on a high, in flight.

Thelma D whines a bit on the downshift and as usual, a small knot of fear flares in my stomach when I pass a small pickup. I've been following it for a couple of kilometres since Arnprior, a small Ottawa Valley town a half hour northwest of Ottawa. Thelma D easily accelerates to 130 kilometres before I shift up to her cruising gear, pull back in front of the truck and throttle down. I release my breath. The knot disappears. For me, a little fear is a good thing when I'm riding. I'm confident in my abilities even with my anxiety at its peak, but fear makes me careful. I've had some close calls in my riding life. Mostly, it's always a driver who doesn't see me before pulling out, cutting me off, or changing lanes suddenly into my side. Once, I heard the high-pitched squeal of brakes before spotting a truck in my mirror, almost sideways in his attempt to stop behind me at a red light. He stopped in time, but not before I drove onto the sidewalk.

Experience tells me to always be aware and be on the lookout for the person that's going to kill me. I hope to see them first.

I settle into a speed that is a few kilometres over the limit. An easy pace where I can make good time, but not a speed that would attract the attention of the police. Thelma D is a big bike and she doesn't lack any power with her V-twin 96 cubic inch displacement, nearly 1600 cubic centimetres in the metric language of Japanese or European machines. She runs strong and steady, keeps her line when chosen and isn't easily buffeted by large trucks. A blessing when you've ridden bikes that can be thrown several inches off their line when meeting up with tractor trailers and their accompanying gusts.

In the past year, I've outfitted her with a windshield, backrest, luggage rack, and saddlebags. All the components are quick detachable and I can have her stripped down to basic machine in less than five minutes. I like the detachable units because she's much easier to clean and I'll be able to knock off her luggage quickly when I'm settling in for the day. Some riders like the bare bones, sleek look for cruising at night once you've reached your destination. Right. I'm thinking I won't have the energy for much more than a shower and bite to eat after riding all day. Besides, where I'm going, cruising will take me out of most towns in less than two minutes.

3.

TYPICAL OF OTTAWA'S SUMMER WEATHER, the start of the day came with a heat-filled, skin-drenching humidity that hung on me like a wrung out rag. There have been daily heat warnings and health cautions issued for the elderly and those with asthma to stay indoors in air conditioning. The heat wave, with its deadly oppression and temper-inducing flares, is only expected to get worse. I picked a great time to leave.

In contrast to riders with full-face helmets and body armour, I wear a half helmet and on hot days like today, tattoos, jeans and a T-shirt is my armour. For me, it's all about staying cool, not worrying about personal protection. I'm not sure how the armoured riders manage in the oven created by the asphalt, concrete, and steel of the city.

In the week previous, I pondered and worried about all the *"what ifs"* for this ride. I finally gave up, only last night, after convincing myself that I'm as prepared as I can be for this trip. I've packed my leather jacket, rain gear, toothbrush, deodorant, a camera, several pairs of riding jeans, three pairs of gloves, four pairs of riding glasses, and ten pairs of clean underwear. One for each day I'm expected to be away. I would have only packed five pairs and did some washing, but Paula insisted. She's a woman who appreciates clean underwear and doesn't understand why anyone else wouldn't. Besides Paula packed my bag so I couldn't really protest.

Yesterday, I washed and cleaned Thelma D to get her ready. She's a beautiful motorcycle, painted a deep sunglo red with a metallic gold sparkle. Her chrome-spoked wheels and engine trim gleam when she is freshly washed and polished. Being new, with only 2000 kilometres on the odometre, she'll be strong and dependable when I need her. My machine won't let me down, but I am worried about myself. I'm afraid that I won't have the strength or the stamina to ride every day. I tell myself that I'll only go as far as I can manage and if there are days that I can't ride, then I won't. I'll bunker in somewhere to rest and read, or watch television. The thoughts reassure me, but I still have twinges of anxiety thinking about the days of riding ahead of me.

Anxiety wouldn't have been in my vocabulary after I quit my secretarial job in 1979. I couldn't sit inside at a desk anymore so I went out west on a whim to wash dishes at a Banff resort. When I returned to Ottawa I couldn't afford a car, so I rode a 400 Kawasaki everywhere, at any time, day or night. It was my only form of transportation and I stretched the limits of the riding season, cruising in the early frost and late snow. I loved that little bike.

My happiest riding memories during the early years of the '80s, were when a bunch of us girls would drive our motorcycles to softball tournaments in the summer. Most of us played hockey together in Brockville and we had a pretty good team this side of Toronto. Our group won a couple of provincial championships with girls gathered from Kingston, Cornwall, Ottawa, and the rural areas scattered between them. In the summer, our hockey crew entered softball tournaments to help raise money for the season because the winners were awarded cash prizes. We were all good athletes and made out pretty well. For me, it was summers filled with partying and playing, drinking and driving my way through rural Eastern Ontario, often camping and sleeping in the same fields I played ball in.

I don't play softball anymore and I've only been back on a bike for a year after not riding since the mid-'90s. My last bike was a desperate looking Honda 650 I'd bought used and fixed up. I sold it when I needed the money to build a back deck after buying my first house. That decision helped heal a rift with my partner at the time. I had bought the bike without her knowing.

To get primed for this ride north, I went on a friend's annual spring run in early June. My long-time pal Frank and his best friend Mike organize the day. It's a time when all their crazy friends get together and try to outrun each other from checkpoint to checkpoint. I've attended a couple of times and on the years I didn't ride, Frank made sure to get me a T-shirt they always had made up to celebrate the day. This year was the thirty-seventh and the annual shirt was a bright grass green, and it had the route mapped out on the front so you wouldn't get lost if you couldn't keep up with the crazies.

There were a couple of FLH Harleys and metric cruisers, but most riders preferred the dirt, dual-purpose or sport bikes to run through West Quebec's rolling hills and curving roads. It was 750 kilometres of intense riding with stops for fuel and food. It was after being driven down and passed by a psycho BMW rider, hauling his husky-like dog in a box on the back of his bike, in a curve, on a hill, into oncoming traffic, that my bladder and I decided to quit the run early. I heard later the dog made it.

My partner Paula and I went to the after party in Frank's garage for company, conversation, and bowls of chili. It was there I had a chance to re-connect with Trudy, who I first met thirty years ago when we both played hockey in Brockville. Like myself, Trudy came back to riding after a long layoff and now rides a Suzuki 600 Bandit. When we were leaving, I scratched out my phone numbers in the space provided by the Algonquin Park portion of one of the many maps that Trudy pulled out of her back bag. We agreed to get in touch to further catch up and make plans for a ride.

While I was writing out my numbers, Trudy was telling Paula the story of being kidnapped and taken to a "peeler" bar located at the crossroads of a small community just south of Ottawa. I had completely forgotten about the episode, but yeah, we did. We tricked more than kidnapped her though. One of our teammates, Donovan, asked for the keys to her bike and then hit the kill switch after driving off. Trudy couldn't start her machine, never thinking to check the controls. We all stood around and pretended it was her fault for giving her keys to Donovan, a party girl who measured her fun with equal amounts of drinking and driving. It was Donovan who introduced me to the ruse of opening the bottom flaps of a case of beer, instead of the top, so it would appear intact and unopened if you were ever pulled over by the cops.

At the time, I drove a 1981, 650 Honda Silver Wing. In those days it was a smaller version of the Gold Wing, not the big scooter design of today's model. We convinced Trudy to hop on the back of my machine and several of us drove out of town on the pretext of going to a great place for a bite to eat. We coerced, coaxed, and finally persuaded Trudy into the popular basement bar, which did serve food, although it was overpriced, tired, and mostly fried.

Donovan was chatting up a scantily clad dancer by the bar and we had just started on our first couple of jugs of beer when I heard scuffling and some loud swearing. I turned in time to see Trudy disappear under the table between two chairs. Her reaction wasn't from seeing her first stripper, but from watching her brother walk in with a couple of his buddies. After hiding her in the washroom, where she ranted and raved about how she'd be kicked out of her house, we managed to smuggle her out unseen, and were generally satisfied that Trudy wasn't really a lesbian, just a pretender.

Remembering that night makes me laugh, but it also makes me think that maybe I'm the pretender. Thinking that I can just hop on a bike like I'm twenty or twenty-five years younger than I am, and take off like I don't have a care in the world, heading north, then west, and returning south. The decision to make this trip wasn't impulsive, and it was certainly not as rash and fucked up as my weekend trip with Lenny, but it might prove to be a foolish one. After buying Thelma D, taking her and myself on a road trip became an embedded hope that I couldn't shake. Once I decided that what I needed to do, in order to figure out a redirection for my life, was a long ride by motorcycle, the hope became a tentative plan.

It's hard to tell when the lack of enthusiasm crept into my life, but some time in the last couple of years my life had stalled. Indecision and fear of dying choked the life from activities I've always enjoyed. The drive to finish the building of my house at the lake had come to a standstill. The first summer of construction was uplifting and energizing. After a contractor did the foundation, friends, family, and myself took over the building, cutting, and installing floor joists, laying plywood, and framing walls. Before

FIRST GEAR: A MOTORCYCLE MEMOIR

the fall came, I hired a guy to help me install the trusses and the metal roof, then I was able to install some used windows I had picked up cheap. It was one of the best summers of my life, but now the building sits unfinished in house wrap and vapour barrier. I use the excuse I can't find the money, but I could if I wanted. I didn't even finish painting the house in the city after I had done two rooms, because I didn't know whether I'd be there to enjoy the new colours or not. So why bother.

I was bewildered at my own outlook and muddled through, until one day I decided finally to put the plan in place. If it took an ass-numbing ride to figure out how to get some siding on the house, or a roller in the paint tray, I would do it and somehow shake out a revelation for myself. Maybe the disinterest, my lack of commitment, came from my belief that I didn't expect to live this long. It's possible, but now that I've started this ride I don't want to die until I've figured out where I'm supposed to be going.

Near Cobden, I downshift Thelma D before I get to an intersection where a car has stopped to pull out onto the highway. I slow to make sure the driver sees me and when I pass in front of him I give a slight nod as a way of saying thanks for stopping. With his car in my mirrors, I accelerate back up to cruising speed, one potential killer down.

4.

FOR THE LAST TWO HOURS, I've been running steady on Highway 17 through the Ottawa Valley into Renfrew County. Even with the heat, it's a glorious day for riding. Sunny and bright with little traffic. It's the kind of day where you can settle, relax, and ride for the joy of it. Your mind clears and the faint aroma of pines, wild grasses, and hay blend with the trailing exhaust of cars and trucks. The wind peels back your anxieties and troubles and leaves you free and ready for any speed bumps. Even though I described riding as being on the edge of chaos, it is also a place where I am in control. Crazy impatient drivers and big trucks out of control are exceptions. I have my feet up on Thelma D's highway pegs, my shoulders and arms are loose, I'm breathing regularly, shaking off the last remnants of my earlier anxiety.

Part of my confidence today comes from having travelled this highway many times in the past. When I left Deep River after graduating high school in June 1977, I went south for work. With no car, I'd hitchhike back and forth when I couldn't afford the bus fare. I only got in trouble a couple of times where men picking me up wanted more than I was willing to give them. After an uneasy time with a trucker who had greasy yellow-white hair, a harelip, and nicotine-stained fingers, I started to wear boots so I could hide a small knife in them.

Bam Bam, the Shih Tzu puppy I'd gotten from my uncle, used to hitch rides with me. Bev took care of him one weekend I came home to visit and he never left her. That was okay because she was in a better position to look out for him at the time, and I believe she needed the company.

I flex my throttle hand. It's numb and stiff. I try to hold the grip in a number of different ways and that helps for a bit. Thelma D has a screw control located under the right hand controls that I can turn with my thumb to hold the throttle in place, a very primitive cruise control. I used it once and found it to be cumbersome and confusing. My mind and body couldn't get used to having her not decelerate after letting go of the grip.

Finally I release the grip completely and Thelma D slows immediately. After taking a few seconds to flex my hand I clutch, drop two gears, and throttle back up. It's been my experience that it'll be numb for a half an hour or so and then my hand will be fine for the day. I just need to be patient with it.

In contrast, the numbness in my feet and thigh may never disappear. I twist and roll my feet, flexing my toes in my boots and rub the upper part of my left thigh. No, still numb. I'm hoping it doesn't start creeping through my legs. If that happens, then I'll have to pull over, call for help, and trailer Thelma D home.

In a half hour I'll be in Deep River, where I grew up. It's a small town on the Ottawa River that was built to house the workers that the Atomic Energy of Canada Limited needed for their nuclear plant in Chalk River.

I was three years old when we moved there from Sudbury. When our family dissolved, my older brother John and I went south and my two younger brothers, Craig and Mark, and Bev, went back up north to Sudbury. Eventually Bev would move out west, settling in Vancouver with her boyfriend, Frank. I only found out she moved when I went to visit and couldn't find her.

Thelma D and I are passing by the small city of Pembroke. It too is on the Ottawa River where it's joined by the Muskrat River and was home to the Eddy Match Company until 1998. The business rose from the humble beginnings and efforts of Ezra Butler Eddy, an American entrepreneur, who made matches by hand from discarded wood. I picture this determined man hunched over his workbench, working by candlelight to take care of his family, and I am humbled.

The large sprawling plant had also marked our arrival to Pembroke when we used to travel here from Deep River. Now the highway bypasses it completely, as it does other towns and villages along the Trans Canada Highway through the valley. Eager travellers and the transportation of goods to and from the north in a timely manner, weighs more with the power brokers than slowing down and taking in the sights, smells, and attractions of small town Ontario. Some blame the bypasses for the blight in small town, main street commerce. Others, in more recent history, blame Walmart.

Pembroke is also home to a Junior "A" hockey team, the Pembroke Lumber Kings who play out of the Memorial Centre. When I was a kid I used to watch Craig play hockey for Deep River at the grand old arena. He was a really good defenseman and would have been great if he hadn't been forced to leave home. There was a rumour around the Midget C team, promoted by Bev, that he was being courted by a Junior team in Niagara Falls. It was more Bev's dream than Craig's I think, as he was more interested in girls and making enough money to live and party than playing hockey.

The old arena had lower tunnel-like sections under the stands. Between periods or games, I'd explore them pretending I was in a cave. Sometimes I had enough money to buy some French fries to take with me. There were lots of nooks and crannies, but I never found anything more interesting than old nets and mops, brooms and pails. Occasionally I'd run into men wearing work shirts and pants. Most let me go on with my quest. Once I was told to get lost by a man dressed like the others, waving his cigarette at me. His voice sounded like two stones being rubbed together.

Bev didn't have to drag me to watch hockey in Pembroke. Some days I was already in the car waiting for her, because pretending, exploring, and playing in the arena was always better than being left at home with Eric. I felt safe on my own, alone in the tunnels. I was too young at the time to even think that I'd find other measures of comfort in Pembroke later in my life, and that they would come from the justice system.

A few kilometres more and I cross the Petawawa River where it makes its way to join the Ottawa. From the bridge you can see a fence installed just above the rapids. It's there to prevent paddlers and boaters from entering the Canadian Forces Base, located in the small town of Petawawa at the juncture of the two rivers.

When I was in full party mode as a teenager in the '70s, it was a cheap place to go drinking if you could hook up with a soldier to get into the mess. They weren't that hard to find and were always up for a party.

The landscape changes from a mixed forest to flat stretches of sandy soil with stands of red pines. Kilometres of power lines, strung with large orange balls, line the highway. The presence of the army is evident with gates blocking side roads and warning signs on fences that parallel the highway. Elevated viewing shacks and bleachers mark the start of maneuver fields. The road is straight and long and urges me to accelerate and fly a little faster. I push a bit and Thelma D responds quickly and easily, a satisfying loud exhaust growl that only a Harley voices. Satisified, I back off, telling myself it'll be a long day in chaos and I need to save my adrenalin.

Heading out of the sand and pines I come to the Petawawa National Forestry Institute, 100 square kilometres of forest still called the Station by some locals. It was initially established in the early 1900s to protect and manage the forest of the Petawawa Military Reserve, but it quickly evolved into an internationally recognized research, scientific study, and educational facility. I had never been there on a field trip as a student, but I experienced some of my education in its parking lot when I was sixteen.

* * *

My defiance is gone and my confidence broken. I stand in front of him defeated, slouched with my head down. My arms are crossed about my mid-section and I'm kicking at the sand with my sneakers. He tells me that all he had been trying to do was to teach me how to be a young woman. He makes it sound so normal, like it was something that had to be done and he was the one that had to do it. He asks me if I understand and I nod my obedience. We get back on his motorcycle and he drives me home.

* * *

Loser, stupid, fat cow. No, I'm not. I am worthy. Loser, stupid, fat cow. No, I'm not. I am in control and life is what you make it. I am worthy. Stupid fucking self-help mantras.

The ugly voice came when I was a young girl. At first it was soothing, insisting, caring even. After, it entrenched itself into my nature like an anchor to a seabed, and it became mean, sarcastic, biting, and sometimes hurtfully honest.

"Fuuuuuck," I yell. The sound of my shame, my anger, my sadness dissolves into the wind before it can take shape. It is getting better, but on some days it's hard to keep telling myself to think positively. Self-trashing was a legacy given to us by our parents. My brothers and I were never good enough, or smart enough. We had to work hard and when we didn't, or when we were disobedient, we were beaten down. Eric mostly delivered our physical abuse, especially after Bev broke her paddle on one of the boys.

The trashing creeps in and takes root. I can't let go of the message loop in my head that tells me that I'm not worthy, that I'm going to die, that I deserve to die. I'm going to wipe out on a corner, a car is going to run into me or I'm going to get cut off and side swiped on the highway, or my front tire is going to blow out while I'm in the fast lane and I'll crash and get run over.

When I was a younger, brash rider I had no fear. I rode with a *bring it on attitude*, and I erased the self-trashing by not caring whether I lived or died. What wasn't erased was suffocated by alcohol. Driving my motorcycle while drunk was one of the reasons I gave up riding for a decade in the late '80s. This was a good decision because it might have saved my life, but it didn't stop me from drinking or taking risks or indulging in depression-inducing behaviours. It took a few years, but I learned that letting go of riding didn't solve any of my problems.

I yell louder with each shout challenging the wind making my voice hoarse. My throat is tender, my mouth dry and I need a drink of water. I shift Thelma D roughly back and forth through her fourth and fifth gears. She whines several times in the lower gear before I back off and remember it's not her fault.

I slow down to half the speed limit and settle myself with some controlled breathing and try to let the tension go by working through a checklist: legs, core, shoulders, neck, and arms. After a few moments, my breathing slows and I'm able to find some peace. I let the wind whisper to me. The sound is sweet and the breeze lingers on my cheek like a loved one caressing me with her hand, calming, forgiving.

5.

PLANT ROAD COMES INTO VIEW, and I slow down to ride through Chalk River, home of Atomic Energy of Canada Limited or Chalk River Laboratories, known as The Plant.

Chalk is a lonely little town where the highway is the primary artery. There's a main street and some housing and of course, the labs and workshops of The Plant, but you can't see them from the highway. The place was named after the chalk a logger would use to mark logs with, or depending upon your source, the loggers who used chalk to mark logs. When I was younger I always thought the name had something to do with the colour of the water in the area.

Looking left from the only set of traffic lights entering town, I can see the Chalk River Hotel. It looks different and I realize it has been renovated and turned into apartments. The old establishment starts a run of scattered buildings along both sides of the highway. There is a gas station, some small businesses, and a couple of restaurants, one of which is chronically busy because it is the bus depot.

When I was sixteen, I had a boyfriend in town. Peter and I spent a lot of nights with friends closing the hotel, then at last call making the run to Swisha, where we could all drink for another two hours. He, his dad, and grandmother lived on Plant Road and like everyone else's father it seemed, his worked at The Plant. It all went to hell with him during my last year of high school. Peter got violent and I got pregnant, a bad situation.

Eric worked as a machinist at The Plant from the early '60s until he retired long after I moved away. Like most people who worked in Chalk, he chose to have his family live in Deep River. There were more services, shops, grocery stores, and of course, the Yacht and Tennis Club. Not that we were members. Bowling and snowmobiling were a better fit for our family.

An offsite work force needs transportation and every workday morning in Deep River, like clockwork, buses that resembled big green beetles would leave their garage den and creep around town picking up workers, skilled labourers, clerks, managers, engineers, and scientists to take them down the highway to work in The Plant. The beetles would return at night, spitting out people along the routes in their neighbourhoods before burrowing back into their shelter to wait for the next morning's run. Their presence was predictable. They took Eric away every day, but they also brought him home every night at five minutes to five.

It takes only a minute to drive through Chalk River and I'm already thinking about seeing my grandparent's house. They emigrated from Denmark as a young couple and had originally settled in Sudbury, eventually following our family south when Eric got his job at AECL. My grandfather built their house on the highway between Chalk River and Deep River himself, a tiny white bungalow with two small bedrooms. It had a white picket fence that separated the front of the property from the highway. The grounds were always neat and tidy with a well-tended yard, complete with small shrubs and flower gardens.

My grandfather was a putterer who loved to build stuff like his snowmobile shed that had two openings, an exit and an entrance. He built in an arm that would swing in to support the back of the machine keeping the track off the ground while in storage. So all he needed to do was open one end, drive in, support the back of the machine, close the door, and then open the other to drive out when he wanted to go snowmobiling.

He constructed a three-hole putting golf course that surrounded the house and small garage. Holes were made out of soup cans with small metal poles and flags. He and my brothers spent hours hitting a golf ball around and around. I tried to play, but it didn't capture my attention. What did amaze me was the pit he had dug in the back of his property to service his car, a Datsun 510. He felt he had been shafted by the mechanic at the garage, so he shovelled out a hole, shored up the sides, built steps down, and constructed identical ramps on either side of the opening. When it was done he boasted that he didn't need to take his car to a shop, because he could easily change his own oil, and make his own repairs. I wanted to play in it and pretend I was working on a car, but I wasn't allowed.

When I was a teenager, my grandfather became this crazy, often cranky old man, who'd drive his moped down the side of the highway into Deep River, wearing big goggles and oversized gloves. He was easily identifiable by his ladybug orange helmet. Depending upon his mood and level of entitlement, he'd take up the whole lane giving no quarter to cars, trucks, or buses. If they wanted to get past him, they'd have to use the other lane. He was no better when driving his car to town. He'd brag about how he would race the cars that tried to pass him. He insisted that they didn't need to go faster than him because he was doing the speed limit.

Travelling on the same road, I think about him on his moped. It's a miracle he was never driven off the road, to be found later in the ditch by the pickers who scoured the sides of the road for beer bottles.

In a good mood, my grandfather was fun to be with. I'd go visit him with my brothers and he'd make us open-faced cheese and sardine sandwiches on thin rye bread. I hate sardines. My brothers loved them. Sometimes we would drink Fresca, my grandmother's favourite drink. He gave it to us knowing she'd be mad when we drank it all, but it was one of the rare times we ever got pop, so we never said no. Other times he would make tea for us. I remember him telling us that if we wanted the tea to cool quickly we needed to leave the spoon in it, because it dissipated the heat. To prove it, he would make us touch the spoon before he put it in the tea. It was cool. We'd feel it after it had been in the tea for a minute. It was hot. It seemed like he had to prove his theory every time the kettle boiled. I never minded going through the routine repeatedly with him because, at these times, he was a caring, laughing, nice man, proud to share his knowledge.

There were the other times when he was a mean, vindictive old man who had no time for anyone. We knew to tread lightly around him when he was ignoring us. During those times we tried to be out of the house, exploring the bush behind his house, because if we hung around, eventually he'd start yelling at us, putting us down, and calling us names. It's easy now to see where Eric got some of his rage and hatred from, a direct pipeline of anger from grandfather to father to child.

Eric might have got his coldness, need for preciseness, and attention to detail from his mother. She kept a vegetable garden in their backyard that had precise neat rows, and when we spent any time at their house during the season she'd have us on our knees weeding the plot. She'd check our work often and point out any areas we missed, then have us fix them before we got permission to stop. The garden was her pride and I was always afraid I'd pluck a plant that wasn't a weed or somehow mess up the perfectly formed, raised sections of black earth that smelled like worms and rain. She never talked much, except to give direction and make corrections, but it was easy to see the disappointment and disapproval in her face after I made mistakes in her garden. It was much harder to see any love and kindness in her, even when I got it right the first time.

Their yard in the back was also host to the occasional dinner and the most memorable for me was the catfish. Eric had pulled the twenty-pound-plus bottom feeder from the Ottawa River. Since Bev didn't know how to cook it, or pretended not to, my grandmother got hold of it and insisted we all come to share in the bounty. I didn't want to go because I hated fish, and couldn't imagine eating anything that looked that slimy and ugly.

When we got to their house the dreaded fish was laid out on a platter in the centre of a folding table on the concrete patio. A sacrifice being worshipped by lawn chairs that had been set in a precise circle by my grandmother. The setting made it look like we were expected to pay homage to the slippery black, grey-bellied centerpiece that resembled the joining of a small shark with a humpback whale. Just add whiskers, cook, and serve to the unwilling.

When I smelled the portion on my plate I was reminded of the garbage dump where we went to watch the bears forage for food at dusk, near Driftwood Provincial Park. I knew I'd be in trouble if I didn't eat it, so I pretended to chew and then spit the pieces into my napkin. I used to do the same with peas, French-style green beans, and Bev's special chickpea dish. The toughest part was trying not to swallow while pretending to chew. Once Bev smiled at me raising a brow after putting down her beer. She knew what I was doing. I went through several napkins and made a couple of trips into the house, where I'd pull the soggy tissues from my shorts and hide them in the kitchen garbage. I was really glad my grandmother chose disposable over her usual cloth napkins.

She was so pleased with her meal that all of us kids got some of her Fresca.

6.

THELMA D AND I SLOW as we come to their old house. Along with Bev, who died in August 2001, both my paternal grandparents have departed this life and it shows. The picket fence is gone and the property is looking worn out and used. The grass is thin and brown, bare in some spots, and the little bungalow needs a good scrape and a paint job. You can tell that someone had at one time painted the window and door trim a light blue. A similar hue was used on the garage door and it too needs a touchup. A rusty old truck with a flat tire and flaking paint is parked beside the gravel drive. The pines and spruce that divide the property from the neighbours are much taller and wider than I last remember.

It was in this driveway beside the tall pines, on a summer afternoon in the mid-'70s, when my grandmother showed John and I newspaper clippings that she had saved for years. The clippings were from the *North Renfrew Times*, Deep River's local newspaper. Mostly I remember her fingers shaking, as she pointed to a picture of Bev and read the article to us in a stilted, angry voice. The clippings detailed how Bev had defrauded her employer by forging signatures and cashing cheques. The reporter went on to describe that Mom had been charged and convicted of two counts of theft and fraud and was going to go to jail. Her employer was the *North Renfrew Times*.

Bev applied for and received a pardon for those crimes. Years later, in the late '90s, when she was diagnosed with colon cancer, she sent me her pardon papers along with some other certificates that she'd earned in grade school for spelling and poetry. When I asked her why, Bev told me she didn't want Frank, her companion then for twenty years, to find the papers if she died. I wanted to say, well you'll be dead, so what could possibly happen, but I didn't. She was sick and I suppose even in death, people want to keep a certain image of their persona intact. So I kept her papers in silence, another family secret. I don't know why she didn't just destroy the documents. Why did she want me to have them? I was more touched by her sending me her certificates of achievement. I still have them. They remind me of a young dark-haired girl, innocent, caring, and full of pride for her school work.

Less than a kilometre from my grandparent's house is The Jehovah's Witness Hall. My grandmother was a Witness and she spent a lot of hours at the Hall. I would have thought that being close to her friends and place of worship would have made her a happy person, but I can't remember a time when I saw her truly cheerful or contented. Even when she was gardening, she seemed cranky and dissatisfied.

To be fair, I never witnessed her interactions with friends inside the Hall, because we weren't believers, so I didn't know how she was with people of her faith. Her other son, my uncle Ken and his wife Linda, are Witnesses and they always seemed to be happy. Maybe it was because they only came for visits and lived in a Jehovah household. It's possible my grandmother's anger and disappointment came from trying to faithfully follow the directive that Witnesses are not supposed to fraternize with non-believers, and she was surrounded by a family of them. Witnesses are allowed a little more flexibility with relatives, but I could see how the never-ending struggle to balance conviction and family might result in anger and resentment.

There was never any anger, though, only persistence in her voice when she would speak at length trying to persuade us to believe and read the Witness publications she'd bring to our house on visits and holidays. Every Christmas my brothers and I would each get a crisp new five dollar bill and a little booklet. I'd say thank you, sit down on the carpet by the tree and pretend to read. Early on in this ritual, I'd given up trying to understand the meanings written down in undecipherable paragraphs and tiny fonts. I also couldn't reconcile the Witness belief that only those who were like my grandmother would be saved. Only the true believers like her would find glory. That didn't seem right.

Eventually the booklets would pile up in a little stack on a basement bookshelf before being thrown out by Bev on one of her infrequent cleaning frenzies. I'm not sure if my grandfather was a Jehovah's Witness because he seemed not to care about the pamphlets. He never pushed them on us and I never saw him read one. When my grandmother wasn't around, he'd boast that he only went with her to the Witness Hall for the free food.

I put the Hall behind me with the thought that my grandmother must have felt very alone without any close family believers. Her support system was a narcissistic control freak that made fun of her faith. If she was truly lonely, then why did she push John and I away by telling on Bev? Is that what she wanted? I don't know, but her shaking fingers and angry voice only made me dislike her more.

7.

For the first time in almost three hours I get off Thelma D at the PetroCan gas station in Deep River. It's been fifteen years since I've spent this much time on a motorcycle. It feels good. I'm where I belong.

I walk slowly around in a small circle to work out the stiffness in my legs. Torn cartilage in my right knee contributes a small limp to the circumference of my path. I injured it playing hockey last December and am waiting for surgery, a result of my optimistic fitness plan. With each circle I get straighter and taller, a revolving poster of Darwin's theory of evolution.

I remove Thelma D's gas cap and fit the spout into her tank. There is a slight shake to my hand. I just drove past my childhood home and I'm trying to tamp down all the emotions that are threatening. Between the pumps there is a sudden flash of bright red accompanied by the loud growl of an exhaust accelerating. My chest tightens with a sense of pride mixed with embarrassment, a confusing mix that brings me to another gas station, at another time.

* * *

The heat is stifling and the dead air allows the humidity to drape over my shoulders like a wet shirt in the rain. I'm walking up to the gas station on the highway to pick up a pack of cigarettes. Sweat has started to trickle down my back and into my underwear. The temperature didn't change my choice of clothes and like most mornings I'm dressed in jeans, Adidas Rom running shoes, and whatever T-shirt I could scrounge from one of my brothers or the laundry pile. I'm fifteen years old and the clerk sells me the cigarettes without any hassle. They always did.

Leaving the station, I walk out past a pile of tires and a line of cars waiting for repairs and concentrate on pulling out the first cigarette. Frustrated with my short, bitten-down fingernails, I use my teeth to pull the smoke free. I'm almost out of the lot when Bev in her 440 Charger pulls in and triggers the service bells. It's difficult to miss the '72 Dodge with its bright orange paint and wide black stripes running down the centre of the hood and trunk.

I sidestep quickly to stand beside the phone booth perched in the corner of the lot. I light the cigarette, my first of the day, cupping it with my hand while I take a long drag. I'm not worried about getting caught. Most weekday mornings before school, my brothers and I start the day with a breakfast of coffee and cigarettes, compliments of Bev, and lately her idea of a babysitter is a small box of beer and pocket money. I worry she'll see me smoking and ask where I got the cash. Bev had already raided the envelope that held my paper delivery money, but she didn't know that I had pilfered some of it back from her purse. I take another drag and watch through the dust and grime of the booth windows.

The service bells stopped ringing and the driver's door of the Dodge creaks open. First one and then two platform wedge sandals appear in front of thrush mufflers that look like the exhaust stacks of a transport truck. Firmly planted, Bev first pulls then pushes her weight from the car. Not a tall woman, the four-inch heels put her close to 5'10". Her hair makes her appear even taller. Dark brown, almost black, it is back-combed, teased and pulled up high into a mound of curls and fuzz, held together with bobby pins and hairspray. Her double-chinned, round face is framed with two curls pulled down and pasted onto the sides of her cheeks. It was a look found everywhere at record shops and dance halls in the '50s.

While you can't see her eyes because of the sunglasses she wears, they are heavily laden with eyeliner, mascara, and blue eye shadow. Look closer and you'd see glimpses of the glue that holds her false eyelashes on. Peeking out above her glasses is a set of perfect eyebrows. No colouring outside of the lines.

After Bev closes the door with a solid swing of her hips, she walks around the back of the car, pulling the thick straps of her heavy purse onto the shoulder of her peasant blouse. The top is a leopard print, cut low enough to see her bra and pulled up tight under her breasts, displaying generous amounts of soft puffy cleavage. The blouse ends at a pair of cut-off jeans that just barely cup her butt, and the zipper shows the strain of keeping her extra thirty pounds tucked in.

The door to the station opens and Buck, a lanky teen dressed in work jeans and a flannel shirt despite the heat, comes running out of the cinder block building. His face is pimply and narrow with thin lips, and his hair is shaved up the sides leaving a short mop that drapes to one side. Buck picks up the handle from the first pump he comes to. It doesn't make any difference because everyone in town knows that the first pump is regular and the second pump is regular.

"Fill 'er up Bucky and put it on my tab," Bev says.

"But, but we don't have tabs here ma'am," Buck stutters.

"Don't worry about it Bucky. Mr. Burns and I have an understanding." Bev laughs as she walks for the station door.

Buck's face flushes red. "Mr. Burns isn't here."

"Oh, and be a sweetie pie, and check my oil using that dipstick thing," Bev throws over her shoulder as she walks through the door.

Buck turns a shade redder and moves back to the car, opens the filler cap, and sets the pump handle to kick off when full. I peer out from my hiding spot and we make eye contact. Buck looks away. He pulls the chrome pins and lifts the hood.

I grind out my half-smoked cigarette in the sand that wind from speeding cars and trucks has piled against the bottom frame of the phone booth, and push the butt back into my pack. Diesel fumes from the tractor trailers mix with the pungent smell of freshly cut grass from ditches and fields that neighbour the highway. I think about going to the pier to see who's hanging around. Maybe I'll go to the beach for a swim. If I'm lucky Karen and her boyfriend will be there and they always have something to smoke. The last time it was hash oil. The sound of a hood closing pulls me back.

Buck pulls his sleeve over his hand and uses a polishing motion to wipe his handprints of the hood of the Dodge. He's placing the pump handle into its cradle, when Bev comes striding out of the restaurant tucking two packs of Rothmans into her purse. From my angle I can see a string of scars crisscrossing the front of her left leg, running from her mid-thigh to calf. Her summer tan pulls them out, ugly and white, even though they've long since healed. Whenever asked about them, she would flash the scars like a mysterious, proud survivor and reply they came from a horrible car accident she had with her younger brother Daryl. Sometimes she is driving in the rain, other times he is driving and it was snowing.

Buck is standing at the back of the car twisting the rag in his hands. The knuckles of his big hands are alternating white and red as he squeezes and pulls.

"Is she full Bucky?"

He stammers, "Yes, ma'am."

Bev lifts her glasses up past her eyebrows and rests them in her nest of hair. "How's my oil Bucko?"

Buck has twisted the rag around his hands tying them together in the front of his crotch. "Good."

A little taller than Buck in her heels, Bev grasps his chin in her right hand, pulling him in, making his eyes level with her breasts. She puckers her lips as if to kiss him, and tilts his head up to face her and her large eyelashes. The ends of her fingers with their long, thick nails are haloed in white as she squeezes his cheeks and shakes his head slightly. His eyes are wide and frightened.

"Now do me a favour, sweetie. Remember to tell Mr. Burns to come by the hotel any time I'm working next week to settle up. Okay?" Bev stares into his growing eyes for a moment, making me afraid she just might give him a big wet one. "Ya got that honey?"

Buck manages to grunt and Bev gives him a little extra squeeze before releasing him. He stumbles back stilt-legged, nearly falling, before running through the open bay door of the garage.

"Remember, next week Bucky," laughs Bev as she finger waves to his back over the roof of the car. She opens the door and quickly slips into the front seat with an agility that belies her weight and the height of her heels.

The Charger starts with a deep rumble, its engine and headers making the body rock and the mufflers vibrate. The rear end lifts and it suddenly squawks, accelerating quickly out toward the exit and the phone booth. Expecting to see a flash of orange, I am engulfed in a cloud of dust and when it settles I'm looking at Bev through the open side window. She leans towards me, then smiles and waves before lowering her sunglasses and laying a strip of rubber down the highway.

8.

I RIDE OUT OF DEEP RIVER and think back to one of the first landmarks to greet me riding into town, the water tower. Twice in my last year in high school some resourceful pranksters had climbed up and gotten access to the water tank. They painted a middle dash through the D and then a slash down the P making the sign read BEER RIVER.

When word got out the first time it happened, my friends and I ran or pedalled our bikes out to the highway to better see the prank. Like excited hordes, we made our way south to where the golf course nudges up along the road where we could see the letters clear and proud.

Groups of us huddled together, all looking in the same direction, to admire the vandalism and speculate about how it was done and by whom. There were lots of whispered guesses, laughing and boasting. Smokes were passed around and eventually came back to the owners with squished filters and big heaters. It was just like during breaks in between classes in the parking lot of the high school, except longer. Eventually, like the need to go to class, the groups dissipated and we all wandered away home or to the beach or to the bowling alley. During the following weeks, there were lots of rumours of who did what, but no names surfaced. I couldn't tell you who did it, but I was proud of them.

After I left home, the caper was accomplished a couple more times before some town engineer, or janitor, got the idea to paint over the letters and spell the name of the town using metal cutouts that were attached to the outer rails of the water tank's inspection platform. Now it would be impossible to achieve a name change unless you had a plasma arc cutter, sheets of metal, and an on-site welder.

The cutouts are gone now and the tank is freshly painted. It's a glossy white with large black letters, shiny and wet-looking. It's not too hard to imagine the letters thirsty for additional brush strokes. I'd love to travel through Beer River again.

A few miles north of Deep River, I come to Point Alexander. It's barely a dot on the map, but it is the site of the old Byeways Hotel, now burned down. Bev worked there for years, first as a waitress and then as one of the night bartenders. She got Craig and me a job cleaning up the lounge on Sunday mornings. Our church was a dark and dingy place, that smelled of stale beer and nicotine tinged with a sour mix of body odour and urine the closer you got to the washrooms. We knew it'd be a hard sermon when our sneakers stuck to the floor of the main lounge, squeaking with every step. And like church, the routine was the same. Lift up all the chairs and sweep, wash and wax the linoleum floors. When dry, reseat the chairs and clean the tables.

After we washed the floors, I usually cleaned the washrooms while Craig waxed the linoleum. Occasionally we'd switch. Craig and I thought we had it made with that job. It was a lot more grown up and we earned more money than delivering papers, babysitting or shovelling driveways. We still delivered papers, but the worst was the shovelling, because Bev would get us out of bed at five-thirty in the morning to clear the driveways before our neighbours needed to get to work or school. Then we'd have to do our own driveway. Craig and I were proud of our shovelling work and always made sure that the sides were neat and tidy, with a nice clean flare opening to the street.

Working at the Byeways we quickly learned the trick to getting unlimited playtime on the juke box. I'd sing and pretend to dance while sweeping or swinging the mop around. There was always some extra pop and often there was some food in the kitchen that we'd scrounge. The real bonus came when we'd find the draft kegs left unlocked and help ourselves to a little beer while scouring and scrubbing. There were a few times when Bev picked us up in the afternoon and we were half lit after a few hours of cleaning. We'd sit in the car and giggle as if getting something over on her. Now I realize that she had to have been able to smell the beer on us, but she never said anything.

We didn't always have good times on those Sundays, giggling and laughing. Sometimes we fought and then each of us would take turns calling Bev to complain about the other, until she stopped answering the phone. Craig and I had one of our most memorable fights at the Byeways. Whatever the subject matter was I can't remember, but I wouldn't let it go, pressing and pushing him until he snapped. I can still see him, red-faced and yelling, "Shut the fuck up and leave me alone," while lifting up a cleaver and embedding it into the doorframe beside my head. That ended the argument. I called Bev and begged her to come out to the hotel to pick us up early. It wasn't a good drive home. She was mad, I was crying, and Craig kept insisting that he meant to miss me with the knife.

9.

THE HIGHWAY WINDS AND DROPS as we arrive in Rolphton and I turn right on to Swisha Road. It's the road Lenny drove me home on from the hotel when I was yelling hopelessly into the wind over his shoulder asking if he could see. It leads to a small island in the Ottawa River that belongs to the Province of Quebec. The real name of the place is Rapides des Joachims but the *English* or *les tête carrée,* squareheads as the French call the English, of the area couldn't pronounce it and the name was anglicized and shortened to Swisha.

The road is curvy and narrow, running alongside rock cuts and deep ditches guarded by galvanized rails. Pine, spruce, and birch trees shadow the road creating deep cool spots that refresh and ease the heat of the day. It's tempting to stop and cool down.

Thelma D and I come around a ninety-degree corner with rock cuts on both sides and face a single lane bridge. It's a metal grate structure. The kind you can see through if you look down, and the vibrating bike feels like it's driving itself. I gear down and slow immediately. *Oh shit.* I completely forgot about the bridge. How did I do that? The last time I was on one of these with a motorcycle was crossing the Interprovincial Bridge on my Silver Wing in Ottawa. I swerved and swayed, high up in the air, barely in control and I swore then I'd never do it again. *Fuck, fuck, fuck.*

Stopping and turning around isn't an option. It's only the first day and there's going to be a lot more challenges to come on this ride than a long steel grate structure to cross. I don't know how long it is, but I'd guess about 120 feet or more. Pulling in a deep breath, I try to remember the safe driving tips I recently read in the *Harley Owners Group (or, HOG)* magazine. What to do when approaching gravel, railway tracks, grooved pavement, and metal grate bridges. Slow down, keep your grip loose, don't accelerate or brake quickly, and don't make any sharp turns.

I loosen my hold on the handlebars, and try to push down the anxiety that is bubbling up like one of Bev's seltzers after a heavy night of drinking. Thelma D slows and we hit the bridge platform entering a square tunnel created by steel girders and ribs, riveted and bolted, all painted a washed-out green. My focus narrows to a point on the far shore, where the asphalt and sand come together beyond the opening of the bridge. The rapids of the river mix with Thelma D's exhaust, creating a confused melody, each trying to outdo the other. I sense the white water below me, churning up the earthy scents of moss and wet leaves from the sides of the riverbanks. Her tires are humming with a high-pitched whine and Thelma D starts to vibrate and wind sideways. I steer her back gently, letting her take her own path. She goes sideways again and its then I realize that the grates don't line up with each other and every time we hit a new section her front wheel is pulled to one side or the other. From the back we must look like we're shaking a little tail. I ease off the bars and she doesn't pull as much with the next grate.

Confident now, I let her run, but three-quarters through I over-steer coming back in line and Thelma D starts to head to the right. I tighten my grip and clench my legs into her sides. Still heading right. *No, no, no.* I let my shoulders drop, tell myself to release my legs and to start breathing. The ribs and girders seem to close in on me, tightening and suffocating. I make myself loosen each one of my fingers and re-focus on the earlier point I had picked out beyond the tunnel. *Just let go, stay loose, don't look down.* Thelma D wanders a bit more but keeps her track tentatively. *Almost there.* The pitch of the whine lowers as Thelma D's tires make contact with the asphalt and the sound of her exhaust becomes throaty and deep without the empty space and white water beneath her. *Yeah, yeah, made it.* Slumping with relief, I rub the side of Thelma D's tank, and whisper, "Thank you."

Des Swisha is a five-mile long, island portal for hardcore outdoor enthusiasts. The paved road ends and nature begins. You can fly out by bush plane to hunt and fish camps in Northwestern Quebec. People can also access hundreds of acres of wilderness by bush roads, including a controlled harvest area, where they can fish innumerable lakes and rivers for lake trout, walleye, and northern pike. You can also hunt moose, bear, or wolf and you can canoe-camp along several routes and rivers.

I don't hunt or fish and the only hardcore activity I practiced in Swisha was partying. I was fifteen years old when I started drinking here. I always drank beer and used to order Export figuring that my nervousness wouldn't show if I only had to say one letter to the waitress, I'll have an "X" please. Often a wave and a cross of two fingers was all that was needed. I certainly wasn't the only one. It was common practice for packs of teenagers to come to the small town after a night of drinking in Ontario. It didn't matter whether you were at the Staff Hotel in Deep River, the Chalk or the Byeways, you could always find a ride with someone who wanted to continue to party at Swisha, where the bars were open until three a.m. If you weren't totally sloshed by then and wanted more, you could get beer to go in brown paper bags, subtly served out of the side entrance. Since a serious drinker at the time couldn't buy booze on a Sunday in Ontario, we also used to drive out on the holy day, to buy either large or small boxes of beer, depending upon how much cash we could scrape together.

I pull into the parking lot across from the Second Hotel. Another one of my driving dilemmas, a gravel lot filled with holes, sand, and large stones. The dumping of my first bike I blame on gravel. I was touring home at night on my Kawasaki after leaving a small shop south of Ottawa where I worked part-time, sanding and prepping cars for cash while I was taking a machine shop course at St. Lawrence College in Brockville.

It was dark. I went into the wide curve not knowing that gravel had been thrown up on the road by cars cornering into the shoulder. I couldn't slow down or straighten my line in time to not end up in the opposite ditch, and had no choice but to try and run through the stones. Within seconds the bike went down. I let go. Metal was shrieking and a display of sparks marked its travel towards the ditch. I slid down the road following my machine, scraping my left thigh and hip through my jeans. The shoulder of my jacket ripped open and my helmet thudded and thumped on the pavement before I stopped.

When I picked up my bike, I realized most of the sparks came from having a half-inch of metal shaved off the centre stand. The front signal light was gone, the shifter was bent past the engine case, and the handlebars were twisted. I was able to kick the shifter down, start the bike and drive back to the shop where I worked. Using torches I heated up and straightened out the shifter. I used some wrenches to re-align the handlebars with the forks and then jumped back on and drove the fifty minutes home. I proudly showed off my battered helmet and torn jacket as evidence of my road rash to my teammates at the ball field the next day.

I'm able to maneuver Thelma D around the holes and large stones and turn carefully to face the road. No one I ever hung with knew the true names of the hotels in Swisha. We always called them the First Hotel and the Second Hotel. The First was usually patronized by old men, barely hanging on to their teeth, who enjoyed leering at the continuous loops of bottom shelf strippers, working women who needed the cash, but were worn out, tired or too old for the uptown circuit. My friend Liz and I would go there sometimes when we were low on cash, because we could always get the old guys to buy us quarts of beer if we sat at their table, listened to their stories, and endured the occasional squeeze and grope.

The Second Hotel was the most popular with the younger crowd of drinkers. There was mostly country music in the jukebox, interrupted at times by the Eagles, Stones, and Fleetwood Mac. Occasionally there was a live band that featured musicians whose dreams of making it big were more faded than their jeans. Two pool tables filled the raised section in the back where players could look out onto the dance floor. It was also the bigger of the two hotels, a raised two-storey building fronted by large concrete steps with metal pole railings running up both sides.

It is still white with white trim, the paint peeling in large sections. Some of the shingles have lifted and a few of the windows are broken. The signs are gone and it's obvious the tired structure is no longer taking customers. The side where John and his friends would smoke up is overgrown with scrub and tall grasses. Weeds are growing out of cracks in the parking lot, and even though there are a couple of later model cars parked to one side of the front steps, the building has a vacant unkempt look about it.

Thelma D idles in neutral and I sit there for a few moments, a medley of intoxicated nights of fun and loss running through my head. I was a loud, boisterous, and mostly drunk teenage girl when I spent time here. It was a period that was all about drinking and partying, so why am I feeling sad, like I lost something? Was my life simpler then? It seemed so. Would it stay simple? No. I put Thelma D in first gear and turn her back toward Highway 17.

10.

IN NORTH BAY, I TURN RIGHT onto Highway 11. It will be my first time on this road, either by car or by bike. I've decided to take the northernmost highways on my way up and then return on the southern routes closest to the great lakes. Like most of the riders I know, I never want to take the same road leaving and returning. There is one exception to my plan, and it's between Nipigon and Thunder Bay, where Highways 11 and 17 merge to become one route.

A large lighted overhead sign comes into view. It spans the double width of the highway, and warns of the dangers when driving the northern route. The sign advises drivers to reduce fatigue by resting properly, and to stay alert for hazards. Within seconds I see another sign, this one warning of moose as a night danger. In Eastern Ontario, deer are a constant threat to motorists and riders. I've hit one, my partner has hit two, and I've barely missed several while driving on four wheels. I now consider them to be big field rats. The attitude of urban dwellers gushing, *omigosh, look at the beautiful deer*, disappears pretty quickly when you're a rural driver. I don't want to envision hitting a deer with a bike, much less hitting an animal the size of a moose. It would be like hitting the side of a house. For a couple of seconds, I imagine being in an action movie, and faced with an unavoidable collision with an ungulate: I lay the bike down, twist it at ninety degrees and slide neatly between its quad leg towers, avoiding death and rise amid a shower of sparks and smoke, limping but alive. Keep dreaming I tell myself. Actually, the signs tell me I shouldn't daydream at all on this road.

It has taken me about four and half hours, with stops for gas to travel the 360 kilometres to North Bay. The city has its roots as a railway town with the establishment of the Canadian Pacific Railway in 1882. North Bay is also known as the Gateway of the North, a population of 54,000 that lies on the northern shore of Lake Nipissing. I have passed through the city innumerable times on my way to Sudbury following Highway 17 northwest along the lake. Nipissing won't be visible today because I'm headed into the vast bush region of Northern Ontario. North Bay is the last metropolis with full amenities until the traveller gets to Thunder Bay, 1100 long kilometres through mostly forest loaded with deer, bear, moose, and tired unsafe drivers according to the big warning sign. I plan to be off the road by dark. A move heavily encouraged by all the riders I had talked with before leaving Ottawa.

Ascending Hwy 11 out of North Bay, I'm reminded of my long descent forty-five minutes earlier into Mattawa. The small town marks the end of the Ottawa Valley and it was then I realized, shifting Thelma D down a gear, that somewhere in the last hour or so of riding, I had lost the deciduous maple and oak trees of the south. They had been replaced by the sporadic stand of birch and balsam enveloped by the spruce and pine and fir of the boreal shield. It's beautiful country.

In the 1800s, all of the timber harvested in Northern Ontario and Quebec had to pass through Mattawa on the vast water highway to Montreal and beyond. It was common for men who lived in the Ottawa Valley to spend their winters in the bush, as loggers supplying the trees for the spring timber run on the river.

Now timber and pulp are delivered to the mills using logging trucks and rail cars. The small communities along the Ottawa River that sprang up as sawmills and shanties for the spring run of timber are now only signs marking the highway between Deep River and Mattawa. Stonecliffe is the most prosperous of the settlements with a gas station, bus stop, and agency liquor store. You'll find less than that in Deux Rivieres, Bissett Creek, and Mackey. Walmart had nothing to do with their demise.

Stonecliffe is also where Bev crashed her snow machine. She and Eric had spent a little too much time at the hotel during a club run, and when they left she was going too fast and hit a snow bank. Bev's story was that she went airborne and crashed down the other side of the bank hard on top of her machine. They managed to ride back to Deep River, but the next day the lower half of her face was black and blue, and her chin was swollen to twice its normal size. I wouldn't have believed her if I hadn't seen the cracked windshield of her Skidoo.

On the ride through Mattawa, I recognized another landmark of my early drinking days, the Gaylord Hotel. I shake my head and grip the Thelma D's handles a little tighter when I realize that I've drunk my way through the Ottawa Valley. It's pretty pathetic marking your passage by the holes you've fallen out of.

I slip into old familiar behaviour and start feeling sorry for myself. Why couldn't my memories be different? Why was it me and not someone else, like her ... or her? My recollections should be of normal family fun activities, like picnics in the park. Mom setting out food on a checkered table cloth, ice cold Kool Aid in a glass pitcher, Dad chasing the four of us playing tag, all of us screaming and laughing loudly as we all tumble into a big pile of arms and legs. Then, we all go out for ice cream after dinner. *Stop.*

I know why I acted the way I did when I was a kid, and as that drunk and boisterous teenager. It was because all I wanted to do was to pretend that my life was different than it really was. All I wanted to do was to believe that nothing ever happened, and alcohol helped with my denial.

My wishes for those times may change, but my memories won't and every time I pass the hotels and bars I've partied in, I'll still remember the smoking and drinking chaos. My teenage behaviour, however insane and unsafe it was when I drive by it now, helped me cope and survive a bad time in my life. I'm glad I didn't know then just how long it would last.

A horn blast and an answering screech of tires from somewhere behind me brings my mind back to the ascent of three lanes of blacktop. One lane is devoted for trucks that are having difficulty with the grade and I pass two tractors with their flashers blinking caution. I chide myself when I realize how far away I was. I sit up straight, take some quick, hard in and out breaths, and tell myself to stay in the moment. Listen to the sign: stay alert, stay alive. I accelerate and shift Thelma D up a gear and top the small mountain that leads the way out of the city.

11.

AN HOUR AFTER LEAVING NORTH BAY, I stop for gas at the PetroCan station in Temagami. The warmth of the sun hasn't yet abandoned me or the throng of visitors that have made the same stop. The station has a Subway restaurant and after filling up I park Thelma D by the exit and go in for a sandwich. I order water and a six-inch grilled chicken sub with whole wheat bread. The joy of being middle-aged. When I was in my twenties, working hard and playing hockey, the sub would've been twelve inches long, on white bread with double cheese and meat, a bag of chips on the side, and a couple of cookies for dessert. I try to fool myself and pretend the water is a white chocolate and macadamia cookie. It's not working.

Now that I am sitting, I'm glad I stopped for gas and a late lunch. The protein energy bar I had in Mattawa helped, but I'm hungry and need the rest. It's my hope that the short respite, food and refreshment will give me a few more hours of riding. I'm grateful again that I made the decision to fit the sheepskin on my seat. Lenny's pillow doesn't even begin to compare to it. The skin allows my butt to breathe, and with the heat of the day it has reduced the sweaty-ass factor. I don't think I'd be all that eager to ride for much longer if I didn't have it. With that admission, I promise not to make fun of all those old guys out there riding on sheepskins because I assumed they couldn't hack it. The water is nice and cold and I take the last bite of my sandwich leaving the shop smiling about cookies and ass.

Smiling is good. This morning I was anxious and nervous about not being able to predict or write the outcome of this trip. With

45

a few hours of riding, my confidence is high and my outlook has changed to *let's just ride north and see where I end up*. No hurries, no worries. It's similar to the times I used to hitchhike for rides. You couldn't be in a hurry and if you worried about getting picked up by a psycho, it would be better if you borrowed money or panhandled until you had enough coin to take the bus.

I am greeted by two couples looking at several machines parked by the exit when I reach Thelma D. A big man and a small man, accompanied by two very similar women wearing high-waisted mom jeans and boasting the big hair of the '80s. They are my age and I have an urge to run back inside to the washroom and look in the mirror. Tell me it's not so. I run my hands through my short hair and tug up the back of my Carhartt work pants.

The big man is wearing an Orange County Chopper T-shirt and the smaller man is dressed in a tank top with jeans and cowboy boots. The big man nods using his nose and tells me I'm packed for a long trip, before the small man asks me where I'm headed.

"Thunder Bay," I reply.

"Really?" questions the woman to the left of the big man. Her tone implies that she may not believe me. Why would she think that?

"Well, I hope so."

"That's ... great," contributes the other woman. The hesitation she uses between those two words tells me that she's wondering why I would want to do that.

"Nice bike," nods the small man.

"Thanks, it's a pretty good ride. I like it."

"Is that your parts bus there?" asks the big man nodding towards a burgundy tour bus that has just pulled up across the highway.

It takes me a moment to get it and then I protest, "Hey, Harleys are a little more dependable now."

He laughs and turns to the smaller man, nodding, "Got her."

I match their smiles with one of my own, and tell them, "I used to always drive Kawasakis and Hondas before. This is my first Harley." That seems to buy me a little respect as they stand there with their hands in their pockets, nodding their heads. Why do they keep nodding? What's with that? It comes to me then. I've seen their type before, in the parking lots of the local coffee shop. Packs of riders in bandanas, leathers and chaps, standing around, hands in their pockets, some smoking, all nodding their heads acknowledging each others stories, victories, and defeats. They ride to the coffee shop to talk about riding and often the ride is shorter than the socializing. They are Nodders.

"We both ride Gold Wings." The big man gestures to the small man and tells me they'd be out themselves, but the little man's ride is in the shop. I suppress the urge to nod and give their banter back to them. I want to get going before my body stiffens up and I lose my motivation, so I grimace in sympathy to the small man and unpack my camera. That seems to do it. The couples leave with chimes of, "Safe riding," and a note of caution by the big man. "Make sure to get off the road before dark, eh, guaranteed to hit a moose if you're not." He wasn't nodding, he was pointing.

Temagami is a postcard of the wilderness of Northern Ontario. Everywhere I look there is a picture worth taking. I turn a slow circle and am greeted with a panoramic blend of water, trees, and stone. Deep blue-black waters are outlined with walls of old growth, robust pines, and spruce. Powerful-looking mounds of smooth rock bust out of the water landscape, monoliths coloured with hues of red and pink and shades of grey, charcoal to slate. At this moment, if I were to show a stranger a picture of what my Canada looks like, it would be this snapshot.

12.

THE BOGS, MARSHES, JACK PINES, and moose country disappear behind Thelma D and I as we run Highway 11 into the New Liskeard area. The change to the level landscape is startling and I feel like I'm driving through Southern Ontario, with its large flat fields and monster farms. I'm met by a massive John Deer dealership and wonder if somehow I entered a travel portal, where all travellers with a Grade 12 and some cash are shipped to the Toronto area.

The dealer lot is filled with a herd of tractors. A straight row of bright green super cabs sporting curved tinted windows. I'm sure they all have AM/FM stereos and air conditioning. The cabs are sitting on chassis trimmed in yellow and tricked out with huge rear wheels, tires glossy with the shine of rubber dressing. The machines, lined up neatly from large to super large, are decadent and show off a wealth that is in contrast to some of the earlier communities I rode through on Highway 11.

As with most rural areas I've driven through, there are some rough shacks with lots of junk, dismantled vehicles, and garbage littering overgrown yards. But there are others that gave the impression the residents had battled and beat back the bush to carve out small lots for their families, claiming what little they could from an unyielding Mother Nature. On those scrubbed pieces of land, the house or trailer is clean, level and solid, and while the older structures, though diminished by time and the elements, still radiate a faded dignity. The surrounding yards and vehicles are trimmed and detailed, a no-budget landscaping that brackets older trucks and cars scrubbed and washed so many times, their hazy finishes no longer keep a shine. The impression is poverty walking in hand with pride, showing more determination than money. So unlike the rows of shiny green cabs that suddenly sprout up in this faux farm country of the north I've driven into.

New Liskeard and its surrounding communities were founded on logging and mining, but their contemporary economy and commerce are driven by agriculture. By my first look and a measure of their tractors, a successful one. The town of 6000 mostly English residents is located on the waters of Lake Temiskaming. The lake shares its shores between Northwestern Quebec and Northeastern Ontario and it marks the start of the mighty Ottawa River.

The lake was part of the early trade route. I try and picture the days, weeks, and months it would take for the voyageurs to travel the lake, down the Ottawa River to the St. Lawrence and then along the seaway to Montreal and Quebec City. They'd have to carry all of their supplies, including extra goods for trading going north, and then make the return trip south laden with bounties, like furs and Native artifacts. The voyageurs would need to portage and paddle, distance achieved using only the skill and energy generated by their physical efforts. I'm taking a guess and figure Thelma D and I have travelled in a day what might have taken them a couple of weeks to do. It had to have been body-breaking work that required strength, courage, and stamina.

People adapt to their world and the environment, but I'm not sure I would have survived one of those journeys. Although as a woman, I don't think I would have been invited. An invitation to stop for the day would be welcome because I'm feeling the fatigue of travelling the greater part of the day. I resist the desire to look for a hotel room because I want to make more miles before calling it quits for the day. Besides, running through the New Liskeard area is a nice break from the tension of riding in the bush. I'm hoping I'll gain some energy by being able to relax, while crossing the flat wide stretches. I put my feet up on Thelma D's highway pegs, stretch my legs, and lean back pulling my arms straight. The vibration of the V-twin, combined with Thelma D's bulk, sooths and acts like a hammock holding me while I unwind. Contrary to wooded areas, the open fields provide a welcome visibility, limiting my worry about moose or other wildlife bolting from the curtains of trees that mark the cut of the alley beside the highway.

Near Matheson I pass another large barn and see my first cow since Renfrew. Now that's a toss-up, hitting a cow or a moose, both ungulates, similar weight I'd guess. In my action movie scenario, I don't think Thelma D would fit under a cow. Besides it wouldn't be as glamorous or as exotic as sliding under a moose. The coin flip is taken from me when I see a night danger, beware of moose sign. My rest time is over. I straighten up and pull my boots back to her mid-controls. The bogs, marshes, and jack pines return as quickly as they had disappeared, channelling me towards Cochrane.

13.

A<small>N ENERGETIC YOUNG WOMAN</small>, who seems to be the waitress, bartender, and night manager of the small Cochrane restaurant I landed in, brings me my half-chicken dinner. It came with choice of potato and a side of coleslaw. I chose the baked potato instead of the fries and avoid the sour cream and pats of butter that line the plate. Avoidance is made easier by telling myself I'll have a treat meal soon and I fantasize for a moment about a large, all dressed, double-cheese pizza, the hot and sloppy kind, requiring lots of napkins.

At the table opposite me a young couple leave behind a couple of inches of beer in a cloudy plastic pitcher, and a stack of cleaned wing bones. Must not be true drinkers. A woman with short brown hair in large curls, carrying a heavy-looking shiny purse over a narrow shoulder, comes to the counter for takeout. An older woman, she reminds me of the manager of the Thriftlodge in town.

***

"Sorry, we're full. I don't have a single room available."

"Tell me you're kidding."

"No, I've been full all summer because of the road construction."

***

During my planning, I never thought about road construction and how it might affect my ride. There has been a lot of construction. How many people travel here anyway? It must be the infrastructure, recession-relief dollars at work, the dollars the government brags about on the news every second day. In its television plugs, the smiling, confident faces never fail to mention the infusion of badly needed cash across the country, creating jobs for ordinary Canadians. I'm sure the money the workers spend in the area, and the motel rooms scooped up by construction companies are more than appreciated. No question, but what happens when the roads become pristine?

I pull my bird to pieces and taste the coleslaw. It has too much oil in it. I add a little salt and take another forkful. Better.

Getting to Cochrane meant Thelma D and I driving 750 kilometres, chased by the heat, the humidity, and the occasional tailgater. I was exhausted when I finally pulled into the Thriftlodge. I didn't think I could drive another hour to the next town for a room. I was seriously thinking about finding a hardware store to buy a tent when the manager suggested I try the Westway.

I got confused when she told me, "It's right there on the right, when you turn left up there, back on to the highway, around the corner." Beat tired, I didn't ask her to clarify. How big could Cochrane be anyway?

The Westway came up on my right as promised after a couple of turns and I parked on the interlock in front of the office, but I was not encouraged. It was late, past quitting time for the road crews, and there were several clusters of people along the concrete walkway fronting the motel rooms. There were mostly men, a sprinkling of women, all sitting in lawn chairs, drinking beer, smoking and playing cards on overturned coolers and small bedside tables they'd pulled from their rooms. Competing music was blaring from a couple of open doors and windows. It looked busy. It looked full.

The counter man told me that their very last room is available. The unit I'm getting is more expensive than the others because it sleeps six and comes with its own kitchenette. I didn't really hear the complete list of amenities after he told me a room was available with a swipe of my credit card.

When I rode Thelma D across the lot to the room, a dark-haired woman catches my eye and I think of Bev and how this scene would be just her thing. She'd be outside for the larger audience, drinking, flirting, and laughing loudly with a beer in hand and a cigarette in her mouth.

I come back to my plate. The chicken isn't all that bad, just a little dry. I congratulate myself on not eating the crispy parts of the skin. The coleslaw doesn't work for me and the baked potato sucks without butter, sour cream, and lots of salt.

14.

WEARINESS IS MAKING MY HAND SHAKE, but I'm able to hold the needle level and upright. I tap the side of the syringe sharply with my finger to release the air bubbles captured in the barrel. The pockets float to the top of the liquid and I press the plunger to force them through the needle. There doesn't appear to be any more air captured in the solution, but I tap it again a couple of times to make sure. The clear mixture clouds a little, swirls clear, it's ready.

I load the self-injector and wipe an area the size of a small coaster on the side of my stomach with an alcohol swab. The injector collapses when I force it into my side. I push the trigger. A snap sounds and an arrow shoots down through the viewing window, coming to a stop within a few seconds. There's a bite of pain. I clench my teeth and groan. I clean the pinhead size of blood off my stomach with the same swab. Wrapping up all the packaging, I unscrew the needle, cap it with its protective cover, and put it in my injection case for safekeeping.

The injections I do now, every second day, are bearable when compared to my early days of taking the drug. When I was first prescribed the interferon, I had to do deep muscle injections into the top of my thighs once a week. The needle was an inch and a quarter long and I'd plunge it into my leg, pull it back to make sure I wasn't in a vein, and then empty the syringe. I was good at first, no problems, but then it got more and more difficult. Some days I'd just sit there holding it for an hour, poised above my leg, trying to get up the nerve to plunge it in. Friday became a day I started to dread. The most painful times were when I went through a vein and when I pulled the needle out, the puncture would bleed heavily. It finally got to the point where I couldn't work up the courage to hurt myself anymore, regardless of the benefits of the medicine.

From my pack I shake out a concoction of Tylenol and Ibuprofen. The painkillers will help with any lingering side effects of the shot. The flu-like symptoms have mostly diminished, but after taking an inventory of my body, I need some help erasing the aches and pains of riding. My right knee is throbbing and there doesn't seem to be a part of me that isn't sore or stiff. One part hard life and one part Multiple Sclerosis.

Sometimes I can't avoid telling people that I have MS, and at times I want others to know because it will help explain my withdrawal and lack of energy. Most people have the same reaction when I tell them. Some hug me, but most are not sure what to say, so they don't say anything. That's okay with me, because I've been in the same position and will probably be again, you know, the not knowing what to say when a friend tells you they have a life-changing disease. Somehow saying, *that's too bad*, when someone tells you they have breast cancer or leukemia, doesn't seem to honour the sharing or the trust they've given you by telling.

The tingling and numbness started in the bottom of my feet on a Tuesday in late August of 2003. I was working at Carleton University for a friend of mine rebuilding laboratory furniture from reclaimed tables and desks. She was doing me a favour, helping me make the jump between finishing my teachers program and school starting in September with some much needed cash. Earlier that spring, I had just graduated from the Faculty of Education at Queen's University. I was forty-three years old.

A week before the tingling started in my feet, weird stuff started to happen to my body. My butt crack would go intermittently numb and what felt like a hot rash would invade my groin area. I'd go to the washroom, drop my pants and boxers, pull back my stomach and look at where my legs joined my torso. Expecting to see a red rash, there was nothing. Being a little too chubby at the time and not that tall, I couldn't really get a good look at my ass in the mirror to see if anything was wrong with it, so I gave up trying. Then it would all go away. I thought I was going crazy.

One afternoon, when the numbness in my butt returned, I thought I had it all figured out. Somehow my boxers keep getting twisted under my work pants, and they had wiggled up into the crack of my ass so I'd been giving myself a wedgie. I gave up going to the washroom to check because I wasn't getting any answers. Instead, I would walk through the job site with my right hand down the back of my pants, hitching up one leg and then the other, while pulling down on my underwear. Because I was working in an area that saw only construction workers, no one seemed offended or surprised by my behaviour and, if they were, they didn't say anything.

By Friday, the tingling and numbness had reached almost to my knees. The doctor at the university clinic didn't really know what to say to me. I didn't blame him. Reflecting on our conversation, I think it was my telling him that it felt like someone had stuffed a pair of socks between my butt cheeks that had prevented a quick diagnosis. What he did suggest was that if it got worse I should go to the hospital. By Saturday it was. I was numb from the hips down and had a hard time walking. Actually I was shuffling. I couldn't drive and lost my balance if I closed my eyes because I didn't know where the lower half of my body was.

My predicament didn't get me out of helping with the groceries though. "You can use the cart like you would a walker," said Paula. "No trying to get out of it. Now let's go, I'll drive."

On Saturday of the Labour Day long weekend I went to the Civic Campus of the Ottawa Hospital, and within five hours I had been seen by three doctors, a neurologist, had X-rays, and an MRI. It was impressive. Since there was no need to call in a neurosurgeon, I was sent home by a sympathetic nurse who told me I had an appointment with a neurologist on Tuesday, and if my symptoms got worse, I should come back to the hospital.

I was confused. For two and half days, I thought I was losing my mind. Why would the hospital release me if there was something wrong with me? My thinking was, since they sent me home there was nothing they could fix, so therefore there was nothing wrong with me. If there's nothing wrong with me, why can't I walk? A friend of my neighbour, visiting the lake for the weekend, suggested that anxiety could cause a lot of strange things to happen to the body. He said that I might be stressed because I didn't have a job lined up for the coming school year and this was my body's way of coping. Great, I thought, I'm a fucking whacko. Try selling that to the people in charge when applying for benefits.

I practice my opening line. "Well, you see I'm a little stressed and now my legs don't work."

"Who isn't, honey. Get in line."

On Tuesday, I saw the neurologist, Dr. Clark, who was runway model thin, wearing a pencil skirt and high heel stilettos that clicked on the floor when she invited me into her office. Only slightly younger than her, I refrained from apologizing for my weight, slovenly appearance, and my inability to walk properly.

I was relieved when she told me that they had found something. I wasn't joyful at the time, but I was happy to hear that I wasn't crazy. The MRI showed bright spots on my spinal cord and that was the cause of my numbness and tingling. I don't think she could choke out that it was the cause of my wedgie. She'd pretty much had the same reaction as the doctor at the university when I tried to describe the feeling to her. A blank and controlled stare.

Arrangements were made for another MRI the following day. The hospital had only taken images of my spine and to make a firm diagnosis an MRI was needed of my back, neck, and head. Dr. Clark told me that my difficulties could be caused by either a virus, or Multiple Sclerosis (MS), or Amyotrophic Lateral Sclerosis (ALS), also known as Lou Gehrig's Disease. I started to think crazy wasn't all that bad. Regardless, I would know by Friday. It was a tough couple of days, but shuffling around getting groceries, tipping over in the shower when I closed my eyes, and spending time with Paula got me through.

On Friday, by my appointment time, the results of the MRI hadn't yet been received. I had to wait. Dr. Clark said she would phone as soon as she got them. Paula's small basement apartment in the city was my waiting room. If I wasn't chain smoking on the back patio, I was sitting on the couch listening to some white noise on the television, looking at the phone. Willing it to ring, wanting it to be quiet. It finally rang.

"The MRI showed lesions on your brain," Dr. Clark stated. "You have Multiple Sclerosis." She started talking about sites of disease activity with two confirmed areas and something or other. I wasn't listening. I was processing the fact that I have an incurable disease. I need to call Paula, I thought. I need to call Craig. I need to get Dr. Clark off the phone.

Then I realize that I'm not going to die within five years from ALS, so while having a virus would be preferable in some cases, I'm okay with having MS.

Dr. Clark finishes by telling me, "I'm ninety percent certain that you'll recover ninety percent of your function."

15.

THE EARLY MORNING BRINGS A DIM GLOOM. A murkiness that washes the chrome and colour out of the vehicles parked in the motel lot, making them appear listless and tired, in contrast to the wet black of the new asphalt they sit on. It's raining. Not a heavy rain, but an insistent drizzle that promises to last.

The wet start of the day also brings a cold with a dampness that penetrates my jacket as I walk across the parking lot beside the motel to the Tim Hortons for coffee. My legs feel good and I'm refreshed from the near coma I was in for most of the night after my injection and concoction.

I'm a little confused that Cochrane has chosen a polar bear as their mascot, rather than give the status to hockey player and coffee shop entrepreneur Tim Horton who was born in the town. From what I understand, given my conversation with the waitress, bartender, and night manager from yesterday, polar bears did come south to town for a visit and to commemorate that once in a lifetime event — there are real polar bears at the Polar Bear Conservatory. There is also a large statue of a polar bear and pictures of the bears everywhere in town, including one on the town's water tower.

That seems to be a lot of representation of a bear that's not even native to the area, unlike Horton, who played for twenty-four years in the National Hockey League, which is practically a Canadian religion. And, after his hockey career, he went on to co-found what has become the most popular and prolific coffee shop in Canada, the iconic Timmy's. I must be missing something.

Obviously I am, but right now I'm only interested in getting some caffeine so I can focus on the start of my day. After a coffee and bagel, I finish packing my gear and get my rain suit on. My protection from the rain is two pieces of polyester, black bib coveralls and a jacket with silver reflective piping. The suit is meant more for the construction site than riding, but I've used it before and had good results.

The rain is steady and what light there was earlier seems even drearier when Thelma D and I turn north on Highway 11. I ride the paint and think if I'm able to put in the same mileage as I did yesterday then getting to Thunder Bay today is possible. I'm pretty proud of my first day of riding. No nodding here. When planning the trip, I thought that North Bay or Temagami was a reasonable and realistic destination for my first day. I was quite happy at the time with the thought of taking three days to get to the big city on the northwest shore of Lake Superior.

It doesn't surprise me that I got to Cochrane in one day because part of my personality is to completely focus on the goal in front of me, ignoring other stuff in my life, like rest, food, and managing the small but necessary daily details. It's hard for me to find a balance. If I'm gathering firewood, I do that until the shed is full. If I'm fixing a car, then I don't stop until the car is running. I could give a hundred examples of my obsessive behaviour, but essentially it's difficult for me to multi-task at anything when I'm intent on completing a project. It can be debilitating because I'll work at something until I can't stand anymore and, like yesterday, I can push myself too far, cheering myself on to make it to just one more town, and then one more, and then crash and burn. It'd be nice to find some balance on this trip, but I need to get through the rain first.

Standing in the rain, and driving in it on a motorcycle, are two completely different experiences, and within minutes of starting out I'm cold. I'm only wearing a T-shirt underneath my rain coat and the chill has worked its way through, making the inside liner feel damp and wet on my bare arms. Because it was so warm yesterday, I didn't think it'd be that cold today, even with the rain, so I didn't bother to put on my leather jacket. I drive for another ten minutes and then realize it's stupid to be so stubborn. Maybe I've found some balance already when I decide that shivering and fighting through the cold will only make me tired and miserable.

I slow down and pick out a gravel lane on the right side that has a wide-mouthed asphalt entrance to the highway and signal a turn. The sloped wet gravel further in the narrow lane is intimidating, so I make a shallow turn on the asphalt. Because of that decision, I am more parallel to the highway than I'd like to be and the slope makes it impossible for me to get Thelma D's jiffy stand down on the grade. I stay in the saddle and try to pull Thelma D back down the lane, but because of the grade I can only push hard with my left leg, and my boot slips on the wet grit of the asphalt making me wobble. Fully loaded, she's heavy and I can't get her going backward even after straightening her front wheel. I think about getting off of her, but I'd have to push her back with one hand, while pulling, turning, and braking with the other. It's a maneuver I've done with my other machines, on nice gradual slopes, in great weather and in my prime. I'm sure I could work up the strength to pull her back, but there's not much asphalt to work with and what there is, is wet and slippery and covered with grit. Not ideal.

I try and seat her jiffy stand again, but I'm afraid to pull Thelma D past the point of, you know it's going down and there's nothing you can do about it. I'm reminded of an old timer whose expression was, it's not *if* you drop your bike, it's a matter of *when*. I tighten my grip, ready my legs, and dare a little more slant to my right. My heart starts thudding when I shift Thelma D just a little further. A couple of extra degrees and I'm shaking, but she stays upright. The stand starts to bite on the grit and I kick it forward with the heel of my boot a couple of times, hard. White scrapes mark the pavement when the stand is fully seated.

Relieved I drop into the seat and let her fall into the lean. The jiffy stand on Thelma D is unlike any of the ones I've used before. I'm still not used to it. All of my metric machines had side stands that sprung forward and locked into place with a satisfying clunk. That movement and sound has always been my signal to let the bike fall on the stand, safe. It also seems to me that those stands could be set almost anywhere because they are short and sturdy, and don't require a lot of room to work.

In contrast, Harley jiffy stands are stretched out, long pieces of bar flattened at the end with a welded metal loop that you catch with your boot when you need to use it. The stand is somewhat spring-loaded but does not lock into place with any satisfying click, snap, or clunk. I've gotten into the practice of holding it tightly in place with my boot to keep it seated completely forward before letting Thelma D fall. She's heavy and it's a freaky feeling letting her go and just when I think that's it, she drops a little further because of the flex in the long bar. I guess it's all part of the Harley image, low slung and lean, and once the bikes are properly on their stand, they won't fall. The salesman demonstrated that to me by dragging a bike on its jiffy stand backwards across the concrete floor of the shop of the dealership. I was impressed at the time, but I didn't know yet about the anxiety it would cause me getting to the point of being able to drag Thelma D's ass anywhere. The only feeling I can relate it to is the team-building exercise where you let yourself fall backwards into the arms of your teammates.

Besides my dislike for her jiffy stand, what about that name? I mean who names anything that's Harley related, "jiffy?" It sounds too vanilla, too eager, like Jiffy Park, Jiffy Lube, Go Jiffy. Well, I can whine and complain all I want but it wouldn't have been a problem if I had been more confident in turning her through a sharp circle on wet gravel. Being miserable is not fair to Thelma D, but I see the jiffy stand as a project. It's a separate being from her, an object I need to conquer and master. What I really worry about is that I should've become confident and competent with it by now, especially after having driven her for a half season. This time, having the excuse to kick it into place, makes me feel better, more superior. It's brief satisfaction because I still have to pull Thelma D up over centre to get the stand back in place, and no manner of kicking will help me with that.

The rain starts to pelt my helmet as I pull my leather jacket out of my saddlebag. My T-shirt gets a little wet switching up my gear. I pull on my rain gear and start the fastening process. "Maybe I should have stayed with the polar bears and had a second coffee at Timmy's." I imagine Thelma D agreeing with me.

"Fuck, I hate that jiffy stand." No response.

After all the zippers, snaps, and Velcro are fastened, I'm ready to try the road again.

16.

THE DOWNPOUR IS STEADY AND STRONG, blurring the landscape. It's like looking through a window during a violent storm, making the road ghostly and evasive. The yellow signs showing curves and intersections are helpful, but seem to come too late for my confidence. I'm riding like a wary dog that has been kicked too many times, hesitant and insecure, hoping the next turn won't boot me off the road and into a rock cut. I try to concentrate, intensely, but trees blend into rocks, rocks melt into ditches, and the ditches dissolve into roadside gravel. When a gust of wind batters pellets of rain into Thelma D's windshield and my face, there seems to be no skyline or horizon, just a mass of shades of gray filling the lenses of my yellow-tinted rain goggles. I'm riding the paint and trusting Thelma D to stay the line I give her, but I'm struggling to keep her path true to the road. The speed limit is safe with me this morning.

We are almost to Kapuskasing and the rain has endured since I left Cochrane. I don't know how much longer I can ride in these conditions. It's one thing to be cold and miserable, but to be blind, cold, and miserable is another. I've never been just a fair weather rider out enjoying the warm sunny days and then parking my machine safe inside its shelter at any chance of rain. I have ridden in storms before, but riding has never been this bad. Why am I struggling and fighting for every kilometre? What's wrong?

A line of bright yellow appears as a trickle in the left lens of my goggles. What the hell is that? The streak continues, becoming a slice of distinct and sharply focused trees, rocks, and pavement.

I'm stunned because I realize the strip of vision is a stream of rain that has been driven down the inside of my goggles. I've never worn goggles before, and they have fogged up, adding a layer of moisture to my already limited vision. I didn't realize the extent of the hazing until that line of water lit up the road in high-definition yellow monochrome.

I can't believe it. What a fucking loser.

First, I don't dress properly for the rain.

I'm an amateur.

Second, I can't turn Thelma D into position for an easy landing.

Did I say how much I hate that fucking jiffy stand?

Third, I don't even know enough to recognize condensation on the inside of my goggles.

I'm pissed.

I put myself in a dangerous position, a stupid, correctable situation. What if I drove off the road or into another car or swerved when I didn't have to, wiping myself out and trashing Thelma D?

I'm an idiot. What am I doing here anyway? I should just turn around and go home.

A raging tightness starts to twist and bubble up in my chest and if my goggles weren't wrapped around my head under my helmet, I'd pull over, take them off, and slam them into the ground. Then I'd stomp the shit out of them until the lenses popped from the frame, hopefully broken, if not cracked, scratched, and unusable. After the imaginary stomping, my anger leaves as quickly as it came, but I'm left feeling worn out and totally unprepared.

The goggles pull easily from my face and there's enough room for me to wipe the inside of the lenses with my thumb. I'm amazed to see a bright yellow future ahead of Thelma D and the tightness in my chest eases. The backdrop is still a little blurry because I can't completely dry the inside of the lenses, but the clarity of the landscape is a beautiful sight. After a couple of minutes the goggles fog up again. By the time I get to Kapuskasing, I've had to repeatedly slow down and wipe the lenses. When I get through town, I look for a place to pull over. This time I choose a large parking lot encircling a small convenience store. Lots of room and I'm reminded of that truck driving country song: *"give me forty acres and I'll turn this rig around."*

My gloves are soaked and I have trouble pulling them off. Some of the inner lining comes out with my wet fingers. If I hadn't paid so much for what the clerk said were, "Guaranteed waterproof gloves with triple layer protection," I'd throw them down with the goggles when I get my helmet off.

My inner voices are in turmoil. *I can do this. No you can't. I'm a good person. You're no good. You're a loser. What were you thinking, going on a ride like this?* The positive mantras are slowly losing their space to the self-trashers.

"What a cluster fuck this is," I say out loud. I finally rip the gloves off and shove them under the bungee cord holding my small rear pack to Thelma D's luggage rack. Hopefully, they'll dry some time during the ride.

The waterproof cover of my large pack comes off easily and I pull out a pair of genuine Harley-Davidson photochromatic glasses, and a dry pair of gloves. The glasses darken their tint with the sun, but there's not much luck of that right now. Still they should be better than the goggles now sitting on Thelma D's seat. I'm tempted to toss them into the garbage can by the door to the convenience store, but really whose fault is it? Mine. They fit easily into the space vacated by the riding glasses and dry gloves.

I walk around Thelma D several times to ground myself. The large circles become smaller as I build up my confidence. I feel like a wrestler circling her opponent, getting ready to lock bodies and engage in battle. It seems to work.

I get back on the bike. We soon come to a single storey, metal-sided building. A sign tells me it's the General Motors Cold Weather Development Centre. A large snowflake graces the side of the building, reminding me the weather could be worse. It's comforting to see clearly now, but the glasses don't give me the distinct vision that the coloured goggles provided. Wearing yellow or orange lenses is like having a giant highlighter wipe across your field of sight, creating sharp edges, distinct features, and depth layers. It's what makes the lenses so appealing to riders and drivers driving at night or in the rain.

My inner fight has quieted down and I'm feeling calmer now that I can see. Maybe it's not time to turn around and go home. *I can do this. I know I can. I'm going to do this.* My improved vision increases my speed and I ride with the cautious glow of having overcome a problem.

The radiance sputters out after five minutes when my glasses start to fog up as well. *Fuck, fuck, fuck.* This can't be happening. What's the problem now? I wiggle the glasses on my face using my nose. The foam liner that circles the perimeter of the frame has sealed the glasses to my face, like a sloppy gasket on a fruit preserve jar. There are slots in the foam to assist the air in flowing behind the lens to keep them clear, but they are obviously not enough.

The lesson I learned today is that goggles and gasket-type glasses are okay for dry-skinned, cold-blooded riders who never break a sweat. Do mannequins ride?

I'm not likely to stop sweating and I have another pair of glasses to try, but I don't want to stop again. Instead, I shift the glasses down on my nose and this allows air to pass over the back of the lenses, defogging them. I ride, wrinkling my nose to alternate them in and out, shifting them up and down, fogging and defogging.

Unfortunately, this in and out action allows rain to peg my eyes. I have to blink constantly. This motion connects me to the times as a child when I'd be hurtling down Dump Hill on my flying saucer, squinting into sleet and ice pellets. The best times for me at the toboggan hill were the wild, crazy rides down the ice run trying to break through the fence that bordered the bottom of the hill. I managed to bump it a few times and contrary to my current trip, I didn't really need to see during those runs, just scream a lot, hold on, and hope. Then repeat, by running as fast as I could back up the hill, my saucer flinging wildly side to side, my legs and boots churning up chunks of snow behind me.

17.

CLOSE TO AN HOUR LATER, hope for a cleaner ride comes in the form of a break from the rain in Hearst. The sky is still gray with clouds, not quite full with moisture, but bleak enough to threaten future showers. Thelma D and I roll into a truck stop. The attendant tells me it's the last gas station on Highway 11 for 200 kilometres. The parking area for the trucks is bigger than some outdoor rinks I've skated on, so I'm guessing it must be busy at other times because right now there isn't one rig to be found. Maybe the lunch hour will bring a few customers. After filling up, I park Thelma D off to the side and take off my jackets. The collar of my raincoat was rolled down exposing my bandana, and it acted like a lantern wick pulling in the rainwater, soaking the front of my T-shirt.

My boots are sloppy and soft. They make squishing sounds when I walk into the building. I'm nervous about going into washrooms and am thankful there's no one about, because I can't find the women's washroom so I need to use the men's. It must be age, but somehow the pressure on my bladder seems to increase when it knows a bathroom is near.

There's a lounge with private phone booths and above the couches and chairs there are signs for hot showers, towels available. A hot shower would be wonderful and I'm almost tempted, but it would be unthinkable. A couple of hours of riding in the rain is not a real challenge to a biker who has put in serious saddle time. I'm not saying I'm that person, but I'm not ending my day in Hearst by having a hot shower and a meal. I've always taken whatever weather comes with the ride. This morning the goggles almost changed that. I was ready to give up then, now that I've peed, I'm glad I didn't.

The sky has darkened, threatening Hearst from the south. Looking west there's a glimmer of light under the clouds along the top of the tree line. A red Honda sport bike, with a rider wearing black on black armour chasing the same good weather, blasts past the parking lot. They wave, I gesture back and hope they've filled up. That slight bright strip along the western horizon makes me feel optimistic and I pack away my rain pants and jacket in my saddlebags. My wet bandana joins my soggy gloves tucked into the bungee cord and I retrieve my cheap high-definition sunglasses that I bought at my local Loblaws. They are my last pair, so I'm hoping they'll be good to me as Thelma D and I leave Hearst to drive through the dark side.

I don't know if anyone else calls it the dark side, but it seemed the right call after looking at a map. The dark side runs from Hearst to Longlac, 200 kilometres of nothing but true Northern Ontario bush country.

Before leaving for the north, I understood from some people who have ridden the road, that there isn't all that much to look at, and I was advised that there were certainly other, more scenic routes to follow. Some motorcyclists I talked to think Highway 11 is a waste of gas. Scenery isn't what made the choice for me to run the road. It was because I've never been here before. I've heard of places called Temagami and Kapsukasing and Hearst and Nipigon and now I can say I've driven through them. The drive may not be pretty, but I think it's pretty cool to ride the northernmost highway in Ontario at least once. Maybe time and money would be better spent for the kind of rush I'd get from touring a road that is twisty and curvy with scenic highlights around every corner, but I'm doing the grind and I'll be proud of the ride if I make it through.

There are lots of things in my life that I'm not proud of and one of them was the last conversation with my mother.

* * *

"I'm not talking about that now."

"Why not? You never want to talk about it."

"You know why."

"No, I don't. Tell me."

"I've told you already."

"No you haven't."

"He hurt me too."

"Well what about me?"

* * *

The exchange became harsher with every word said and then we hung up on each other. It was typical of our interactions. We didn't listen to each other and we were always too busy pushing our own victim agendas on each other, both of us holding to positions that were selfish and rarely unyielding. Bev died nine years ago and I have often dictated several variations of a last letter to her.

Dear Mom,

I'm sorry Frank sent you home in a box. When I went to pick you up, I was shocked and then really disappointed and sad. I was expecting some kind of earthy, dark-coloured urn carefully packaged in foam peanuts or plastic bubble wrap for your journey. Instead, you came east wrapped up in a plastic bag like wall compound sold at home-improvement stores, packaged in a nondescript white box. It was a little thicker and stiffer than the kind of box you'd find in the local bakery, but not much different.

I want to let you know that you're safe now and you're with your favourite son, Craig. He's put you in a beautiful urn and you have a place of pride in his home.

Tears start and I can't continue. No matter how many times I try to finish the letter, I can never get past this point. I set my lips, shake my head, and start to count the dashed lines on the road and when they run out, I blink my eyes with every third post of the guardrail.

It doesn't take too many rails for me to remember a proud moment I had with Bev. We were leaving the ski hill west of town and I was in the back seat of our Dodge Coronet. The road out had become slippery with the sun and a couple cars had been unable to make it up a hill. One had slid backwards off the side and into the ditch creating a backlog of vehicles waiting to leave.

We spent the time watching several men working with shovels to free the stuck car, and then push the second vehicle up the hill. One of the men came to the window and asked Bev if she wanted him to drive the Dodge up the incline. His tone implied Bev didn't have the skill to make it. She laughed at him in her big way and said, "No way, I'm driving my own car."

I slunk down to my knees on the floorboard. Bev put the car in gear and left the man standing there. I was like a puppet peeking out the front windshield from just above the back of the front seat. I can't remember if she slipped or not, but the further we got up the rise, the straighter I became, and by the time we topped the hill I was bouncing up and down, cheering and hitting the top of the seat with my mittens.

18.

HALFWAY THROUGH THE RUN TO LONGLAC and the scenery hasn't changed since leaving Hearst. The sun has bullied the clouds aside, a full throttle beam, strong, powerful, it tells of a hot afternoon of riding. My grocery store glasses filter the glare and highlight the scenery at the same time. They make the trees, the ditches, even the gravel come alive with a certain vibration and intensity. I decide they're very optimistic glasses, my happy glasses. Is cheaper really better in some cases? Right now, it looks like it.

The trail taken by Highway 11 is swollen with wetlands, wild grasses, scrappy looking pines, and ragged ground cover interrupted occasionally by yellow moose danger signs. A seemingly straight run with the same uneventful snapshot duplicated every kilometre. It's comparable to rolling through the same reel of film, spliced the length of a football field, and played over and over. Night travel through this murky corridor would be mind-numbing and hypnotizing. It would be like chasing an image captured in your headlights, hoping the scenery will change when you overtake it, but no matter how fast you drive, you never catch it.

It's been hard not to open the throttle and wind up Thelma D, but speeding, even in the daylight, is going to put me in a vulnerable position if something big comes out of the bush. Where the wooded area is densest, it's cut back away from the highway about the length of a rail car on each side, creating alleyways of stumps, rocks, and flattened brush that parallel the highway. The alleys wouldn't provide a smooth landing if you left the road, but at least the strips give you some measure of warning if a big animal does start to cross the highway, like a deer or bear or, surprise, a moose. It's quite possible the buffers also provide a warning system for the wildlife, warning them of crazy motorists who are speeding through their environment and can't be trusted to slow down or yield.

So far through the dark side there have been no signs of moose or crazy motorists, with the exception of one car that shot past me about a half hour ago. Nothing since. This kind of time in the saddle, droning by at a constant speed with the same scenery repeating itself, puts my mind into a lot of different places. I recall one of the latest fantasy series I've been reading by Terry Brooks, and I picture a very large creature, a huge centipede, its undulating body chugging forward consuming scrubby pine, rocks, and dirt without resistance. The arthropod's giant maw is swallowing everything in its path as it wends it way through the dense Northern Ontario bush, shitting out a narrow flattened strip of highway in its wake.

Keeping the fantasy theme going I picture myself as Eragon on a quest and imagine that Saphira is flying above me keeping watch, ready to swoop down and give warning of any dangers that lie ahead. The thought warms and makes me feel safe, but an imaginary dragon isn't going to help me stay in the moment and focused on the road. And she won't, I realize with a flutter of fear in my belly, be able to help if Thelma D broke down.

It's also hard to be present without a lot of physical interaction with the bike. A road that challenges me to brake, accelerate, select gears, squeeze Thelma D with my legs, pick my line, lean into the curves, and pull out of corners while anticipating other riders or drivers, as well as looking out for hazards, is in some ways a much easier road to drive. It's like my body has melted into my machine to survive the ride, and there's always a rush, deep in my groin when I've reached my destination, often wishing I could do it over again right away. Chasing the rush is one of the thrills of riding a motorcycle and I could never truly paint the picture properly. A person needs to experience it, like with a roller coaster the rider doesn't know what the thrill is going to be like until they're in the middle of it. Then again, maybe the ride will make them vomit and wish to never do it again.

I'm trying to stay alert, but this is one ride I won't repeat, even if I conquer Highway 11 without introducing myself to a moose. I'm glad I'm doing it because it'll be an accomplishment when I get through it. I won't be able to brag about it, the same way as if I conquered Tail of the Dragon, an international destination road for motorcycle enthusiasts. The Tail is an eleven-mile stretch of US129 bridging South Carolina and Tennessee with over three hundred turns.

To one day slay the Dragon would be awesome and while I'm not up for it at this moment, I tell myself it takes perseverance and determination to ride upright in a straight line for hours, holding the throttle at the same speed, staying in the same gear, all with the drone of Thelma D's exhaust never changing its tune of a sleep-inducing lullaby. I'm reminded of some lectures I've attended. If I had to choose, I'd much rather fall out of a chair than off of a motorcycle doing 110 kilometres an hour.

Needing a change and a little exercise, I pull my feet back from the highway pegs and stand up on the mid supports, fully extending my legs to stretch them out and catch some air on my chest. The wind pummels me around, pushing me backwards. I harden my core, tense my legs, and tighten up my arms. Beating back the gusts of air makes my body feel alive and strong. After I sit down, I roll my chest forward on to Thelma D's tank and stretch my legs out backwards to compress my lower back. It's comparable to an in flight cobra pose, but I don't hold it as long as I would in a yoga studio. Then I sit upright and twist, stretching my back and shoulders from side to side, shifting one butt cheek off the side of the saddle and then the other. The stretching feels so good I want to break out purring, like my cat Stella does when she pushes her head into my hand for attention. I settle back in and watch eagerly for any sign that says I'm getting close to Longlac.

Besides the prolific yellow fluorescent moose danger placards marking the highway trail, I've seen a few billboards advertising game outfitters, garages, and towing services, but most disturbing to me are the signs about domestic violence. I wasn't expecting them. They are not only on this run. I had seen a couple yesterday after Thelma D and I turned at North Bay. A northern anomaly it seems, but only in terms of signage. One was direct in both its plea and accusation. *Stop the sexual abuse of our children.* No denial or fucking around here. Let's just put it all out on the table and tell it like it is. No small print brochures discreetly stacked in doctor's offices and community centres. No concerned whisperings at Phil and Ann Thropic wine and cheese fundraisers for women's shelters and programs. The brutality of sexual abuse put right out there for everyone to see, if not to acknowledge. No hiding behind closed doors or minds. How many drivers and passengers feel the doors and windows closing in on them when they see one of these billboards?

The signs pull me back to yesterday, before I filled Thelma D up in Deep River, when I drove past the house I grew up in. I parked in front and didn't stay long because there were two people sitting outside. The shell still looked the same, a large two-storey duplex. The house was a little scruffy, but there were new shingles on what used to be our side of the roof. The giant white pine that marked the corner of the front walk was gone, replaced by a front porch. Only two of the four maples remained in the front yard. I helped Eric the day he planted them in a straight, precise line across the middle of the lawn.

The window on the second floor to the right looks into my old room. When I was really young, I used to gnaw on the ledge with my teeth. I left a pattern of chew marks that resembled a bed of clams, all lined up neatly in a single file along the sill. The taste was of old wood, flavoured with white paint that felt gritty and tasted like oil and old rubber. This was in the '60s, so maybe the paint contained lead. That could be pretty convenient for me. I could blame all my craziness and irrational behaviour on early childhood lead poisoning.

I need to put Thelma D in gear but the window pulls me back. The image is there, captured and framed as a still in multiple panes of glass, a dark figure kneeling and hunched over a bed. My breathing quickens, becomes ragged, and I choke on a quick inhale, triggering the recall of my escapes.

I float up and slide out the window like smoke gliding across the clams, now painted shadows. The big pine beckons me close, a gentle gesture from a giant. I settle on a large limb and huddle up to its trunk. The bark is coarse and rough, but warm and welcoming. The tree's ancient spirit and boughs shroud me, keeping me safe until I can float back in over the ledge, unnoticed and insignificant.

The images in the window start to pixelate and break apart. I'm alone. The dark side returns and I concentrate on the centre lines of the asphalt. My breathing is rapid, harsh. I look around quickly and am relieved to see I'm still between the lines and Thelma D's wheels are on asphalt. The sky is blue, the clouds white, and the trees are green. After-shakes threaten to drown me and I feel like I'm being pulled backwards into a pool of water. I tighten my hands on Thelma D's bars until my fingers ache, and pull myself in and out trying to shake myself back into the ride.

"I love my jiffy stand, I love my jiffy stand, I love my jiffy stand."

19.

ALMOST INTO LONGLAC, I MEET an oncoming car, my first in two hours. Thelma D has helped me conquer the dark side corridor of Highway 11. I'd celebrate more enthusiastically if I weren't so numb with the effort of staying alert. It's hard for me to grasp that in these busy times, with overpopulated cities and countries, that a person could travel 200 kilometres on a major highway in the largest province of the country and see nothing. No towns, no villages, no settlements, just a pooped-out strip of two-lane asphalt running through the bush.

On the map, the lonely run between Hearst and Longlac, is part of the apex of the northern portion of the road that has its origins in downtown Toronto. Canada, unlike its European cousins, is generously vast to its citizens and I'm feeling very small. If the country were a football field, in our day and a half of travel, Thelma D and I have gained twenty yards. With that math comes a feeling of insignificance, like I wouldn't be as discernible as one pine among thousands. Incredibly tiny in the larger scheme of life and land, would I even take up a pixel on a Google Earth view? Some might reply that depends upon the resolution.

Why am I doing this again? Maybe I should crawl back home. I'm tired and need a rest because my thinking is getting weird. I shake the thought of retreating because I know where the old thinking has led me in the past. I'm the biggest consumer of my life and I need to stay in the moment, in the now.

There are innumerable self-help libraries and web sites devoted to communicating the clichés about the process of changing the world, changing your body, invigorating your spirit. I run a few through my head. I may feel like a tiny speck now, but I really do believe that one person can affect positive change in the world. I've read the stories about people who have done the seemingly impossible. I've seen and talked with strong, committed men and women who have profoundly changed the communities they live in and, like the voyageurs and pioneers, I admire them. They strike a lot of emotions in me. Sometimes I feel incredibly inadequate and unworthy, other times I'm inspired, ready to run off and get started at some heartfelt cause that will change the world. That hasn't happened.

Some say it should be about you initially. Heal and love yourself first. Then you can go forward. Can't it work both ways? I know that helping people has always made me feel good about myself. There were exceptions when I was younger though. I'd help friends and relatives, sometimes going out of my way to *find* favours to do for them, without actually being asked. Then I'd become resentful and angry when they didn't return my good deed, shower me with gratitude or take out an advertisement telling the world how wonderful I was. Expectations made me miserable. Now that I'm older, I don't have many expectations and the ones I have, I've negotiated and communicated. I'm not expecting this ride to change my life in a significant way, but right now it is all about me and I am hoping to find a way to shake loose the sadness that has crept in around me like the pounds of weight I amassed until one day I really looked into a mirror and started crying. My goal is to finish my life motivated, however long it is, and begin each day in a graceful, honest, and reflective state. Regardless of how the ride will end, and they all end, I know the only person who can make a difference in my life is the one sitting in Thelma D's saddle.

We turn into the first gas station we come to. The lot is opposite the statue of a really large horse. I feel shaky and a drop of sweat is running down behind my ear. Since my return to riding, I've noticed as the day gets longer, my turns get wider and sloppier, more unsteady. By the time I get to Thunder Bay, I'll need more than the forty acres I had this morning in Kapuskasing to turn Thelma D around.

The attendant tells me there's only regular gas available in town. "It doesn't pay to have supreme, it's pretty dear and no one around here'll pay the price of that stuff."

Down south drivers are spoiled with a buffet of fuel choices from major gas distributors within blocks, if not metres, of each other in the larger centres. All coincidentally, showing the same price for gas, regular or supreme. My experience so far in the north is you get what you can, like chicken for dinner, accept what is offered, like a hotel room for six, and be grateful for any kind of gas when the tank is empty.

Having only regular gas available makes sense when most communities of the north are dependent on the internal combustion engine and the fuel it consumes for daily survival. It's a hell of a commute any which way you look down the highway, and transit isn't as easy as standing at a bus stop with your pass or a pocket full of change. People who live in the north are running cars and trucks daily, grinding out long distances. They play or work with four-wheelers, snowmobiles, bikes, and boats. Craig's small camp north of Sudbury is off the grid. He gets there by boat, and uses a four-wheeler with a small trailer to transport supplies. Chainsaws and a wood splitter are used to ready wood for the stoves that heat the various cabins and the sauna. He runs a generator when his solar system batteries run out, shares a water pump with his neighbour, and in the winter he travels to the camp by snow machine.

One summer, some of the residents around the small cove shared the cost of a barge that brought out a loader and building materials. A big expense and a lengthy production, but a package that southerners could put together with a couple quick calls to the local Home Depot and Rentall stores for next day delivery. It makes me wonder if we aren't trading our ingenuity and problem solving skills for convenience and credit? A northerner might say so. Regardless, there is a lot of fuel being consumed and if I were scratching out a living here, I'd want to see my dollar move as much as it could. So regular it is.

After filling up, I turn Thelma D around and park in front of Robin's Doughnuts. I settle into a window seat to enjoy a cold meat sub with lettuce and onions. The whole wheat bread is soft, chewy, and freshly baked, a pretty good sandwich for a donut shop. Before eating, I pulled off my boots and placed them under my chair. I'm hopeful the time I spend in the restaurant will dry out my socks a little and air out the wet leather of my boots.

As I'm getting ready to leave my table, the rider on the red Honda that blasted past me in Hearst tours into the lot. He parks his machine by Thelma D and jogs into the restaurant heading straight for the washroom, like an arrow shot from a crossbow. It doesn't matter if you're young or old, a biker's bladder, ridden down and beaten hard, requires frequent breaks. Finding relief when riding is much easier when you're a guy. All men need to do is find a discreet corner, or tree, or rock and failing that, most are able to just turn their backs to traffic when they need to pee, no awkward embarrassment or explanation required and all done in the standing position.

It is several degrees more difficult for me to pee off road. Discreet locations aside, I first need to undo my belt or two, if I'm wearing chaps. Add Velcro, snaps, and zippers for rain gear. Second, I need to pull them down as one sheath and lastly, I have to make sure the mess of belts, snaps, Velcro, and elastic doesn't get jammed into the top of my boots, halting my squat. It has happened. I've panicked and peed on the back of my pants. Memories of that soggy time now make me a little frantic when I have to off-road urinate. Frantic makes me nervous, and then it becomes a race to separate my sweaty body parts from my riding clothes. It's a little like trying to peel the skin off a really green banana.

Over the years I've squatted in ditches, fields, behind trees and rocks, even between cars and curbs, with and without a lookout. Hidden, while peeing in sand is ideal, but relieving myself in a grassy or mossy ditch, facing downhill behind a rock, comes a close second. The most unpleasant surface to urinate on is asphalt or concrete. It's not pretty and the worst is the back splash from the hard top. If I'm peeing on pavement in a parking lot I'm desperate.

I don't travel with Kleenex, anti-bacterial wipes, waterless soap, and re-sealable disposal bags like some of the female riders I know. Of course, they would rather risk a urinary tract infection, than expose their bare ass peeing in a parking lot. The supplies they carry are really meant for the public washrooms they have to endure. I'm lucky to pull out some single ply napkins that I've picked up from a Timmy's or Dairy Queen for just those occasions. If I don't have anything to wipe with and I feel safe, I'll wait out the big drips before buckling up. I've tried shaking, but that never works, especially as a big girl.

That's why men, like the young Honda Rider have it easy. They don't have to worry about undoing belts, chaps, gear or underwear. It's all designed for them and their organ. They can take their time because they're standing up and who's to say they aren't checking their GPS or maps and really should have brought their reading glasses. Men can also pee well away from their boots, minimizing the splash quotient, and apparently if there are more than two or three going at a time, I've heard they've been known to have contests for distance. And when finished, all they have to do is shake it, no wiping involved. How fair is that?

The Honda man grabs a bottle of water out of the cooler, and after he finishes up at the cash, we stand by our machines and chat about our trips. He's young, tall, and fit-looking and so far has not nodded once. I'm encouraged. He tells me that he left the Maritimes on Saturday and is hoping to be in Vancouver by Friday, in time for his buddy's wedding on Saturday. One week to cross the country. It's already Tuesday; he'll have to ride hard in the next few days to make it.

His bike, a CBR 600, is brand new and he says it runs great, but the seat is terrible, and he's having a problem staying on the bike because his butt gets numb so he's had to take frequent breaks.

He sounds a little down when he says, "It's taking more time than I thought."

"Well, the bike is new and really you wouldn't have gotten the full experience until you put in the time," I encourage.

We talk a bit more about the pros and cons of gel packs, suspension seats, foam, and I show him how I fastened Thelma D's sheepskin to her seat. I look straight at him to prevent myself from nodding while he tells me that it's too late for him to retrofit his bike with anything on the ride to the wedding, but he's thinking he'll make some time and stop at a dealership to see what options he has before he travels back east.

"Really can't go wrong in making your saddle as comfortable as possible. Best investment you can give yourself." I nod ... twice. *Fuck*.

Before crossing the road to the parking lot of the Rexall Drug Store, I wish him luck and tell him to ride safe. The store is brand-new shiny with large tinted windows. I pick up some water and a tin of Dubbin to waterproof my boots. The parking lot is fresh asphalt with bright yellow lines, newly painted, and the concrete walkways surrounding the lot and building are a recent pour. Put the drugstore in any mall in the south with its aluminum stiles, cedar hedges, and stonework and it would fit right in. In Longlac, however, the building looks out of place with the rest of the buildings and structures in the village. They're not quite quaint, vintage or Victorian. Some houses are small and older looking but scrubbed and bright with colourful knick knacks and embellishments, their gardens and grass well-tended. Other buildings I see are dated, and showing their age with additions cobbled together, each one a little fresher than its partner. I get the impression that they wouldn't stand alone, but together they provide shelter and a home.

20.

STIFF-LEGGED, I WALK DOWN the sidewalk to Kelsey's for dinner. Thelma D and I arrived in Thunder Bay at seven-thirty p.m. and even though its now nine p.m. there's still ample light clinging to day. Some of the heat of the afternoon has leaked away and the evening is pleasantly warm. I'm in shorts and a T-shirt, flip-flopping my way past big box stores, strip malls, and car dealerships.

The strip is home to the Econo Lodge I booked into. I've travelled 1500 kilometres in two days. I was ready to get off the road when I got to the city, and the Lodge was advertised as being renovated and under new management. Rooms were being let for $79, a price that respects my budget.

The room was clean, with a new bath insert and tub surround panels, but there are just some substances no manner of cleaning and scrubbing, or renovating, can get rid off. The diminished stink of nicotine, smoke, and stale beer filled the hallway when I lugged my bags up the stairs to my room. One deep inhale brought me back to my pious days cleaning the Byeways. The persistent tang also tells me the old hotel has put in a lot of hard time, and has probably soaked up more beer, urine, and vomit than the new Days Inn & Suites that I passed on the Harbour Expressway will ever in its lifetime.

I'm not fussy where I crash and even if there weren't a budget, I'd pick a place closer in character to the Lodge than the Suites. Much in the same way I'd pick a tavern over a martini or wine bar if I were still a drunk. I think about ordering a cold beer, and imagine the taste and feel of the brew as the first foamy run swirls in my mouth. It flows like smooth velvet and tastes like water would after being denied of it through a morning of working in the hot sun. Saliva builds and I have to swallow quickly once, then twice.

It would be so easy to start drinking. Booze is everywhere and most people assume I drink, and are often surprised when I say no thanks and ask for club soda or ginger ale instead. Sometimes they ask if I was always a non-drinker and they laugh when I tell them that I used to drink and that I was really good at it. It's easier to tell them that, than to share that I was a drunk, an alcoholic, and that I eventually ended up in rehab before relapsing again. I don't tell them that.

It's hard not to think about drinking. It's what I did for thirty years of my life, starting at thirteen when I had my first mickey of lemon gin. Even though I vomited most of it up behind the apartment buildings where I delivered papers, and I never drank gin again, it gave me a taste for wanting more. There is a slogan I heard often at Alcoholics Anonymous meetings: *one is too many and twelve is not enough*. At the time, I thought it was a little sorry and self-defeating, but now that I'm sober, it is my truth. One drink would really be too many and if I had one, I wouldn't be stopping at twelve. And if I were drinking again, I'd be smoking. One swallow, and I'd be back on the elevator at the same floor I got off of, taking me to the ultimate intention of every addict. Death.

At Kelsey's, I hobble through the main dining room and slide into a large corner booth. Two tables away is a big man with long black hair tied back in a ponytail. His black T-shirt is stretched over a huge belly, and both of his arms are covered in dense dark hair and tattoos. He's wearing a jean vest patched with the full insignia of Hells Angels. Sharing his table and a couple of plates of food is a slim woman with long blond hair. Dressed in jeans and a black tank top, her bangles jingle continuously, as her arm flutters around the table like a bird pecking at its meal. He's concentrating on what I think is the biggest burger I've ever seen.

Their presence brings me back a few minutes to the strip club down and across the street. A makeshift fence bordered the sidewalk, shielding the dancers as they smoked outside the club.

Six inch heels and tight calves below, and long hair with large lips above. Everything else hidden by the fence is up to your imagination. There were several Harleys in the parking lot, and a loud Softtail throttled in behind the fence, then left in the time it took me to shuffle past the club. Drug deal?

The big guy is joined by two other men in full colours. The trio reminds me of the large, aggressive looking men that were with the bike gang that Lenny, Stan, and I spent a couple of hours with, drinking at the old Sturgeon Falls Hotel. I wasn't at the men's tables, but spent my time with two women playing pool. Both were slim and attractive, with long hair that was closer to blond than brown. Like with the blond woman and her bangles, silver jewellery adorned their fingers and ears.

I didn't say much to them other than, "Your turn," and if I wasn't drinking hard, I was chewing my nails and trying to hide my yellow skidoo helmet by kicking it beneath a couple of chairs I had pushed together. There was nothing I could do about my runners and polyester hockey jacket, which were in stark contrast to women's black leather chaps, boots, and riding jackets. It was Stan who told me afterwards that if we had taken up their invitation to tour with them, I'd be made available to the men who wanted me. He said it was that way with girls who hung on to the fringes of the gang. Then he made it sound like he and Lenny had rescued me. I'm not sure if I was grateful for their decision, or just too hungover and with not enough beer in me, to care. I suppose if you became someone's main squeeze, like the blond woman here seems to be with the big man, you'd be okay and protected from the rest of the pack.

The two men who came in later get up and leave quickly, as if to get ready for something. The big man stands and takes his time, re-tucking his T-shirt and adjusting his belt. I sneeze loudly as the pair is leaving and the woman looks over at me, smiles, and says, "Gesundheit."

21.

LIGHT HAS FINALLY GIVEN UP its grip on the day by the time I make it back to the Econo Lodge. My legs are weak and buzzing with fatigue and I pull myself up the stairs using the handrail. The strain on my shoulders brings me to the time as a young teen when I had to heave myself up the ski hill because the car engine that ran the towrope had stalled. I grin tiredly when I remember how the new attendant re-started the engine and put it into a higher gear than normal and the rope was going much faster than it should have been. I was jerked almost off my skis when I grabbed the line, but I held on. It didn't take long for me to be propelled into the mound of thrashing bodies at the top of the hill, all entangled in a mix of jackets, skis, poles, toques, and mitts.

Somehow I make it up the last stair, but heaviness accompanies my every step to the room. Even the smell of stale tobacco and spilled beer seems more washed out, somehow less now than before. How am I going to make it through another week of riding? Am I being foolish? Maybe I should turn around and head home tomorrow. Isn't it enough that I conquered a pretty desperate start to the day, and rode the dark side?

* * *

After leaving Longlac, Thelma D and I run through a hard, heavy flash of warm summer rain. It lasts for a few minutes, and shortly after we meet the most stunning view of spectacular cliff faces. The facades are hundreds of feet high, like vertical quilts of stone in a rainbow of soft muted colours, draped from the horizon to the shoreline. Closer to shore, they resemble waterfalls of rock and granite, a cascade of falling stone mosaics.

Unable to stop along the highway, I pull over as soon as possible by the Mission Bay of Helen Lake. It's disappointing that I can't see the faces of the cliffs from the rough parking area. I'd have to ride back to see them again. I don't turn around, but close my eyes to bring back their images, to imprint and collect them, as you would those things that can't be purchased or gathered. Their brilliance will stay with me for a long time, ready to be pulled out, their awe and joy experienced again, maybe shared with others.

My mood dims a little at the thought that my happier collections always seem to fade slightly with each opening, eventually disappearing. Unlike the brutal moments that have been seared into my head, never forgotten. I wonder why that happens? Is it just me that I can't seem to forget? Is forgetting possible, or will I always remember the feel and touch of his hands pushing into me, his lips on me, his beard rubbing and chafing? Is it because my capacity for remembering joy and happiness is broken? I push hard to bring back the cliff faces. It takes a few moments, much quicker than in the drunken years, and I return to their magnificence.

Turning from the water, I face a small white church sitting across the highway. Trimmed in a light aqua blue, its paint is washed and scrubbed to a dull finish, but the building itself is square and sturdy. Centered above the church's front entry is a large round window, its circumference divided into six slices, shaped like a simple daisy of large leaves. A tiny white cottage with a small red chimney is tucked tightly to its left. Some of the wood shingles on the cottage and the church's bell tower are missing, and those that remain are twisted with weather and age.

The surrounding land is showing its age by having given up most of its spruce and pines to the logging industry. The terrain is now mostly a mixed second growth of aspen and birch trees and some kind of shrubby brush that I can't name. The stubborn heritage of the old growth forest is revealed by the small spruces and jack pines struggling to hold on to a mostly rock hill behind the small building. Their roots cling like claws to the spare earth gathered in the crevices. While crooked and misshapen, I admire their tenacity and unwillingness to let go. Much like Bev's stubbornness when she was trying to save her life by going through years of chemotherapy, enduring any treatment with the hope that a cure would come in time to save her life. She hung on to that small chance with a determination and a will that I respected. I was proud of her, but it pissed me off. Why didn't she use that strength and perseverance to protect her kids and drive Eric off? She did it for her life, why not ours? How does that matter now that she's dead? It shouldn't, but sometimes I lapse and revert to needing answers that I know will never satisfy me, even if she was alive. It's who she was and it's an old expectation I need to let go of, before it brings me more than misery.

A cure never came and Bev died at sixty-two, having lived only five years longer than her mother did. My maternal grandmother died when I was in high school of lung cancer at fifty-seven, and while Bev was originally diagnosed with colon cancer, it had spread to her lungs and then fatally to her liver.

My middle name comes from my grandmother Marjorie. My brothers and I always called her Grandma Marj, and before she died, I connected with her and we wrote letters back and forth for a couple of years during her illness. She had moved out west to be with her third or fourth husband, or boyfriend, I'm not sure which, and settled in Stewart, British Columbia. She had a career as a nurse in the east and finished her working life driving a truck. I was pretty proud of her. My most vivid memory of Grandma Marj was spending the afternoon by myself with her when I was seven or eight. She took me shopping to a department store where she held my hand. I felt special and safe.

Both women faced their deaths with a willful need to live and an unwavering fight that lasted years. They brawled as hard as they were able to endure and it wasn't enough. They both died young and left before I could find out why mother and daughter felt the need to put the greater part of this country between themselves and their families. I had always hoped, like with some people who faced troubles that would crush others, they would each come out of their battle with death stronger and more vibrant than ever. Bev especially. I wanted her alive and willing to share and talk, to be a mother. I realize now, standing here, that that was a false hope. It was never going to happen, but I can at least be proud of their fight. I had also hoped, mostly through my drunken years, that if given time, Grandma Marj, Mom, and I would have gotten to that easy place. The spot where there is an understanding and respect for each other. I used to picture an afternoon of three generations, a time spent with easy hugs, quiet words, and knowing smiles of encouragement, of having survived. Together. It was a fantasy. Realistically, the scene would be more like the three of us fighting over the chair that had its back to the wall, while getting seated in a dark tavern, before lighting cigarettes and ordering Canadian Club whiskey and draft beer.

I shouldn't, but I can't help doing the math, adding five years to Bev's age when she died and look at my own mortality. How will my death come? Will I cling to my life and the hope of a cure like Bev and the roots of the jack pines? Or will I say fuck it and head to the beer store, dying a drunk who gave up when it mattered most?

A sharp gust of wind over the lake sprinkles my neck with tiny droplets. The tingling of spray is like fingers lightly stroking my skin and a shiver runs down my back and through my legs making me wish I had Grandma Marj's hand to hold.

Straddling Thelma D, I pull her up and start the twin engine, giving more throttle than she needs. I'm drawn back to the stylized celtic cross rising from the small bell tower of the church. Captured by the harsh winter winds, it is tilted backwards and to the right. I feel a certain kinship with the lonely icon. Battered by sleet and hail flung inland from the lake, its will bent but not broken, and stubborn like the remaining shingles on the church roof, not so willing to be defeated.

The buzzing in my legs pulls me back to my room. The numbness from my first MS relapse still holds my toes, and part of my left foot. It's the ten percent that didn't come back. Not unexpected, but the sensation seems like it has crept up closer to my knees. Shaking my legs and wiggling my feet only confuses my tired brain. Moving on, I check the numb spot on my left thigh that came with a recent flare up. I prod around it, like a finger checking the middle of a sponge cake to see if it is done. It feels like the numbness has claimed some more real estate. What will I do now if my legs give out? How will I get home? *Stop whining and complaining, there are more people in world with greater problems.* I'm hopeful that sleep and rest will reinvigorate my legs and the numbness will have retreated by morning. If not, I'll deal with it over coffee.

Before slumber pulls me down, I view my collection of larger than life statues and structures that marked many of the communities along Highway 11. The freshly acquired images run through the backdrop of my eyelids, bright and clear. It feels like there was an informal competition or agreement to create something to put out alongside Highway 11 to represent the residents. There were the usual animal themes: polar bears, oversize Holsteins, fish, horses, and of course, moose. In Moonbeam, there was a giant flying saucer, a huge raptor filled a lawn in Mattice, and one of my favourite slowdowns — a three-storey high snowman, wearing sunglasses and holding a fishing pole in Beardmore. The figures seem to be a quirky northern tradition that reflects the culture of taking pride, working hard, and persevering with a sense of humour and adventure. It sounds sappy and trite, but I hope to take some of their character and strength with me for the next few days of riding.

22.

"JUST WHERE A WOMAN SHOULD BE. On her knees," the parts manager says as he smiles, and touches the zipper on the front of his pants.

I put my head down and start to cry. My tears catch up with the rest of the stains on the sleeves of my coveralls, making them invisible. I'm grateful. It's my second day of cleaning out the rails of the frame machine in the body shop of the car dealership where I work. My arms and shoulders burn with the effort of pushing and pulling a scraper along inside the rails to loosen up the dirt and debris. It's a task that can only be done on your hands and knees. A job for the shop's apprentice, a job for me.

Part of my work as an apprentice is to also get coffee, hustle parts and supplies to the journeymen and painters, and to keep the body and paint shop clean. I spend a lot of time on the end of a broom, but the worst part of my job is cleaning the frame machine with its two hundred feet or more of slotted rails embedded into the floor. The rails are like two railroad tracks running parallel to each other, flush with the floor and gapped approximately an inch. They provide a way to attach and secure damaged vehicles to the floor using a combination of chains, anchors, and wedges.

During the frame straightening process, thousands of pounds of pressure are exerted on the rails by hydraulic pumps and pullers, and to prevent injury and mishaps they need to be kept clean. Red plastic inserts used to cover the gaps, but they've disappeared, and after months of sweeping, the rails have filled with dirt, dried Bondo bits and shavings, chunks of steel, bolts and nuts, clips and anchors.

I use a screwdriver, an L-shaped scraper I made out of a piece of heavy scrap steel, and the narrow crevice tool end of a shop vacuum to remove the debris. I scrape back and forth and then vacuum out the loosened material. Some times I have to use my fingers to get at chunks of steel, broken plastic or bolts that jam the opening or the vacuum, making my hands red and raw with cuts and scrapes. I can't wear work gloves. I tried, but I couldn't get my fingers in between the rails. Light cloth gloves worked, but they didn't protect my hands from the curled pieces of steel, tapered to a needle point that stung my fingers over and over, just like the hornets did when I stepped into their nest while camping at Driftwood. This time I can't run away crying to Bev to make it all better.

Crying also won't help the constant ache that accompanies my lower back or soothe my sore legs. My knees act like sponges soaking up the never-ending dampness of the concrete floor, making them throb and cramp. Standing during breaks helps with the stiffness, but my joints feel hot and inflamed. An ice bath would help, like the big tub full of ice and water that I had to put my leg into at the physiotherapy clinic when I was rehabbing a knee injury from playing softball. I moaned and groaned at the time trying to submerse my leg inch by inch, but I wouldn't complain now. I go on a quick run of two feet of easy scraping and vacuuming. If I'm lucky and work hard I'll finish tomorrow.

***

I finished. It was a tough, shitty, crappy job. Having a co-op student in the shop would have been perfect timing, because in the hierarchy of trades the only person lower on the ladder than the apprentice is the co-op student. The shop manager told me that he'd never seen the frame equipment look so clean. I gleamed with his praise and it filled me with a lot of pride to take on a rough job and finish it, instead of bailing on it like the last apprentice did. I got through it by ignoring the parts manager, and telling myself that all the miserable work in the shop was given to me the apprentice, and not to me the woman.

There's a shuffling of boots on pavement behind me.

"Hey, if you have time, we'll wait for you to shine our bikes," a voice calls out laughingly.

Standing up, I take a step toward the man, holding out the bandana I had been using to clean Thelma D. "Here you go, help yourself." I get a little tight and resist the urge to add fuckhead.

"No, no, I'm good, just asking," he says, backing away with his hand up.

A few minutes ago the man, Rick, had walked toward me in the parking lot of the Lodge, stood and watched me clean the dust and water stains off of Thelma D's chrome while he drank coffee.

Rick and his buddy Hal are from Haliburton and are also in the process of packing up their machines for a day of riding. It was natural for us to talk when we first met, attracted to each other by the unspoken two-wheel kinship. Both men are grey-haired. Rick is a little taller and slimmer than Hal.

Hal is a big-gutted guy dressed in the typical riding attire of a Nodder, wearing boots, jeans, belt with big buckle, T-shirt, and a black leather vest.

Rick is wearing black jeans and a black T-shirt, and is riding a red and white 1100 Yamaha V-star, tricked out with a Mustang seat and some custom touches to the grips and mirrors. Hal's ride is a very nice black Harley-Davidson Road King. The men are heading along the route I came in from yesterday, towards Nipigon and Highway 11. They seem impressed when they hear Thelma D and I spooled off 750 kilometres each day of riding. Five hundred kilometres is their maximum. According to Hal, "We just do the speed limit and stop a lot."

Rick and Hal are leaving the lot. I wave and realize I was a little harsh with Rick, and feel bad that I didn't play the game with him, because he sounded playful, not mean. I should have just asked him to get me a real coffee, not the weak-coloured brew served by the motel, and by the time he came back I'd be finished with his bike. I also wouldn't have the urge to call him names like I wanted to do that day with the parts manager looking down on me. My reaction to him today would be much different. I work through giving it back to him.

Starting with, "You'd be so lucky, not a chance, now get lost."
Or, "Go troll somewhere else, I'm busy."

Or one of my favourites, "Is that your zipper or your weenie?"

Of course, there's the plain and dependable, "Go fuck yourself."

It's blunt and direct, but a little severe when you want to soften the message and give the guy a way out with a laugh and the opportunity to leave the conversation with no lasting resentments. That might sound wonky, but it worked for me. Most of the men in the shops I toiled with would appreciate and understand any one of those comebacks. The unspoken rule on the shop floor was if you gave it out, you had to take it. No matter your sex. Not all the men I worked with played the game. They punched in, did their time, and worked quietly and earnestly before clocking out. Never an inappropriate joke, slur or comment from them.

* * *

When I worked for the City of Ottawa during the '80s, in their municipal garage complex, I was the only woman in the workshops. There were other women in the complex, but they worked as clerks and assistants in the office. I'm not sure, but I think they tired of me dirtying up their washroom with my work boots and coveralls, and one day there was a flurry of construction and soon I had my own locker room, complete with a shower and stalls. It was in another building than the one I worked in, and even though it meant I had to get dressed in the winter to go to the washroom, I appreciated the private space.

I'd still sneak into the men's room on those days I was too lazy or didn't have the time to take a hike. The guys I worked with didn't mind. I'm sure if they were bothered or wanted to let me know they knew I was patronizing their private space, I would've heard about it. It doesn't take much for me to imagine, "Did you put the seat back up?" or, "How do you shake that equipment?" Then I'd need to give the banter back to them. Play the game.

With other men, the joking, tricks, and wordplay seemed non-stop, especially when they had an audience. Waiting in the garage for a shift to start, there was usually a crowd and pinching each other's bags was a frequent game they'd play. The unsuspecting guy would shriek, grab his testicles, and jump around. The culprits laughed, clapped each other on the back, and imitated the jump throughout the poor guy's shift, over and over again. They razzed each other constantly and if you were in the garage you were a target.

In the lunchroom of the main garage it could be unbearable. For me it wasn't necessarily the jokes, but it was the attention and having everyone look at me. I was conflicted, because I fully participated in playing the game, and at times it was difficult for me to accept and participate because I knew it was sexual harassment, plain and simple. According to the rules it should be reported. Did you feel uncomfortable? Yes. Did you report it? No. Am I a hypocrite? Yes.

With that admission, I felt I did my job well, fit in, and left the City of Ottawa after four years with no problems with either co-workers or bosses. In fact, it was their letters of reference that helped me get a teaching job at Algonquin College. Did growing up with three brothers help me tolerate the game? Or did the desire to fit in overwhelm the right? I'd say it was a combination of both, but what I do know for sure is that if I didn't have a teaching job lined up, I would have continued to work for the City of Ottawa. It had been a good job and it had paid well, much better than what I would have been making if I had kept working as a secretary.

It's empowering for a woman to drive and repair fire trucks and police cars, to operate and work on heavy equipment. I even loved using the sidewalk sweeper to clean the floor of the main garage, because I got to drive it around and around in wicked circles and figure eights, trying to make each one tighter than the other, until one of my co-workers turned the gas off and I was left wondering why the sweeper had stalled.

It's comparable to going to work every day with a group of big brothers, who while they teased and baited you, would break the pattern of their life in an instant to help if you needed them. The job also didn't require sitting, typing or shorthand skills, and I had my own toolbox. I loved it.

23.

THELMA D AND I ARE IDLING behind a red Dodge 4 x 4 waiting to turn left onto Highway 17. We get an advanced green arrow and the truck's dual exhaust billows black smoke as it loudly accelerates through the intersection. I throttle down and back off Thelma D to the cusp of the carbon cloud. The smoke, while not completely opaque, carries the greasiness and smell of unburnt fuel. I think the driver must have a blown engine and wonder why he's still driving the machine.

When the cloud dissipates, I pull Thelma D back within a couple of car lengths of his bumper. As soon as I settle in, the Dodge growls and races its engine. Its exhaust spews twin streams of black smoke like fire launchers from under the back bumper. I back off again, and then when clear, close the distance, this time a little more cautiously. The scene repeats itself and it's then I realize the driver is doing it on purpose, baiting me and Thelma D, reeling us in and then piling on the greasy carbon fumes.

"What a fucker."

The rear window is tinted, so I change lanes trying to catch up to the truck to see who's driving. I want to put a face to the asshole. He won't let me gain any ground and every time I get close, he accelerates, pulls in front of me, and lays on the smoke. This dance happens two or three times before I finally back off several car lengths to let him know he's won.

The truck slows down, and whoever is driving throttles the engine on and off, blowing out intermittent torrents of black carbon taunting me to come back and duel.

I slow Thelma D to a light trot in first gear, slowing traffic, and stereotype the driver instead.

Definitely boy behaviour, longish hair, sparse goatee, ball cap, T-shirt, jeans, white, late twenties to mid-thirties, soft through the belly, marginally employed. I wouldn't be surprised to see a Confederate flag tacked to the headliner of the cab. The kind of guy who is a chronic jokester, but behaves poorly when the joke is on him. When caught, will complain like a child, "It's not my fault, he started it." Possibly still lives at home so that he can put all his money into his toys.

He tries to pull me in with a few more loud complaints before I turn off the highway to head for the Harley-Davidson dealership. I wave, flip him the bird, and the Dodge accelerates away filling the highway with a final curtain of dirty exhaust.

"Take a bow Dodge man, I'll be picking black snot out of my nose for a year."

After I settle Thelma D on her jiffy stand, I unsaddle and see that I have stumbled onto an interview being conducted with a guy standing in front of his Road King parked by the Harley store. There's a nicely dressed reporter and a big camera on a tripod. I'm not close enough to hear what's being said, but I ask a man who is leaning on his blue BMW 1100 RS, watching.

"That's my brother Doug. He's doing an interview for ALS research. I'm Mike." He offers me a card.

"We're riding across Canada to raise money for research and a cure for ALS."

I nod as I read the card, staying focused on it while I search for the right words.

"For obvious reasons I'm not allowed in the shot." Mike jokes, as he gestures towards his flat twinned, German-made machine.

"We're from Massachusetts, but our parents come from Canada and we want to give something back up here. The money we raise in Canada will stay in Canada. Besides it's a nicer drive," he says with an east coast accent.

Awkwardly, I stumble out with, "That's pretty cool, where'd you start from?"

"We had our bikes shipped out to Vancouver, so we'll finish our ride on the east coast and then drop down home."

"It's your brother with ALS?"

"Yeah, he was diagnosed a year ago and he wanted to do this trip before it got too bad. All we had to do was make some adjustments to lighten the pull on his clutch."

Emotions are racing through me. I'm sad for Doug because his outcome isn't good and yet I'm happy I'm not him. I could have been him and I'm not, thank you. I berate myself for being selfish and think of what he must be going through. Every day his own body is destroying itself, the disease insidiously creeping through his nerves, subtly laying waste to all the cells in its path. A ravaging that is both devastating and irreversible. Knowing that, he gets on a bike and drives across a huge country, one he doesn't even live in, raising awareness for research and a possible cure that he will never get a chance to benefit from. How unselfish, courageous, humble, and committed. I'm taking notes.

Doug never comes over to where I'm chatting with his brother. Instead, after the interview he leans against the building eating a breakfast sandwich. He doesn't look up from his meal as I walk past him into the store and I let him have his privacy. I think that having to put up a cheery front on camera when facing a death sentence would be draining for anyone, each interview and question triggering mortal emotions.

When Thelma D and I leave the lot, I honk, wave, and yell, "Good luck, Doug." He looks at me from buttoning up his bike, and waves back.

Later, a few kilometres north of Thunder Bay, I come across two cyclists struggling up a hill. They are packed heavy for a long ride and their bikes are wobbling back and forth with the effort of climbing. Their hamstrings are corded tightly and calf muscles bulge noticeably with every push.

I think of Doug. Maybe I should have interrupted his solitude and given him a big hug, gifting him with some of my strength by osmosis, for his coming journey. What vigour and power I had this day I would have gladly given him. Would he have accepted? I'm not sure I would in his position. To accept would mean to acknowledge the premise that you aren't as strong as you used to be, and that you are dying. Dying young and too soon. To state, answer, and repeat the standard response in an interview isn't the same as an intimate interaction. Personal closeness with another, acknowledging hurt and pain, for me has always led to a state of fragile vulnerability where I'm at my weakest. I wonder why that is? How is it possible that I can talk dispassionately with a stranger about challenges and defeats, but when I put it on a personal level it falls apart?

Accepted or not, I think a hug would have been a silent, simple way of me saying thanks to Doug for the lesson in humility and selflessness.

What do you say about that Dodge man?

24.

SINCE IT'S ONLY MY THIRD DAY on the road, I've decided to keep heading west and I'm driving the stones towards Dryden. My destination for the day is Kenora and the terrain is familiar Northern Ontario, prolific bush, rock, and endless skies, shades of which travel through the blue spectrum from sunrise to sunset.

It's not long before I start to see the familiar moose danger signs. They've changed back from the deer warnings on the yellow placards between Nipigon and Thunder Bay.

We're blessed with another beautiful day for riding. Cool, but made comfortable by the warmth of the sun. My arms got sunburnt on the first day of travelling, so I've worn my leather jacket the last two days. My nose and cheeks are paying the greatest price for the overexposure and are starting to blister. I didn't even think about putting on sun block and now I can't get enough moisturizer. My face is sucking it up as fast as I can lather it on.

After scrolling through another 120 kilometres, I stop for gas and a break at a complex near Upsala. The restaurant is a well-used building with a red metal barn roof and a red-roofed front porch. The word *restaurant* is written in white lettering on a red canopy that covers the small front stoop.

In one of the windows there's a neon *open* sign and lots of others advertising ice cream, caramel cones, and an ATM machine. To the left of the door, two old men dressed in green work pants and plaid shirts are sitting at a rickety card table smoking and drinking what I assume is coffee in washed-out beige ceramic cups. To the right in another window is a large sign posted by the health unit that states *No Smoking Under The Canopy*. I imagine the old dial type pay phone gracing the wall beside the sign is to call in complaints.

Several cars of differing vintages are parked near the restaurant and across the gravel lot there is a large two-bay garage, steel-sided and trimmed in red. One bay is large enough to accept tractor trailers and heavy trucks. It's empty. A white Chevy short box is up on the hoist in the adjacent bay, its service interrupted because the mechanic, in grease-stained blue coveralls, is outside the shop changing a tire on a trailer.

The trailer sides have been extended upwards with plywood and an orange tarp is tied over the load, secured with streamers of yellow poly rope. Its tongue is attached to an overloaded mini van with a kayak tied to its roof. A young man in shorts is looking over the shoulder of the mechanic and a couple of kids are playing by the door of the vacant bay.

I gas up and park Thelma D to the right of the restaurant sign. I have to use the washroom. I look hopefully around the building for the universally marked rooms. There are none. They're inside.

"Just my fucking luck, a goddam restaurant in the middle of nowhere, in hillbilly heaven," I complain.

My breath quickens. Tight tendrils of anxiety start to twist and rise from my stomach to my chest. My pulse increases with every beat and my hands start to sweat. I take off my helmet and try to fluff up my hair as big as possible. For a brief moment I consider using some spit as a quick gel, but decide against it. My jacket comes off next and I lay it over Thelma D's seat. I pause briefly.

Stretching tall I breathe deeply, arch my back slightly, and thrust out my breasts while clenching my thighs together. Keeping my chin up, I exaggerate my hip action and walk into the small convenience store that fronts the restaurant. I almost sag in relief when the first sign I see is an arrow pointing to the women's washroom. It's pointing away from the busy restaurant to a corner of the store. *Thank God.*

There are two banks of shelves stacked with food and camping supplies. I want to put a hand on my hip, as I sashay through the aisle runway, backdropped with canned soup, beans, and Kraft Dinner, but I think that may scare off the young guy working the cash. *Don't want to make RuPaul too proud of me!*

After I get to the washroom, I look around quickly before I open the door. When I see that no one is in the small room, I unclench my thighs and breathe out loudly. Pirouetting backwards into a stall, I unzip my jeans and am peeing before I get seated completely. I'm hoping I can get my business done before anyone else comes in. I need to be quick. In other instances I've waited five minutes or more while other women do their business and leave before I can come out of the stall.

In a busy place like the mall or the arena, sometimes it's impossible to wait because the in and out traffic is so heavy. When that happens, I psych myself up, stick out my tits, open the stall door, and hope for the best. Making no eye contact.

Paula told me recently. "You really have to stop doing that. You look like a fag doing drag."

Isn't that poetic? My angst in going to the washroom is as a girl who looks like a boy, doing drag to look like a girl.

Just as I finish peeing I hear footsteps clumping my way. *Crap, crap, crap.* I wait quietly, sitting on the toilet and listen to the foot falls closing in. Breathing carefully in that way I used to, when playing hide and go seek as a child, I pick up an underlying scent of urine masked with a heavy pine smelling disinfectant.

Someone has written on the door of the stall at eye level, *This is not the road to happiness, Happiness is the road.* The *i*'s have all been dotted with hearts. *Yeah, that may be, but I'd be much happier on the road with visibly marked unisex washrooms, like the kind they have at Starbucks or places where they don't have the money or the room to devote one to each sex.*

I hope the young woman who scribbled the cliché doesn't find out the hard way that the road can trample and beat you down, and when you run out of money and places to stay, your choices can get a little sketchy and risky. *Geez, I sound like a know-it-all crone.* I'd be more confident for the survival of her soul, possibly her virginity, if her hearts weren't so girlishly hopeful.

The footsteps stop, scuffle around the outside of the door and then retreat. Must be just someone who needed something in this corner of the store. Great! *Hurry, hurry.* I shoot out, rinse my hands quickly and dry them on the front of my pants as I push the door open with my shoulder. I take a moment to prepare myself for an audience, by pulling my shoulders back, raising the tilt of my chin slightly, and walk back through the store as gracefully as I entered, with a sashay and a wiggle. *Who am I fucking kidding?* I can never get it right. I always end up with a bad Liza Minelli or Cher impersonation. The kind you get on amateur night in cheap, shabby, out of the way gay bars looking to attract any kind of cash flow on Tuesday nights.

The gas man is at the counter figuring out the cost of Thelma D's fuel. He had to use a calculator, because the pump is broken and it only displays the number of litres dispensed, and not the total price.

When he handed me the handle to fill her up he said, "We don't get much call for the good stuff, so I'll have to go inside to figure out the price."

There was a hand-written chart, Scotch taped to the side of the rusty middle pump, but it only showed the figures and sums for the cost of regular fuel. It reminded me of my own times table and how I'd carefully run my fingers along the ruled columns of penciled numbers seeking out the answers at the crossroads of my digits.

When I handed him back the pump handle he told me, "I'll get right on that for you, just come to the counter inside when you're ready sir."

I smile big and toddle to the counter to settle up. He looks down after looking at my breasts. When he hands me my change his eyes are confused, disappointed even. It's as if he can't seem to reconcile the image of boots, double front Carhartts, wallet chain, tattoos, and a big ass Harley-Davidson flame belt buckle with being female. I want to console, somehow explain, but I don't.

The young man in shorts is trying to corral his kids into the van while I saddle up. The two old men are still sitting and smoking, and the mechanic is back under the white Chevy. Thelma D skids a little sideways on the gravel when I accelerate out of heaven, onto my own happy road.

25.

SINCE I WAS TEENAGER, I've often been mistaken for a boy or a man. It's why I stress about going into women's washrooms. It wasn't too bad when I was really fat. A person could tell I was a fat woman. No man boobs here. It's worse now that I'm slimmer, but when I was young and fit, working in an auto body repair shop it was constant.

Once, going to work I was stopped by the police after going through a yellow caution light. The officer thought I was using my sister's license and told me to, "Turn around, put your hands on the roof, and spread your legs."

Before complying I unzipped my jacket to show him my breasts.

He blushed and then stuttered, "You should be careful when going through a yellow. You could get hurt." He let me go with that warning, no ticket.

By my early twenties I had been booted out of women's washrooms several times by mistaken managers in low-rent bars and cheap eateries. The most embarrassing time for me was when I was in trade school. I was there for a week before I had to tell the teacher I was a woman. During our conversation after class, I stammered, "If I was as well endowed as my mother there wouldn't be a problem."

At first he didn't understand and then after some reflective moments I could see the light come on. "I have a niece just like you." Without my knowledge, the next day, he gathered all of my classmates together, and announced that he was, "Proud to welcome the first woman ever to the Auto Body Program at Algonquin College."

All of the guys started looking around at each other, all wondering and whispering to each other. "Who's the girl?"

It wasn't long before twenty sets of eyes like magnets locked on me, an opposite pole. Afterwards when we were on a break, one of the guys I had coffee with every day said, "I knew it. I just knew it. I looked down your shirt the second day we were here."

I'm still gender misidentified. Last year I was in an off-chain fast-food restaurant and asked for the key to the washroom. The young man behind the counter gave me the men's room key. I hesitated, but couldn't get up the courage to tell him that I needed the key to the women's washroom. There were people in line behind me, so I took the key and walked into the small hallway where the men's room was. I stood outside the door for a minute or so working through the process. *Unzipping, pissing, shaking, zipping, quick wash of hands, wipe on jeans, good to go.* I even wondered quickly if men peed in circles, or up and down, or side to side, before I walked back and handed the key to the young man, saying, "Thanks."

I don't blame people for thinking I'm a man. It's partly my fault because I don't dress like a girl. Bev tried really hard when I was in my early teens to *femme* me up with makeup and dresses. When I ran away or refused she called me a *butch*. I didn't know what it meant at the time, just that it sounded like it was a bad thing. It would come to haunt me.

She caught up with me once when I was seventeen. I had to go on work experience at The Plant, and she was quite clear, "You are not going looking like that."

I wanted to graduate, so I had no choice but to spend a week working as a secretary, playing dress-up with four other girls. On the first day we were going to lunch and when navigating the steel steps that led away from the building I twisted my ankle, tipping off the high-heeled wedge sandals Bev had forced my feet into. I went down hard, like a puppet whose strings were just cut. My blouse ripped when I landed on my shoulder and my skirt somehow got twisted around above my waist. My nylons were damaged beyond repair.

Since then I've refused to wear a skirt or dress. Actually that's not quite true. I once dressed in drag for a lesbian-only Halloween dance at a local community centre. I made my hair big with lots of hairspray, glued on eyelashes and fingernails and carried a purse for my cigarettes.

I now know why girls go in packs to the washroom. Besides catching up and gossiping about who's doing who, I needed guidance for refreshing my make-up and lipstick. A gal pal followed me into a stall to unzip my skirt in the back. I couldn't grasp it because my nails were too long. Pulling cigarettes also became a chore and by the end of the evening I was worn out. My lashes were falling off, I had lost a couple of nails, and my feet ached from waddling around in heels. I don't know how women do it.

It was bizarre to be so completely out of the wrapper that it was funny and non-threatening for me, but it's not even close to my everyday garb. I'd leave town if I had to dress like a woman. I've always dressed down to be invisible, to blend in, to draw no attention to myself.

People don't really *see* me, and because I wear boy clothes and ball caps they sometimes make the quick assumption that I'm a man. I can't dress like a woman with feminine patterns and cuts. I've tried with the occasional top or girlie haircut when inclined to find my more feminine side. It didn't work.

I'm definitely not the lipstick lesbian type of girl, but I don't want to be a man either. There's no mistake here, and Bev was right, I'm a butch, but her putdown made it impossible for me to find and celebrate who I really was until much later in life. After getting rid of the shame, I'm proud of who I am. To be clear, it doesn't mean I see myself as being born the wrong gender. Taking hormones and growing a beard, while waiting to have my breasts cut off and a dick made, is not a state I yearn for.

26.

THE SIGN SAYS THAT WE'RE COMING up to Ignace, home of Git 'R Done 24-hour towing and wrecking service. I see one of their rigs a few minutes later. It's big. Big enough to tow or recover tractor trailers or buses. The machine is black with a sleeper cab, and double duallies make up the rear chassis. Someone has recently cleaned and shined the wrecker and it sits proudly beside the highway. A large hook graphic on its side points me west like a crooked finger.

Ignace is in Thelma D's rearview mirrors when I decide to pass a truck pulling a camper. The way is clear and it's time to run. I twist the throttle and accelerate. The camper's brake lights come on and I see a small fawn run across the highway, disappearing in front of the truck. The camper starts to shudder and sway. I pull in the clutch, drop two gears, and hit both brakes hard. Thelma D screams in protest, but she trims her speed without skidding and her front forks collapse to their limit, dropping her front wheel. My butt leaves the seat and I come over top of the tank, the momentum sending me and my face toward the windshield. *This isn't going to be good.*

I tense both arms to absorb my body's forward motion and I duck so the front of my helmet will hit first. My left arm starts to crumple and before it fails completely, Thelma D jerks to a stop. My helmet nudges the plastic shield before my body rocks backward. I stare at the back of the camper, which now looks like a large white wall. The frantic ticking in my chest is almost indiscernible and the urge to urinate rushes through my groin. *Holy fuck.*

The baby field rat made it across the road. I see its tail giving me the finger as it flicks and waves, before jumping over a fallen fence at the tree line. The little rat is learning young.

Backing off the big white wall completely, I ride slowly, breathing in and out in time with the big twin's easy rhythm. I pick up the sizes and colours of the shoulder gravel, the height of the grasses in the ditch, and the alignment of the fence posts. It takes a few moments, but my tremors decrease in direct proportion to the increase of Thelma D's revolutions. By the time I hit 100 kilometres an hour, I've settled back into the ride and start riding the paint heading to Dryden.

The small city comes into view by mid-afternoon. The life force of the community, a large pulp and paper mill plant, takes up most of the settlement's meager skyline. It's a jumble of buildings, all different sizes and shapes with smoke stacks, walkways, ramps, cranes, and storage stalls making the mill look like a large misshapen monster. I see it as an oversize creation made from dozens of metal parts that have been welded, patched, and jigged together for a *Mad Max* sequel. Every part is painted the same dreary shade of blue-grey and a lonely line of smoke rises from the middle stack of the tallest building.

There's a Tim Horton's entering town and I break for lunch. Another pit stop means another washroom to conquer. I'm tired and a little cranky and I'm not sure I'm up to sashaying. *Fuck it.* Maybe all of my public pee problems would go away if I wore a sign that says *I am woman.* What's the rest of that Helen Reddy song? *Hear me roar, I'm too big to ignore.*

I'd sing it but I can't carry a tune and I've always been lousy with anything musical. In grade school it was suggested in vocal class that I change to instrumental. It didn't help and I hated the recorder because I always squeaked no matter how hard I pressed down. I spent high school singing "A & G" instead of "Angie" by the Rolling Stones, but I knew all the words to "Delta Dawn." It was on the big yellow bus's permanent playlist when travelling through the valley to sports tournaments.

Humming Tanya Tucker's big hit, I take off my jacket and turn my back to the front windows to re-arrange my breasts in my sports bra. The tucking and pulling reminds me of the first time

I tried to buy a brassiere alone. Shortly after I started work in Ottawa, I went to a department store on Sparks Street to buy one. Bev always bought them for me so I didn't know what size I needed and couldn't ask for help.

I quickly grabbed three different sizes, thinking one of them would be right. It was in the line up at the cash when I broke. The wait seemed unbearable and the longer I stood there, the more I felt people were staring at me, judging and whispering. I kept looking around, shifting from leg to leg, and soon I found it hard to swallow. I could feel my face getting hot, and suddenly it was fight or flight time. I jammed the bras into the closest rack and ran out of the store.

After I had worn out the bras I had moved to Ottawa with, I never wore another one again for thirty years. I tried a couple of more times, thinking that as a grown woman I should be wearing one, but I always choked before I could ask a stranger for help with sizing and fitting. Somehow, it was all too much for me. When I was young, it wasn't uncomfortable because my breasts were pretty firm. I also wore tight tank tops as an undershirt, and they helped with support.

No undershirt can help me now that I'm fifty years old with a major weight loss. My breasts look like wide flat zucchinis or two halves of a butternut squash. I had two choices, either tuck them in or roll them up.

Or, there was a third choice. I could start wearing a bra. The decision was made for me when I hired a personal trainer for my forty-ninth birthday. It was my goal to lose fifty or more pounds before I turned fifty. I succeeded, but it was the jumping while doing burpees that told me wearing a bra would be a good thing. My trainer always politely looked away at every *slap* sound my breasts made against the top of my belly. Poor guy. I started imagining those annoying flapper toys that were a rage some time ago, and I had to admit that flinging them around at my age was very unattractive.

To my delight, like I'm doing now, I found out that I can arrange my breasts and nipples in various positions when wearing a sports bra. There's the fucked up look with the nipples uneven and pointing in different directions. I haven't had the nerve to try it yet in public. Then there's the perky, pointing upwards look that speaks of young energy and stamina. My favourite is the comfortable, middle of the road mom look, where the nipples are centred and nicely spaced. The final look is a low slung, heavy-breasted one where the nipples are pointing to the promised land. I believe a sloppier, stretched out, worn bra would work best for this display.

I've also come to realize, that regardless of the time you spend, and the position you put them in, it never lasts and after ten minutes my breasts are smooshed into a *uni-boob* and my nipples are cross-eyed.

I finish adjusting my boobs to the mom look and as I turn to go into Timmy's my back starts to naturally arch. *Fuck it.* I start to sing the Reddy song. Out of tune, but audible.

27.

THE SIGN TELLS ME I'LL SOON be coming to the exits for Kenora. The highway is a divided one and the ride from Dryden has been spectacular. The road dipped and dove, cutting smoothly through hills and valleys, a camouflage of plush green carpeting inlaid with dark green, almost black shadows. The landscape is crisp and fresh, even the rocks seem clean and unblemished.

For the last hour, Thelma D and I have been running into the sun trying to introduce ourselves. The closer we seem to get, the longer our shadows become behind us, like pulled out bubble gum. The sky is a pale blue, almost white at the thin line of the rise we've been aiming toward. Hypnotic with steady speed and gentle curves, the ride has been a soothing, relaxing tour. No speed bumps for us. Others weren't so lucky.

An hour earlier, the unlucky operator of a tractor trailer stained the pavement with spilled fuel and broken chrome. Deep gouges slashed across two lanes of asphalt where his rig had slid across the road. Diesel was still settling into the gashes when I guided Thelma D around the carnage of broken plastic and fiberglass like a slalom skier. We would have stopped, but several motorists had already filled up the side of the road. It looked like the tractor was heading south when the driver hit the shoulder of the road, and then overcorrected. He lost control and jackknifed into the northbound lane. The rig flipped on its side and broke through the guardrails, coming to rest facing down the gravel hillside.

Determined to keep riding, I've passed the exits for Kenora and Thelma D and I are almost to the Manitoba border. Do I have the energy and the stamina to make the run? I check my legs and they feel okay. Not strong, but not weak either. My eyes are a little droopy and scratchy, a sure sign of fatigue. I'm tired, but this could be a once in a lifetime decision for me. Who really knows where the border is anyway? It's in the middle of nowhere. It's a Welcome to Manitoba sign in the bush, but if Thelma D and I go to Winnipeg, everybody knows where that is. It's halfway across Canada. Wouldn't that be amazing? If I remember the map correctly, it's only about an hour and a half past the border. Doable in the daylight, but I'm wavering. I could really use a hot shower and a bed. Maybe I should turn around, because trying and not making it would really suck. There can be no maybes. If I say I'm going, I'm going, no turning back until Thelma D and I get to Winnipeg.

The last gas station before the border comes up on my right. I signal to pull in and fuel up. Standing beside Thelma D, I release the trigger slightly, slowing the rate of fuel so I can think about making the run. Should I or shouldn't I? The pros and cons race through my mind, back and forth like the screech of a handsaw on thin laminate. *I'm tired. I can make it. I need the rest. I need the run. Think balance.* I screw in Thelma D's filler cap. Winnipeg in three days, how cool is that.

Thelma D is cruising in sixth gear as we blow past the Ontario border into Manitoba. I'm thrilled, and for a moment, I feel like the young and bold rider I used to be, cruising the roads and fields looking for adventure and a softball game to play. The asphalt of Highway 17 changes from charcoal to the beaten grey of Highway 1. The terrain flattens and the pines and spruce are traded for poplars, birch, and aspens. Those gradually disappear the closer we get to Winnipeg, replaced with miles of flat land filled with fields and tiny landmarks, making the horizon almost invisible, impossible for me to discern.

The wind coming from the south is knocking me sideways. Staying on the road means I have to crab my machine constantly, tacking Thelma D like a sailboat. She's holding her line, but an occasional hard gust sends me to the side, close to the gravel and its slippery stones. It's not unmanageable, but it's hard work to constantly lean and steer into the wind. My grip is tighter than it normally would be, making my shoulders and arms tense and tired. And, because I'm gripping Thelma D tightly with my legs, the heat from her engine feels like a radiant heater that is too close for comfort. I'm hot and fatigued.

The divided, four-lane road is a *countrified* version of the four lane highways found in Ontario. The speed limit is 100 kilometres an hour, so that means cars and trucks scream by Thelma D and me at 120. There are entrances and exits like a driver would find on a two-lane secondary road, all indicated with minimum signage. Cars and trucks are leaving, entering, and crossing the highway at high speed from gravel roads that intersect the highway. I feel like one of those steel balls in a pinball machine, waiting to be pinged unknowingly by an unexpected force.

Wind gusts and vehicles running the adjacent roads send dust across the highway, limiting my vision and filling my mouth with grit. I've passed small scooters and bicycles on the side of the road pulling homemade plywood trailers. Two dirt bikes have torn across the road in front of us without stopping. A handwritten sign tells me that I can exit left for fresh berries. Riding Highway 1 is frenzied and intense. I can't help but think what's next? A pair of mules pulling logs stacked in a wooden wheeled cart? The effort of concentrating and staying aware is pulling the energy from my torso, siphoning out through my shoulders and arms, making them feel weak and limp.

Suddenly, I'm startled by a dump truck pulling a piggy trailer, turning with speed from a side road. My stomach twists when I think the driver is going to pull out in front of me because his truck isn't slowing. I feel like I'm going to puke. I check my mirror quickly and take the left lane. It won't make that much of a difference if the truck doesn't stop, because a rig that size would take up both lanes turning. Thelma D and I would be lost. We'd be like a June bug smacking and cracking open on the front bumper. To be scraped and scrubbed off later, eventually being discarded as a couple pieces of organic dirt washed out in a detailing bucket.

Fine sand scratches my teeth when I clench my jaw, breathing tightly through my nose. Waiting. The truck stops abruptly with a jerk, stirring up a cloud of dust that envelopes the cab and dump boxes. He waits until Thelma D and I pass. When I look in my mirror I see him pull out and cut off the car behind us.

The truck and car join my travel, and soon a caution sign in the hands of a flag person is waving at us to slow down. I stop and become head of the line for the next run through. The flag person is a young woman with a blond ponytail hanging from the back of her orange hard hat. A reflective vest covers her jean jacket and sweatshirt hoodie. She smiles at me and then turns her attention to the radio in her hand. A collapsible chair and cooler sit on the gravel beside her.

There are several pieces of heavy equipment working along the adjacent road. Trucks hauling belly dump gravel trailers, yellow graders and big bucket loaders are busy moving and shaping tons of material. It looks like the highway is being widened with new deep ditches. Shifting up, with a light touch from first gear, I put Thelma D in neutral and we settle in for a wait.

***

I think of Dodge man, *asshole*, and Doug, *amazing man*, and the cyclists, *driven*, and two pairs of people I saw walking along side the highway after leaving Thunder Bay. Within a couple of kilometres there was a teenager and a woman, and then two men striding, almost marching. They were on the opposite side of the road with the traffic going south and all were wearing identical white Pro Life T-shirts.

The letters were in a large dark font that filled the front of their shirts. I close my eyes.

***

"It's my baby too," Peter yells, as he punches my locker door shut with his fist.

I clench my books tighter to my stomach. I'm trembling and can't stop crying. "Stop it, please just stop it." I wipe my nose and face with the end of my sleeve.

Other students have stopped shuffling books in and out of their lockers, and are looking at us, taking in the drama, but no one interrupts.

Peter leans towards me, and hisses in my ear, "I'm not going to stop. You can't do this, it's my baby."

His height and width make me shrink backwards until I feel the outline of a combination lock pushing into my back. He lifts his hand and I flinch, thinking he'll hit me again, but he won't because there are people watching. He feigns as if to strike me before dropping his arm. I stumble.

"Leave me alone, I have to get to class," I whine, while walking backwards away from him. He stands there tracking me down the hall with a look that won't let it go. I watch him as long as I can before turning. I know that look and it's not over.

***

Eventually the mess I was in dissolved. I'm glad I didn't become a mother. I wouldn't have been a good one. I was sixteen when I got pregnant and would have been a mother by seventeen. I didn't know how to be a mom. What I'd learned from my parents was how to drink and smoke, lie, cheat and steal, and how to be violent and abusive.

I'm not saying there weren't happy times in my childhood, there were. I was pretty active as a kid and played tag, marbles, hide and go seek, street hockey, and built several tree forts. One of my favourite activities was body-surfing the ditches that ran along the front lawns of our neighbourhood when they filled with water after a heavy summer rain.

When I wasn't outside playing, I loved watching *The Flintstones* and *Hogan's Heroes*. On Sundays after bath time, my brothers and I would fill up the carpet, side by side, in front of the television to watch Walt Disney. Packaged in our pajamas we'd elbow each other for the centre spot, sometimes complaining until Bev sorted it out for us. If we didn't, it only took one word from Eric for us to quiet, eyes straight ahead waiting for the popular program to start.

Walt Disney or ditch-diving was fun and distracting when I was a child, but they weren't enough to shift me, even slightly, from the path of self-destruction that I started earnestly in my early teens. If I had kept the baby, I would have ruined another life, and I was happy I didn't have that guilt to carry with the denial and anger

I was absorbed with through my twenties. I also didn't need any more blame than what I put on myself, drowning most of my thirties in depression. It took decades of living and maintaining the cycle of dysfunction before I realized that I was empty, had no relationship skills, and needed to change. It was only in my early forties when I realized that if I wanted to function, even dare hope to thrive in healthy relationships, I needed help. I reached out, got some, but there are moments still today, when I revert to old behaviours and realize I have more work to do.

Peter did come back that day. He followed me home from school in his car, taunting and threatening me. I managed to get inside our house and lock the door. I thought I was safe. He broke the window to open the door, and found me hiding under the stairs in the basement. He kicked me and hit me and kept yelling that I wasn't, "Going to get rid of his baby." My brother Mark was in the house, and Peter only left when he threatened to call the police.

I got in trouble with Eric over the broken window, and I don't know what happened with Peter after he left our house. I'm assuming there must have been some kind of agreement or understanding between our fathers, because he never bothered me again.

Peter and I had started dating when I was in Grade 11 and were together during the first part of my last year of high school. I'd come home in August from a summer job at a fishing lodge south of Algonquin Park. Since I was going to be gone and unsupervised for the summer, Eric decided, and Bev agreed, that I should go on birth control before I left. I came home after the summer, thirty-five pounds overweight. It was the first time in my life that I'd ever been that heavy. Bev blamed the pill and pulled me off it. She didn't tell Eric. I always thought that she did it to help me so I kept the secret with her, but looking back I don't know. Did she do it because she wanted to get back at Eric?

Bev had no choice, but to tell him I was pregnant a few months later. I was sitting on my bed waiting for him just like the times when my brothers and I were smaller. We'd have to sit quietly, sometimes in pairs, our dread increasing with his every step on the stairs and the turning of the doorknob. We knew he'd had a bad day at work when he took off his belt and told us to pull down our pants. Why did he hate us so much?

Eric opened the door, shortly after five, red-faced, his big body and heavy frame tight with anger. His strides became blows and I put my hands up to protect my head and face.

Bev didn't intervene. She never did. Was she jealous? Or was it some kind of devious orchestration? It's hard for me to accept the idea that she could have been anything other than what she always claimed to be: that she was weak, scared of Eric, and beaten as well.

In a twisted way, it was easier for me to understand Eric's reaction than Bev's. It was violent, brutal, and up front. The depth of his fury made me think that he was angrier than usual because I had been intimate with someone else.

Before leaving, he grabbed me by the shoulders and shook me, hitting my head against the wall, "If you don't have an abortion, you can't live here."

Bev made me an appointment and a few days later Dr. Young hinted that if I confessed to "Drinking alcohol and doing drugs," that there was a good chance of having a therapeutic abortion approved.

It was a lonely time for me in the hospital. I was scared and frightened. Bev dropped me off and left after I was admitted. It made me feel like I was being punished. That all the fighting, all the turmoil in the house was my fault. This was only reinforced when they put me in a room at the end of the hall, away from the other patients. A nurse, who whispered to me like I was some kind of secret experiment, weighed me in at 204 pounds, took my blood pressure and pulse, and then gave me a good night enema. I was exposed, embarrassed.

That evening to pass the time, I had taken one of Bev's novels to read. It was becoming a habit of mine to read through her collection of slave and civil war historical romance novels. I'd spend hours fantasizing and dreaming about another life, filled with undying, forbidden love and gallant heroes. Of course, there were bad guys and threats to the lovers, but in the end it always worked out. I've long since ditched the romance genre, but I am addicted to reading suspense and mystery novels.

The procedure was done the following morning, and I dreamt during the anesthetic buzz that there was a jar on the stainless steel cart with my name on it. That was a mind fuck. I can still pull up the visual in my collection of not so happy images. Bev came and went through the discharge process with me and then drove me home. There was no hug or questions about how I felt, or if she could do something for me. Instead it was ignored, like I'd been gone over night to a sleepover with the bunch at the Brady's.

The young woman in the orange hard hat could pass for one of the Brady Bunch. She tilts her head, smiles at me, and flips the sign around. We can proceed with caution.

I hear the satisfying clunk as Thelma D shifts into first gear. I have come to love that sound. Only a Harley, never a Honda, has given me the reassuring *thunk,* as metal meets metal in the gearbox. There's no tentative searching for the gear, no having to feather or half lift the lever to find position. Thelma D shifts easily through all of her six speeds, but she's especially decisive in first, when her motor shifts slightly and she urges ahead, telling me she's ready. I lead the trail of cars and trucks behind me to the sound of Thelma D's exhaust. The vibration of her twin cylinders are joined together with the hot metal smell of her pipes, like a well-practiced and familiar choir. Her refrain surrounds me with a wrapper of calm and steadiness, while her rhythm caresses and soothes my being. I'm going to be okay.

28.

IT'S STILL LIGHT WHEN I PULL into the Comfort Inn parking lot. Relieved to have made it to Winnipeg without crashing, I tease myself about finally finding some balance. I make a wide and shaky turn into the carport that covers the main entrance. Thelma D settles on her jiffy stand, her engine ticking and exhaust cracking. I'm vibrating with fatigue and the excitement of having made Winnipeg in three days. I'd jump and click my heels, but I'd fall over trying. I get off Thelma D and walk back and forth slowly, to help loosen the rigidity of my legs and hips.

Gerald is on desk duty for the evening, and he takes care of the paper work and credit card for a room. He's a chubby young man with fashionable short hair, wearing a sweater vest with a nametag. I ask him if he can recommend a restaurant. He tells me of a place he likes to frequent. "Just a wonderful place to eat, gorgeous food and excellent service." All said with the lisp and accent of a drag queen in full bloom.

"Sign here please." He points with a finger flutter.

Definitely gay, geez, I hope he knows. He must.

"Where is this place?"

"Well, it's not too far going towards downtown."

"Can I walk?"

Gerald twists his head slightly towards a lifted shoulder, lips pursed. Typical queen. "No, it's too far to walk, at least it is for me." He hands me my room card.

"Is there anything closer, because this bitch is not getting back on her bike?" I reply with my own brand of butch, doing drag with a bad lisp.

Gerald snorts, then laughs with his hand over his mouth before he tells me there's a restaurant a couple of blocks down that's, "Halfway decent."

I pull Thelma D around and park her in front of the sliding doors of the room. I'm settling in with the last of my bags when Gerald calls to ask, "Is the room to your satisfaction?" I tell him he's a sweetheart and everything is perfect, even though I haven't looked at anything, and right at this moment I couldn't really give a shit. As long as there is a bed and a shower I'll be good.

Before my shower, I prepare my injection. I know the longer I wait, the more tired I'll get and then I won't want to do it, using all kinds of excuses to put it off until tomorrow. Paula had me promise her that I'd do my shots when I was supposed to. So I pull out my kit and go through the familiar routine to load the auto injector. Push, click, plunge.

The hot shower has not managed to erase the gritty feeling in my eyes. I stand tiredly, cleaning my ears with a Q-tip. It comes out of my ear, black with soot. Dodge man really does get the last laugh. Bastard.

29.

DEPRESSION CLAIMED MOST OF MY LIFE in the '90s. The decade was like living in the grip of a crazed King Kong. He'd hold tight and crush me to the point of death. Then let me go, batting me around like a cat would a ball, before picking me up in an even tighter hold, bringing on a darkness I couldn't shake. I felt like one of those weird sponge-squeeze toys that never quite gets its shape back.

When I was fully captured by his grip, I'd settle into my basement like water looking for the lowest point and remain secluded for weeks. If I had to, I only went outside in the mornings to stock up on cigarettes, beer, and ice. I woke up every day with the single thought of, *how am I going to feed my addiction today*. Nothing else mattered. I'd start days by hitting a pint after I'd had some coffee.

Denial was my daily companion. It allowed me to truly believe I had a choice about my drinking. It helped hide the fact that the need for alcohol was driving my thoughts and controlling my life. Even when I went into rehab years later, I was very reluctant to admit that I was powerless over alcohol, which by then had become entrenched as my best friend. Being with my best friend didn't make me a happy drunk. I was depressed, hurting, and lonely. Looking back, I'd describe myself as functioning. I managed to keep a job and get through most days. But it wasn't pretty.

When I was fully absorbed by the darkness and the booze, I never sat out in front of my house drinking beers and chatting up the neighbours. I was afraid of people, afraid to talk to them, to have them see me. The need to hide and cocoon was overwhelming.

* * *

The concrete floor of the basement laundry room is cold and damp. I curl my toes and lift my bare feet from the floor to warm them. The hard plastic rim of the bucket gives my weight back to me, pinching my lower cheeks.

I inhale deeply before taking my first tentative sip of the day. A few seconds pass. It stays down. Eagerly I take another, deeper drink and wait. I tell myself this could be a good morning. Then the lurch starts deep in my gut. I swallow several times in succession, hoping this will push down the heaves I know are coming.

No choice. I stand quickly, pull up my pants, turn, go down on my knees and hang my head over the bucket. A couple more gags and I spew the first sips of the day into the pail. My body goes into a convulsive state of retching. Every heave is stronger than the one before it. My stomach clenches painfully. The muscles in my shoulders and neck tighten up like twisted towels, making me afraid I'm going to rip or tear something. A warm wetness fills my thighs as my bladder gives. My eyes feel like they're going to burst from their sockets with every violent expelling of bile. It burns my throat and leaves a taste that will stay with me for the rest of the morning.

Finally the heaves stop. My gut gives up its rejection. I slouch and rest my head on my arms, facing down over the pail. The muscles in my stomach, shoulders, and neck feel like they've been torn apart. I feel wasted, tired. My wet jeans are darkening the concrete floor and I'm starting to shiver. Tears and snot join the saliva I spit into the bucket. After a few minutes I slide back and lean against the furnace. The gentle whir and vibration of the fan motor caress my back, like a mother would do for a crying baby.

After a few quiet minutes, I use the bottom of my T-shirt to wipe my face and look for the bottle.

* * *

There was no window in the part of the basement I used for my drinking. It became like a womb for me, a place where I felt safe, hidden. No surprises. Upstairs became the place I slept or ate in the evening. Since eating interfered with my drinking, I only ate one big meal a day. It was spaghetti, pizza, lasagna, meat with potatoes or something similar with lots of starchy carbs and unhealthy doses of fat. That ritual, combined with the huge amount of calories from the beer, made me obese. I was fat.

After dinner, I'd have some more beers and try to sleep, but my daytime depression would revert to nighttime anxiety. The attacks would creep in slowly, like a snake winding its way through blades of grass advancing on its prey. The first signs were a slight quickening of my pulse. Then tiny tremors would begin in my chest and abdomen. I'm not sure whether the recognition of the attack coming or the attack itself was the trigger, but it would happen suddenly, and like the snake striking, my heartbeat would rise, pounding loudly in my chest. Every beat rebounded in my head and the aftershocks pounded out in echoes through my ears. My heart was breaking and it would explode out through the top of my head.

I thought I'd die in my bed. My heart would fail and my life would be over. Sweat would fill my hands and breath evaded my lungs. I'd swallow gulps of air and that only made me choke. Other times my breath was erratic and shallow and I could only gasp.

Getting up and walking around or watching television only served to distract me for a short while. Reading calmed me. When the assaults would drive me from my bed, I'd sit on the toilet where I'd consume pages and pages of paperbacks. If I didn't have a book, I'd read all the fine print instructions that accompanied Tampons and cough syrup and other pharmaceutical items found in my bathroom drawers and medicine cabinet.

I'd unfold the flimsy sheets that somehow became the size of the poster boards I used in school projects. The fonts were so tiny that concentrating on them brought me calm. Squinting my way to serenity. The difficult part came afterwards, when I tried to fold the page back to its original form and shape. Why did I feel that need? Was it because I didn't want to acknowledge that these thin sheets of tiny typeface were saving my sanity? I did know that refolding them held them in place for me the next time. It was reassuring. Is that what my life had come down to? Dots of ink on paper stuffed in tampon boxes?

There were lots of reasons why I was depressed and anxious, but like the blades of a fan, they all ended in a centre of fear. I was afraid all the time. If there was a knock on the door or if the phone rang, my stomach would twist and surge like I was riding a rollercoaster. If someone wanted to talk to me, then I must be in trouble; I must have done something wrong.

When I had to be out in public, I'd keep my eyes down and averted. If I saw people I knew, I'd turn away or stay in my car, pretending to adjust the radio, or look for something in the glove compartment. My mind would race with scenarios about how I did them wrong. It sounds like a bad country song, but I couldn't get my thoughts in reverse. I'd think that my dog must have barked at them over the fence, or I had promised to help them with a project and didn't show up, or I didn't go to a fiftieth birthday party when I said I would, or...?

There were times when I couldn't avoid people I knew, and I'd find myself apologizing to them at some point during our conversations. If I hadn't done something wrong, I'd apologize for my clothes, the state of my hair, for the bad weather. Fuck, I was a mess. So it wasn't surprising to me that the big gorilla squeezed really hard one day, and it all came crashing down. I was hospitalized.

30.

THE ROOM IS ASTONISHINGLY WHITE and bright. I struggle to get upright in bed, supporting myself on my elbows. I blink furiously trying to focus on the scene to the left of me. *What the hell?* A slight woman with wispy, blonde hair, her gown pulled up past her hips, squats and pees on the floor. *What the fuck?*

A nurse dressed in colourful scrubs, a frown etched on her face, stalks in. She scolds the woman, takes her by the arm, and pulls her out the open door. The woman's gown opens in the back and her pale white ass flashes quickly.

I try to put the pieces together as a slim guy in a light grey uniform comes in and mops up the puddle on the floor. It's all coming back. I'm in the psych ward of the General Hospital, admitted last night because three days ago I failed in my attempt to drink and drug myself to death. *Well, isn't this just fucking great. I've landed in the loony bin.*

I look around and then start checking to see if all my body parts are in place and working. I'm flexing my arms when I realize I'm wearing the same gown as the blonde woman. My temples start to pound and I hold my head to quiet the shakes. The inside of my left forearm is burning. *I am so screwed.* Crawling back under the thin covers, I pull the pillow over my head and try to pretend I'm somewhere else.

Mid-morning, I venture out of my room cautiously and hesitantly, like I did as a kid when I'd sneak into the house after a night out partying with friends. It doesn't take me long to explore the ward and within a couple of days I fall easily into the daily routine of walking, smoking, and eating, and because I'm in a psychiatric ward, meds, tests, and assessments.

Lining the walkway through the ward's common room are several wooden, high-back recliner chairs. The padded seats and backs are covered in a washed-out, aqua-blue vinyl. Two of the chairs hold old men, both white-haired, gaunt, and unshaven. Their arms are restrained. Straps hold their wrists to wide wooden armrests. I walk past them toward the smoking room, and can't help but stare. The men emit a sour milk odour, tinged with urine, and masked with what I think is lilac.

The first old man, narrow-faced with a big chin, tells me to "Fuck off" twice. The second man stares at me and jerks his arms and head side to side. Saliva has dried white in the creases at the corners of his mouth. I avert my eyes and pick up my pace. I found out later from Shelley that the two men are stricken with Alzheimer's and dementia. They swear a lot and yell at people. The men have also been physically violent with family members, patients, and staff, and that's why they spend most of their time restrained. Especially when they're in the common areas of the ward.

Shelley is my painfully thin roommate. She is a drama queen, stick girl in her early twenties suffering from bulimia and anorexia. She was sure to tell me that she has to eat under supervision and she can't, "Like, go the washroom, for like, thirty minutes after I eat." Every statement she makes sounds like a question.

I light a cigarette the moment I walk into the smoking room and sit down in a chrome-legged chair near the door. *What names can I give the two old men? What was the series that plays on one of those retro channels? "The Odd Couple?" Felix and what's his name? The slobby guy? No, they don't fit. Fred and Barney might work. Nah, the old men aren't cartoon types. How about those two old guys in the balcony on the Muppets show? They'd work. What were their names?*

After several cigarettes I'm walking the halls with Larry. I met him in the meds lineup. He's around my age, mid-thirties, slim with a clean-shaven boyish face and a dark, curly mullet showing the first signs of grey. His blue and green plaid shirt is worn with an open collar and the sleeves are buttoned at his wrists. His jeans are tight, reminiscent of the '80s, and worn high on his waist, splitting his package left and right. A habit of pinching and pulling has created a frayed spot, the size of his thumb, at the right side of his crotch. I wonder if it's his penis or his testicle that he frequently needs to tug on.

We walk in a horseshoe configuration, from one set of closed doors through a loop, ending at another identical set of closed doors, on a parallel hallway. The stroll reminds me of my early years in high school and walking the halls at lunch. A flock of us girls would giggle about boys, and who's going out together, and who wants to go out with whom.

If Larry and I walk slowly, we can stretch each trip to ten minutes. First we pass the nurses station, walk through the common room, and then glide by the smoking pit. We haven't yet earned the privilege to leave the ward, so walking and peeking in patients' rooms is pretty much the only entertainment option we have, besides smoking, sleeping, or watching television, and then sleeping some more.

We get to the common area and walk past the old men in their matching recliners. *Would Simon and Shuster work? It might.* The room is a huge space that the hallway expands into. A bank of windows fills the longest wall. It provides daylight and a view of the parking lot if you get close enough to look down. A television is playing in a small alcove off the back of the room. The blonde, wispy-haired woman, who christened my first morning, is sitting on a small sofa looking out the window.

"I get to leave tomorrow," Larry tells me.

"Going home?"

"No, no, I get to leave the floor unsupervised. I've been here five days and I guess they trust me enough to let me downstairs."

"That's good. I wonder how long I'll have to wait."

"Ask your doctors when you see 'em."

"I don't know *when* I'll see any. Besides I don't trust what they have to say anyway. Usually it's all a line of bullshit."

"Sometimes, but they're pretty good in here." Larry hitches his leg and pulls aggressively at his crotch once, twice.

A couple of weeks before King Kong flattened me, my family doctor sent me to see a psychiatrist.

* * *

I am the only person sitting in a row of plain chairs lined up, perfectly spaced along the wall, opposite the office door. There is no receptionist. I relentlessly chew my fingernails and bounce one leg after another, alternating them like beats on a bongo drum.

The office isn't how I imagined. I thought it would be more like the other therapists offices I'd been to. Warm and welcoming, sometimes fake and pretend, like they really wanted to help if you could pay. Here there isn't a plant, magazine or picture in sight. There are a couple of signs posted. One says to remove your shoes and place them on the mat provided.

A woman is sitting at a desk through the open door. I keep looking down at my shoes and can't work up the courage to take them off like the sign directed. I tell myself that it'll be okay; they're clean and I wiped them really well.

The doctor is a small, older woman in her late fifties or early sixties with grey hair forming a queen mother hairdo. She has a grim face with a sharp nose, no chin, and two thin lines for lips. Her skirt and its matching suit jacket are the colour of oatmeal sprinkled with bits of brown sugar. The outfit reminds me of the used sectional couch I picked up cheap from a friend. She calls for me. There is no smile.

* * *

"After telling me to have a seat in her office, the first thing she asks me is if I didn't see the sign, and if I did, why hadn't I taken off my shoes," I tell Larry, "Then she asks me to please respect the rules, and to remove my shoes and then asks if I have insurance and my health card. No, 'How are ya doing?' 'How can I help?' ... nothin'."

"Did you take off your shoes?"

"Yeah, and I held them in my lap the whole time. Well, actually it wasn't very much time at all, because I was out of there in less than five minutes."

"What happened?"

"Well, after she wrote down my insurance stuff, she asked me why I was there and I said that I was having problems because, uh, my dad had ... had abused me when I was young."

Larry looks away and pinches himself.

"So, you're not over it yet?"

"What?" asks Larry.

"That's what she said to me. 'So, you're not over it yet?'"

* * *

I sit there stunned, feeling like I'd just been slapped. I don't know how to reply, so I stammer, "I guess so." My leg is bouncing faster, up and down, frenzied. I twist the laces of my running shoes together, until tears blur my vision and I stifle back a sob that is starting so deep down in my groin, it feels like I'm going to throw up.

* * *

"I mean, how can she say that? Of course, I wasn't over it, how do you get over it? Oh wait, sorry, here, take a pill, twice a day for a week and call me in three days if you're not better." I look at Larry, not expecting an answer and not getting one.

We pass through the common room where Starsky and Hutch are being fed lunch by candy stripers with plastic spoons. I allow myself a little smirk and think at least Starsky, the chin guy, can't tell me to fuck off with his mouth full. A young woman wipes bits of food and saliva from Hutch's face.

We walk quietly for a couple of minutes before Larry asks me. "What'd you do ... after the getting over part?"

"I sat there and didn't hear another word she said because I kept trying to figure out a way of getting out of there. It took me a couple of tries, but finally I just counted to three and took off."

* * *

I run out the office holding a shoe in each hand. My shoulder hits the door to the stairwell and I bolt down the stairs, nearly knocking over a large woman in a long, dark overcoat struggling up the stairs with a bag in one hand and a cane in the other. I don't stop to say sorry. On the bottom step, I sit down and try to get my shoes on. My socks are dirty, covered with grit and sand. I try to keep pulling them on before I tell myself to stop and loosen the laces.

***

"So, I booked it out of there, got some beer and went home."

***

I crawled back into my basement with my cooler, cigarettes, and pee bucket. One day became the same as the next. I would drink, smoke and cry in my beer over the debacle with the psychiatrist, and then sob over flicks with happy or unhappy endings. I'd cry over how Bev didn't protect me. How she didn't take care of me and how if she had, my life would be different, it would be better.

The big crush came during the night I found myself really, truly empty. My being had fled me, and what was left was so afraid, so fearful of life that there was no point in walking back up the stairs. I was lost and desperate for someone to save me, but no one came, and in the end there were no clichés, no tomorrow's another day, no horizon to ride to, no first step, there was nothing, and that's when I decided to see how many painkillers I could consume. The pills were left over from a prescription I had from a knee surgery. There were plenty to take because at the time I had toughed out most of the pain with booze instead.

***

"They took me to the Riverside hospital and after I downed a pint of that charcoal shit, I ended up with a nice doctor holding my hand, asking if I meant to kill myself."

"Yeah, I know about the charcoal. It's bad stuff, gross, man."

"No kidding. Nothing beats looking like a member of the Munster family, spewing black liquid out your ass."

Larry laughs. "I asked for a beer chaser, the nurse didn't think that was funny."

"I'll have to remember that line."

"It's all yours." Larry smiles with a mouth of crooked teeth.

"Anyway, the nice doctor tells me they've paged the psychiatrist on call and they'll be coming to see me shortly."

I dare a look at Batman and Robin as we track through the common room. They've finished lunch and are looking a little docile and sleepy. I imagine them in another place at another time. Taking a nap after spending the afternoon fishing with their grandchild, puttering with the lawnmower or playing chess in the park.

"So, I'm sitting up in bed and I see this short little woman with curly grey hair and I start to think no way, that's not her, it can't be, someone tell me it's not her. Sure enough, it was the same psycho doctor, the one I went to see."

"Fuck off."

"No, I couldn't believe it. I mean what are the chances? I went bonkers and started yelling to the nurses down the hall where she was standing. That's the fucking psycho doctor I told you about. She's why I'm here."

Larry starts to laugh. He peeks into a room where a young woman is sitting cross-legged on her bed. "That's fucked man. What'd she do?"

"She just stood by the door, and then left when I told the nice doctor that I'm not talking to that bitch, and when you have a moment, tell her I'm not over it. Oh yeah, and tell her where she can shove her shoes. She'll know what I'm talking about."

"So how'd you end up here?" He pulls at his crotch while lifting his leg.

"You know Larry, they aren't going anywhere."

"What?" He turns to me.

I point to the split below his zipper. "Your balls, or your dick, or whatever you keep yanking on down there."

"Sorry, bad habit." He reaches for them again and stops. We're outside the pit and he nods. "Need a smoke?"

"Yeah."

"Here, on me." He gives me one of his cigarettes.

"Do you know the names of the two old guys on the Muppet Show? You know, the ones in the balcony."

"Statler and Waldorf?"

"Yeah that's them." A perfect fit.

I left the hospital with a prescription for antidepressants and an appointment for an art therapy class that met weekly at the hospital. After attending one class, I decided that frantically colouring everything in shades of red, orange and yellow wasn't going to work for me.

Fuck the big monkey. I'd go to the police instead.

31.

THURSDAY MORNING BLOSSOMS WARM and sunny, with a near cloudless sky. It's my fourth morning on the road, and the riding gods have blessed me, Roger, and Joanne with another good day to ride.

Their silver BMW GS, parked beside Thelma D, is packed and outfitted for a long heavy ride. It boasts engine and chassis guards, and auxiliary lighting. A GPS is bolted to the windshield above the handlebars, and communication units grace their helmets. Heavy duty tapered aluminum cases are fitted to its sides, and a similar large case creates a backrest for Joanne. Web-like tie downs hold additional canvas bags to the top of the cases, and two bags drape the gas tank under a top tank bag.

Roger is a fair-skinned, tall, sturdy looking guy with a thin blond mustache. His sunburn matches mine. Joanne is quite a bit shorter with a round face that seems to be constantly smiling as she tells me about their motorcycle adventures during a two-week fly and ride trip to Chile. I hear how they drove to Lake Titicaca and saw the lost city of the Inca's, Machu Picchu. The highlight of their trip came when the group was hit with a microburst or mini tornado. Roger said he saw it coming and laid down the bike, but the energy and force of the wind that accompanied the burst pulled up the machine and flung Joanne over thirty feet into a nearby field. Her face radiates as she tells me the first thing she said when getting up was, "Did anyone get that on tape?"

They are from Southern Ontario and are riding out to the coast, then dropping down and making their way across the midwest to a BMW rally. Both are outfitted in matching protective gear. Shades of silver, dark grey, and patches of black match their machine. I'm impressed with their commitment to riding and they haven't nodded once. Why is that? Maybe it's against the Beemer code to hang out nodding in coffee shop parking lots. It makes sense to me that that directive would be in their machine manual.

What does really impress me is that even though we belong to the opposite poles of motorcycling, Harley versus BMW, we have no inhibitions in sharing and talking about the fun and excitement of riding and touring. No question, there is a continental divide between our choice of machines, but if it hadn't been for the bikes we wouldn't have met. I wouldn't have heard or seen the happiness in their faces as they talk about their riding experiences.

Two wheels brings all riders together, rich, poor, young, old, male, female, domestic, German, Japanese, sport, dual purpose or cruisers. It is the inexplicable need to ride and explore that attracts us when our paths cross. That desire, combined with the essence of the saddle, the one we hold in our spirit during the winter season, makes us instant comrades on the road, regardless of age, gender or make of machine. I find the companionship comforting and I don't feel the need to hide from or avoid other motorcyclists. In the same way as knowing you are in the right gear, I sense it is because they understand a small part of me and are accepting.

I watch Joanne and Roger leave the lot before turning back to Thelma D to install her sheepskin. We're parked in the sun, and like the side of a cheap toaster, her seat is already hot to the touch and I can smell the vinyl gassing off of it. The day is going to be scorching. My plan this morning is to visit the Canad Inns Stadium where the Blue Bombers play and then swing by the Harley Davidson dealership before leaving Winnipeg.

I'm hopeful that I'll roll through easy miles today, because my three-day adrenalin fix is depleted. Happy to be turning around, I need to bank some energy and rest my legs through the next few days of riding. Now that I'm heading towards Craig's camp on Lake Onaping, I'm excited to get there because it's been almost a year since I hugged him. I miss the big man.

32.

I TEAR OFF SMALL SLIVERS FROM my nail using my teeth, then spit them out the window. I'm sitting in my car waiting. Waiting to put it into drive. Waiting to work up the courage. I'm hoping today will be the day I drive to the police station. A large chunk of nail comes out of my thumb and it starts to bleed.

Eric hated that I chewed my nails and was constantly berating me for the tendency. Bev tried painting the ends of my fingers and nails with some clear stuff that tasted really bad. It didn't help.

One morning Eric made me get up early and he wound scotch tape around each of my fingers before he went to work.

"That tape better be there when I get home."

I spent the day like a scared, hungry little mouse, afraid of going for the cheese, but unable to stop myself. My classmates asked questions about why my fingers were taped up. When I answered, their bewildered looks reflected my own confusion. If it was for my own good like Eric said, why did it feel so wrong and shameful?

Over the day I chewed little bits and pieces off each of the strips on every finger and thumb. At five minutes to five, the tape had been pared down to mostly uneven narrow strips that no longer covered my nails. I had spent the time after school repositioning them, hoping they would somehow miraculously appear. They hadn't.

Eric cuffed me a couple of times across the back of my head after he saw the wreck I had made of the tape. He wasn't in his usual rage, the one I expected. He was pretty apathetic and I remember thinking his lack of response was worse than the spanking I expected. I'd had a chance to make myself good and I had failed.

It only helped reinforce one of his favourite sayings; he would tell me that since I was born on Pearl Harbour Day, December 7, I was really just another disaster.

Sucking up the coppery taste, my shoulders drop. I roll up the window and turn off the car.

Maybe tomorrow.

33.

THE RIDE OUT OF WINNIPEG on Highway 1 at noon is pretty much the same insanity as the run in. The only exception is now the wind is hitting my right side instead of my left.

Exchanging waves with a rider on a blue machine, I think of Carol and Peter, who I met this morning after filling up. They were on an older Gold Wing that was rigged up with so many homemade attachments that it looked like something a tinker would push down the street with its flags fluttering brightly. Once I showed an interest, Peter proudly showed me the coffee holders he fastened out of some pieces of flat strap aluminum. He demonstrated the swivel arm rests that Carol uses, before lifting the layers of the double seat he put together with some kind of gel pack cradled in a hammock sling. It was obvious how proud he was with his welding when he showed me how he had designed and fabricated a small platform that fitted into a hitch receiver mounted just past the rear wheel. It allowed them to carry extra luggage out the back of the bike. I've seen similar set-ups on the back of vans, but never on a motorcycle. I was impressed, and when I told Peter he beamed, nodded, and stroked his graying beard.

Peter and Carol were both large people. He was taller than Carol in his khakis and black riding boots. A jean shirt draped his belly protruding out from a black vest. She was rounder, made more so by the oversize black riding jacket she wore. The grey of her short, thinning hair matched his beard and they both wore glasses. I don't think I'd have been wrong to guess their weight, combined with the load already on the machine, would exceed the recommended capacity. After taking a couple of pictures, I asked him, "Is the extra load of the platform hell on rear tires, and wouldn't steering the bike be a little soft?"

"No, the steering is fine."

I caught Peter giving a quick glance to Carol, and when she nodded, he pulled a card out of his vest and handed it to me. The card was pretty plain and it had their names and member numbers printed below Christian Motorcycle Association, in large font and underlined. Christian Nodders. I learned they were from Minnesota on their way to a rally in Brandon. I turned the card over. It read:

> **Salvation** – *A plan so simple a child can understand.*
> *For we are all children in God's eyes.*
> Confess to God that you are a sinner deserving of judgement. (Ref. Romans 3:23 & 6:23)
> Believe in your heart that Christ died for your sins and that He rose again. (Ref. Romans 10:9, 10)
> Now pray this prayer: Lord Jesus, I am a sinner and need Your salvation. I believe You died for me and rose again. I now call upon Your name and ask You to save me. Thank you. Amen. (Ref. Romans 10:13)
> "Jesus said to him, 'I am the way, the truth, and the life; no one comes to the Father, except through Me.'" (John 14:6)

I was uncomfortable, and sensed both of them watching me as I read the card. Managing to make eye contact briefly, I said, "Thank you," before pushing the card into my camera case. Then it got all strange and uncomfortable, probably more for me than them. My enthusiastic tinkering conversation with Peter about his ride deflated and fell flat.

"Good luck with your rally," I said as I turned away.

I don't believe in God. I believe people need to believe and have faith in God. I don't understand God. Someone might argue that since I don't understand it, how can I not believe. That's fair, but I can understand better the human need to believe. I've hung onto the slim wires of hope for a better life, while trying to save mine.

For me, believing is the idea of looking inward for strength. To crawl from day to day, never giving up, pushing through each night with the goal to only survive, so I can start a new day. I've done it with the hope that the future will grace me with happiness and rest. For me, that is not the same as believing there is a God. I believe in my own strength and my will to walk upright on most days. During my hard times, I didn't hear or feel a spiritual lifting. I've heard God works in mysterious ways, but so far in my life there has been no helping hand from God.

People have said to me that there had to be someone looking over me, because I have lived where others might have died. As a new teen I started drinking, smoking, and doing the odd recreational drug. I hitchhiked frequently, and I put myself into vulnerable and dangerous positions. I drove drunk. I rode drunk. I drank more than a person should and lived. I don't know whether that is God or a higher power, or maybe it is as simple as my fate was never to be decided then. Maybe I was just lucky and fortunate.

With the exception of Eric's mother, my family didn't attend church or talk about religion. I wasn't taught to believe and if I had, I would have asked God why he let people like Eric loose on the world. I know that question is a simple one, requiring a very complex answer, but I'd still like to know, if there is a God, why he showed Eric the path to my bedroom. I've also been told that God has placed these burdens on us to make us stronger, better, and more devoted. It's impossible for me to believe that the way to Christ was through Eric's groping hands and lashing belt, and that somehow if I survived, I'd be stronger and ready to serve in the eyes of the Lord.

I get defensive when I think about the scripture on the card, where it says that if I want salvation, if I want to be saved, I have to confess to being a sinner and be open to judgment. Why do I need to be saved, and from what, myself? I've been there, and though I might have prayed to a God I didn't believe in at the lowest point, it wasn't Christ who saved me. It was me.

And what do I confess to? Something as simple as stealing cans of flaked ham to mix in with my Kraft Dinner when I was a broke student, or should it be a sin of a more profound impact on another? There might be a lengthy line-up for this latter failing

I'm afraid, but will confessing save me if I'm not a true believer? I don't think it will, and frankly I'm not willing to be judged by someone I can't see or talk to. To believe in the words of salvation, delivered by priests and pastors, and bearers of small white cards, makes it hard for me. Who are these chosen, unique mediums, messengers of God? What makes them special, and why are most of them male?

I don't hate men. I've worked with mostly men the majority of my life and I love my three brothers. I love women, but I'm not a radical lesbian feminist, even though I have difficulty keeping up with the removal of my body hair. I've said that I don't want a dick made for myself, but I'd consider taking one for the power it represents in the world. I'm fantasizing here because I don't think you can just get one, put it in a jar, and then flash it around when you need to get a business loan or to tread on the glass ceiling or to set the price of gas or to....

I grew up with guilt, anxiety, and fear as my devoted trio of dependable companions, and judgment is their father. That's enough for me. Should I tear up the card into little pieces, and let it flutter from my hands like confetti at a wedding, sprinkling the highway behind Thelma D? No, because that would be disrespectful to two people, on two wheels. Besides, I can only admire their will and belief, that they ride every day towards being better people.

34.

THELMA D AND I MAKE THE RUN back to Kenora. Other than a large deer lifting its head while grazing in a field about 20 kilometres before town, it was pretty quiet, an uneventful ride through spectacular country. Kenora is settled on the north shores of Lake of the Woods. The area fills me with the same delighted sense I had in Temagami, having been given the gift of a beautifully crafted landscape for my image collections.

I stop for lunch at the Timmy's in town, and like other restaurants, people are comfortable starting conversations about where I've been and where I'm going. An older couple, sitting in a booth across the aisle are treating their grandson to lunch. They warn me of the road construction, wet gravel, and the deer that populate Highway 71 to Fort Francis. Before leaving, the white-haired, stoop-shouldered grandfather tells me in a very sweet way to be careful, and the plump grandmother pats me on the shoulder.

Within seconds, a guy about my age plops in the seat they vacated and asks the same questions. He seems so eager to talk that we don't take the time to introduce ourselves. He's an ordinary looking guy. Brown hair, brown eyes, average weight for his height, wearing jeans and a T-shirt. His ride is a Kawasaki cruiser, and he tells me his favourite trip is to head west into Manitoba and then drop south into the Dakotas. While chomping down a donut with loud slurps of coffee, he describes how scared he was when he got caught in an electrical storm in South Dakota.

"Scary fucking shit man."

Wired, he nods, chews, gulps coffee, and occasionally wipes his mouth while continuously talking. I'm impressed, but in a different way than I was this morning with Peter's tinkering. He goes on about how it is one thing to battle nature when riding, but the real danger comes from other drivers.

"I've bin riding for twenty-five years and I'm still scared, man," he says.

"Yeah, I hear ya." I want to add *man,* but I gave the expression up when I left my teens.

He appears pleased that I'm of a like mind, and this initiates the start of an oral history of his scary riding stories. As he talks, he chews his way through a second donut.

"Right there, in the middle of the fucking intersection man. Can you believe it?"

I blink quickly, and realize I've been daydreaming and haven't been paying attention. I'm glad he looks like he doesn't need an answer and unperturbed, he continues with a scenario of how the police were being called, and something else I let fritter away.

I finished my coffee at some point, so I get up and tell Dakota man that I could talk about riding all day, but I need to get going.

He salutes. "Keep the fear, man."

35.

FEAR FILLED ME THE DAY I told Bev about Eric. It was the end of summer in 1976. We were in the kitchen. Bev was standing in front of the big white freezer that took up most of the side wall of the kitchen. My voice shook when I described how it had all started with bathing as a child, and how it ended with him raping me as a teenager, after I had been put on the pill.

* * *

Bev picked up the phone and called her sister.

"He's done the same thing," she wailed.

Silence.

"Yes, to Lorrie," Bev cried.

I stood dazed and confused, leaning against the stove with my head down.

Bev hadn't hugged or held me. She didn't tell me she'd make it better for me or even asked me how I felt. Instead she turned around, picked up the black phone on the wall with the long twisted cord that let you talk in another room, and called my aunt.

After a few more minutes of wailing and complaining, she hung up and wiped her eyes with a corner of the dishtowel, smearing her mascara even further across her cheeks.

"How much money do you have from the summer?"

"Three hundred and twenty dollars."

Bev told me, between crying jags, that she couldn't handle it anymore and had to get away. She borrowed my money and left the next day to go to Kincardin. Bev had been there for a couple of weeks, earlier in the summer. Looking back now, it's possible she met someone there, or had such a good time it was hard for her to leave. My confession was the perfect excuse for her to go back.

Over the following years, Bev and I had several unhappy and unproductive conversations about her leaving me that day. The times, places, and circumstances were different, but they all sounded similar.

* * *

"Why did you leave me?"
  "You don't understand."
  "You left us."
  "He hit me too."
  "Why didn't you protect us?"
  "I was afraid too."
  "Why didn't you leave him and take us away?"
  "I didn't have any money."

* * *

I left the same day as Bev and went to stay at my boyfriend's house in Chalk River. Bev said she called Family Services about Eric before leaving town, but no one ever came and talked to me. It was in my second week away that Eric came to get me and took me on his motorcycle to the Petawawa Forestry Institute. Shortly after, Bev came back home and I started my last year of high school.

It was a year of hell. The house was filled with fighting, blaming, distrust, lots of yelling, my pregnancy and abortion. I wanted to run away and leave the chaotic mess behind. I almost did, several times, but I was afraid to, because if I wanted to have any future that included a decent job, I needed my Grade 12 diploma. Graduating gave me the focus and the will to survive in the madness. It never occurred to me, at the time, that there might have been other options. All I knew was that if I could stand the craziness for a few months, I could leave with my education.

Eric didn't make it easy. He refused to give his permission that would allow me to transfer to the four-year program. Instead, I had to take the more difficult, five-year university-bound classes. I almost gave up. I didn't, but I rebelled in my own way. I didn't complete the class assignments or turn in any homework in math. My teacher knew what was going on and tried his best to encourage me, but it was hard concentrating on the Pythagorean theorem when all I wanted to do was some practical math, like how to figure out taxes, car payments, and interest. My attitude was who gives a shit about how far I am from the top of the tree if I'm twenty feet from the base. How is that going to help me spend my paycheque?

It was worse for me in English class. I was a failure. When I first started high school, I was an eager student who loved books and reading. I could read and spell but I didn't know how to compose or structure a piece of writing. One of my first assignments took me almost a weekend of writing, re-writing, and then finally copying my work carefully in my good cursive. I was proud and really excited. When it came back full of red marks, corrections, and slashes with a mark of C-, I was devastated. Another time, I put my hand up and answered a question about the meaning of a poetic line. My teacher laughed. I was embarrassed and could feel my face burning. From that moment on, I sat in the back with a sullen look, never raised my hand, and did the minimum amount of work to get a credit. Except for my last year, when I failed. I took a lot of pleasure in seeing the face of Ms. Black when I told her I wasn't taking her final exam.

"Well, you'll fail English and you won't be able to graduate."

"I took Business Correspondence and that counts as one of my communication credits. I don't need your mark."

Even though I was successful in my rebellion and left as a graduate, the year was really lonely for me. Bev worked a lot at the Byeways. John spent most of his time at his girlfriend's and rarely came home. Craig was gone, and Mark was either playing with his friends, or keeping my grandparents company.

I don't remember voting, but it became my job when Bev was working to have Eric's dinner ready for him when he got home from work, at five to five. I'd get him a cold beer before heating up and serving his dinner. Usually Bev would have something ready for him. If not, I made him scrambled eggs with toast. At the time, I could cook eggs, make Kraft Dinner, and boil hot dogs. Afterwards, I'd do the dishes, hustle him his nightly beers, and change the channel on the television when he told me to. Once I refused to come and switch the stations. Eric stalked into the kitchen and pulled me around to face him by my hair. He grabbed my arm and twisted it in front of me, like you would do to open a doorknob.

"If you want to stay living here, you'll do what I tell you to do, the first time I tell you. Do you understand?"

I understood for another week, then I told Bev I wasn't serving him his dinner anymore. He could do it for himself. I quit. Of course, I was too scared to tell Eric to his face, but I figured if he didn't see me, he couldn't catch me, so I disappeared. He was gone to work by the time I got out of bed and I always made sure I left the house before five to five. I'd sneak back in when he was in bed.

I failed one night. It was three in the morning and I had to wake him up by yelling and knocking on the door to get in the house. I was drunk and thought the door was locked. We never locked the door, and I tried using the key that was hidden on one of the porch supports, but couldn't get it to open. He answered, naked and unhappy.

36.

THELMA D'S REAR TIRE SLIPS and slides to the right in the wet gravel. We are following a dark blue tanker truck and along its back bumper is a pipe that is spraying water over the gravel in the construction zone we've ridden into. Since we are in a residential area, I think the spraying must be to keep the dust down. This way, people will be able to keep their windows open and beat back a few degrees of the summer heat.

The dowsing of the road has created a slippery mess to drive on and it's making me tense and afraid of dropping Thelma D.

I'm also angry, because I can't stop thinking of Bev and how she handled Eric's abuse of all of us as children. Our confrontations were always going around in circles, like water flushed down a toilet. It's something I don't need in my head right now. I need to concentrate on keeping Thelma D upright, but I can't seem to let it go. It should be easier than this. Much easier than the years I spent getting to the place where I finally accepted that Bev was just surviving life in the only way she knew how.

I throttle Thelma D on and off, jerking her forward with every twist. Every surge makes her slip to the side. Angry, I want to stop and do a brake stand, hurling stones, mud, and water out from her rear tire. I know the sudden throttling is inconsiderate and hard on Thelma D's transmission, so I stop and focus on my breathing.

Leaving the wet gravel of the construction behind, I accelerate on the dry pavement and think about adding to Bev's letter.

Hi Mom,

I know that I can't change my history and the only power I have is to change my future. I accept what happened and the choices you made, but on some days it's really hard, especially when I'm tired, like I am today. I'm not sure I understand why you stayed with Eric and pretended our life was normal. And I know I don't understand why you didn't protect us, but what I do know, is that to keep my sanity, I had to let go of the hope that my life was different.

It was that desire that allowed me to stay a victim, to give me the excuse to stay a drunk and spout "poor me," to others who would listen. It was the wish for a different past that took my pride, my future, and stalled my determination to have a healthier life. My life changed for the better when I let you go and learned to trust myself. It was then I understood that the power to change is mine alone, not yours. My energy should be devoted to riding forward, rather than dwelling on a past that I was a passenger in.

I'm riding my own bike now, Thelma D. You'd really like her. I still have my blips of anger like today, but I'm getting better by thinking about the good times instead, like camping at Lake Dore or at Driftwood. Do you remember that time when I came crying out of the lake with a bloodsucker on my leg? You heard me yelling for you and had the salt ready by the time I got to the camper and had it off in seconds. Or that other time we went picking blueberries together and....

Fuck, I can't keep writing letters to Bev. My vision is blurry and my nose is running. I'm lucky I haven't driven Thelma D off the road. Why am I crying anyway? I know why. She's been gone for almost ten years and I miss her. I still love her, for being my mother, for bringing me into the world, and for being Bev, the crazy woman.

My vision blurs a little more, so I pull Thelma D over on the bridge at Sioux Narrows to take a break and blow my nose. There's just enough room on the paved shoulder to tuck her safely in beside the concrete walkway. The mid span of the bridge is framed with heavy steel uprights that are boxed in with cross beams and angled supports. The sections lean in toward each other like dominoes would, both sides meeting in the middle creating an inverted V shape.

I look out over the wooden guardrails down the narrows. Small red-sided cottages huddle together in a small bay to my right. Long docks reach out from the shoreline, like tines on a pitchfork. Several boats are tied off and a catamaran is anchored in the cove, rocking gently with the breeze. A boat speeds under the bridge and I follow its wake, rocking the buoy markers dotting the narrows.

As kids, my brothers and I were all swimmers, and we spent most of our summers at the beach. We'd run and play for hours in the slippery sand and water. There were contests about who could run the fastest along the gravel pier, and how many revolutions you could spin completely before needing to come up for air. Who could swim the farthest underwater and how many clams could you retrieve out of the drop off under the second raft. One time, I managed to come up, ears popping and gasping, with fourteen clams. Some clutched to my belly, and others stuffed into the bottom of my suit. It was the most collected that day.

When my brothers and their friends got rowdy, they'd start whacking each other with the corners of wet towels dipped into the sand, creating angry red welts on their legs and backs. At the end of the day we'd come home tired and sunburnt. I loved the beach.

The drone of the boat breaks through my dreaming, and reminds me that I need to move on. My eyes are dry and like my nose, my head is clear and happy. We head towards Fort Francis.

37.

I SIT IN MY CAR WAITING, chewing bits of skin off the inside of my cheek. The heat of my morning coffee has burnt the raw areas, making them even more painful and sore, but I can't seem to stop.

Today is the day. Today I will drive to the police station. Today I will fuck the big monkey.

Exhaling loudly, shaking slightly, I put the car in drive and leave my parking spot. I drive out and stop at Ogilvie Road.

I turn right toward the beer store.

Maybe tomorrow.

38.

"**Y**UP, DROVE RIGHT THROUGH THE FENCE into a field. That was the end of my motorcycle career," the waitress says, a big smile on her face.

"Now I ride an electric bicycle. That's plenty for me," she adds, while removing the dishes from the table.

Tall and fit, the woman serving me is probably pushing sixty, and very well put together. Her clothes look like she just put them on, even though it's at the end of her shift. I'm impressed. A wide gold lamé belt circles her waist and gold jewellery graces her neck, wrists, and fingers. I wouldn't be surprised to find an ankle bracelet under her pressed black slacks.

It's just past eight p.m. and I'm in the restaurant at the Adventure Inn and Conference Centre in Fort Francis after clocking in approximately 475 kilometres. My legs are telling me it was 400 kilometres too many. I'm drained. When I first got to town, I had to turn around a couple of times. It wasn't a confidence-building activity and I'm happy now to be sitting, showered, and full on a chef salad topped with chicken.

I drop my head forward, and support my jaw using my palms and fingers like a saddle, and close my eyes. There are days when I wish someone would hurt me. Not a kill-me kind of hurt, but enough hurt to damage me visibly. They could run me down with their car or batter my legs with a baseball bat. That would work. People would know then. They would see that I'm somehow damaged. Why do I need them to know? *Stop*. What is wrong with me? *I'm so fucking tired of being tired*.

I don't normally think this way, but today's run has pulled out every ounce of energy I had, draining me like a primed siphon hose in a Cadillac's gas tank, and when I get really tired, I tend to get a little dramatic and over the top with self-pity. *No kidding.* I don't really want anyone to hurt me. I've done enough of that myself.

Since I was diagnosed with MS, one of my biggest challenges is the continuous struggle to overcome the debilitating fatigue that invades my body. Like a junkie, I've worked my way through the available medication. Nothing works for long, and over time I've felt my body and strength fade into a lesser, weaker version of me, a monochrome of sorts. Tonight, I feel like one of those photos made to look old.

The tiredness is really hard to describe. It's not the fatigue you feel when you have completed your first ten-kilometre run or triathlon. I wouldn't know what that feels like, but I've seen the joy and elation that accompanies the exhaustion that runners bring to the finish line, and this isn't the same kind of tired. Runners are rewarded with endorphin buzzes and recovery time. In the full grip of MS fatigue I'm never blessed, and although I've enjoyed the rush of finishing the last few days of riding, I haven't felt that today. Today I'm tired and grumpy. Maybe I should give up, ship Thelma D home, and catch a bus south. I'd still be exhausted, but someone else would be driving.

The fatigue is also not the same kind of tiredness you get when you've stayed up all night to study for an exam and then aced it. You are still grinning with the accomplishment and tired, scratchy eyes on the way to giving yourself permission to sleep all day in a worn-out, blissful utopia. I know what that feels like and it's not the same kind of exhaustion. Right now there is no joy or elation, no rewards or accomplishments.

My reward tonight is a weariness that is lonely and depressing. It is being overwhelmed just thinking about walking back to the room, knowing I'm far from home and the means to get there is another day on Thelma D. It's just like when I want to vacuum or clean or do the dishes and I'm so tired I can hardly spit. To erase the guilt and ease the depression, I have become proficient in the art of negotiating with myself. *You'll be okay. It's not your fault. Rest and then do one thing, then rest again if you need to.*

If others are involved, like when I miss work or a social activity, I obsess with the need to explain myself to them. Self-doubt and guilt have turned me into the crazy person with the chronic disease who won't shut up about it. And there are other times when I remain silent and play the martyr, hoping for compassion and understanding that I'm somehow unable to ask for.

I sit up straight in the booth, rub my face with my hands, and then run them through my hair from front to back. Wouldn't it be glorious if I could erase the lesions on my brain with the same swipe of my hands? My last MRI showed a couple of new lesions in my brain, and on the spinal cord in my neck. Some days, afraid of my forgetfulness and confusion, I imagine a giant Pac-Man munching on my central nervous system, taking away my sanity.

Most days when I am only ordinarily tired, I don't complain about having MS. My life is full and I am grateful for all the disease has brought me. It took some time, but since my first acute episode, I quit smoking and stopped eating poorly, on most days. I lost twenty pounds, hired a personal trainer, lost seventy-two more pounds and am now healthier and fitter at fifty than I have ever been in the past twenty years. Sometimes I wonder if I had not been diagnosed with an incurable chronic disease, would I have made this kind of commitment to myself? I'm not sure.

What I am sure of is that I need to get my ass out of this booth, and bob and weave down to my room. The longer I wait, the tougher it's going to be. Maybe I can have Goldie come over and apply Newton's first law of motion on me, where an object at rest will stay at rest, unless an unbalanced force is applied to it. I think she has the potential to push hard.

Goldie must have sensed my thoughts and arrives at the table with another big smile accompanying the cheque. The cook left after the food arrived, and I thank her again for staying late and tip her generously. I consider asking her for that shove, but I make it out of the booth, and put one foot in front of the other, down a carpeted hallway that smells very familiar.

The Adventure Inn is a larger cousin of the Econo Lodge in Thunder Bay, only cheaper by ten dollars a night. It boasts the same renovations, and it's obvious the hotel has had some rough customers. The window in my room is cracked. The seal is gone creating a whitish blur along the split and a foggy view that is very similar to my second morning of riding with hazy goggles. A new shower liner is poorly installed, and the seams of the recently applied wall coverings are crooked. The carpet has only been cleaned, and contributes its own essence of a strong industrial cleanser to the smell of stale beer and nicotine. I fall asleep before I can think too hard about the scrubbed, faded stains on the bed covers.

39.

THE FORT IS HOME TO A large mill, Abitibi Bowater. When I drive by the plant I pick up a sulphur stink, a heavy scent that has pushed aside the sweet essence of pines, grass, and fresh water that surrounds the town.

With the plant in my mirrors, the odour changes to the wonderful scent of fresh bread and bacon. The aroma is making me salivate. I'm tempted to stop for a large homestyle breakfast with eggs over easy, sausages, home fries, white toast with butter, but I can't. Breakfast is one of my trigger meals and in the past has started daily binges. I love breakfast, but there's no love back in a high-fat, high-carb, and with my excessive use of salt, high-sodium meal — only poison.

I was able to quit my other best friends, smoking and drinking, but quitting food is impossible and fatties like myself use any excuse to consume poison in large quantities. I rationalize overeating by telling myself I'm tired. I deserve it. I need some comfort. I need love. I need to forget.

Losing weight for me didn't come just from hiring a trainer and white-knuckling it from one pathetic little meal to another, five times a day. It came from me realizing that food, while comforting, was nourishment first, and if I wanted to look and feel good then I should eat good food.

The opposite was very true for me for a long time. I wasn't healthy and it was a direct consequence of what I ate and drank. It was life changing for me to finally understand that I should embrace food, and if I wanted to live long in good health, I should love myself enough to nurture my body, not kill it. So my diet became whole foods, good fats, lean protein, and some fruit with lots of vegetables. I even ate vegetarian for a year before acceding to the fact I was given vampire teeth for a reason.

The smell of fresh baked bread becomes stronger and the conversation starts in my head.

The fatty chick is telling me. *You know you'd feel better if you stopped. Breakfast is just what you need to start the day. Can't you taste the butter?*

The skinny bitch replies. *You don't need this. Don't stop. Do you want to eat your way out of your six hundred dollar Harley leather jacket? How would that look?*

But, you'll feel so good afterwards, full and happy. You can always fast for the rest of the day. Think of the home fries with ketchup and salt. Imagine the eggs dripping yolk and the sausages melting in your mouth. It's going to be so good.

Stop it. You don't need a thousand calories for breakfast. It's stupid. Do you want to blow up and pretend that you're actually just fluffy, not fat? Do you?

Don't listen to the skinny bitch. Stop now, park Thelma D, and treat yourself. You can eat better tomorrow.

Don't be a loser. Have some strength and grow a set. Be strong.

Maybe the restaurant will have baked beans and you can smother your home fries with them. Wouldn't that be a treat?

Fuck off fatty.

The girls start a commotion, each one talking over the other, creating a noise in my head like the sound of rushing water. My mouth is salivating again. It's fatty girl fucking with my head. I slow Thelma D and stop at a light, her exhaust joining the noise in my head.

Even after inhaling a protein bar, I swallow hard thinking about the high-calorie, fat-laden breakfast spread mere seconds away. Shaking off the girls, I listen to the love and ride away, leaving the commotion and noise behind me.

In the zone, I ride straight to Kakabeka Falls, a distance of 320 kilometres without stopping. By the time I pull into the attraction known as the Niagara Falls of the North, I am loopy and lightheaded from a lack of food and water. That's not love. It was hard to concentrate, especially in the last half hour. It was also difficult for me to keep Thelma D at a steady speed and ride my line. A couple of times, road snakes grabbed her front wheel, and took me for a long wobble, shaking me out of my loopiness. The long cracks, filled with black stuff the consistency of dried-out chewing gum, can be dangerous and misleading.

There are several clusters of motorcycles in the lot and I park Thelma D beside a medley of three: a brand new Honda Goldwing, a Yamaha old school cruiser with tassels and leather bags, and a Suzuki sport bike loaded with a sleeping bag and another roll that looks like a tent.

My throat is parched and I'm lightheaded. I retrieve a bottle of water from my saddlebag and gulp most of it down before I take off my helmet. After the water, I eat another protein bar, chewing quickly and swallowing large chunks.

What was I thinking, riding this far without stopping, not even for gas? What was I running from? I feel like I've been in a race and now that it's over I'm not sure what it was all about. One landmark I remember seeing was a sign marking the Atlantic watershed line. I recall it because I thought the sign was a typo as it's a long way for water to run to the east coast. It's the same feeling I've gotten when driving a familiar route, where I space out and once I get to where I was going, I can't remember getting there. The usual landmarks and attractions missing and completely wiped from my memory, like drops of water wiped off a counter.

Standing there, looking around and back at the highway, I sense I should understand something. A tingling is there on the edge of some synapses connecting, a tugging on my brain, but the more I grasp for it the more it seems to recede. A familiar feeling, like wanting to be smarter than I really am, surrounds me. I let it go.

My head clears and feeling stronger, I take the short walk to see the falls. The parking lot is user pay and the bike I've parked Thelma D beside has a ticket stub tucked into its seat. I don't pay and hope that if someone were to check they'd think that Thelma D and I are in the same pack as the cycles beside us.

The horseshoe shaped falls are not quite Niagara Falls, but they are still extraordinarily loud for their size. Water falls over steep ledges before breaking apart on steps of natural stone, creating a mist that cools me and whispers its power, its energy. To a purist, the falls at Kakabeka may be even more spectacular than Niagara because they run through an area of nature that is generally untouched, with the exception of the walkways and viewing decks. Here there are no concrete walkways, steel railings, tour boats or novelty stores eagerly waiting to take your money. I spend a few minutes at one of the first lookouts, before turning back. The guys who own the cluster of bikes have returned.

It's pretty easy to connect the bike with the man. The youngest, Tim Junior, is rummaging through the pack on the back of the sport bike. He's wearing a T-shirt with the sleeves cut off and his tanned arms and shoulders are tight and defined with sinew and muscles. It only takes a quick glance to see he's a younger twin of his father. Tim Senior is wearing black jeans, a dark blue T-shirt, and has his almost white hair fashioned into a true mullet. It's impressive. He rides the cruiser, and Heinz, who is slightly taller and softer through the middle than both father and son, is the owner of the Gold Wing.

The guys are on a three-day run from Manitoba to northeast of Thunder Bay, landing at Eagle Canyon. According to the trio, it has the longest suspension bridge in Canada, and is home to a pretty neat zip line that takes the thrill seeker for a half-mile ride. My body aches in a phantom way when they tell me they are camping. That explains why their bikes are overloaded with gear, most of it wrapped in green garbage bags and secured with a rainbow of bungee cords.

It takes a lot of stamina to ride hard all day and then set up camp afterwards. I thought about it briefly while planning my trip. For about two seconds, before I came to the realization that camping would probably kill me. It's been over thirty years since I slid around the floor of Lenny's tent, and while I have done a lot of camping since, I've only tented once when travelling by bike. It was a weekend trip on my Silver Wing, and it rained steadily from Friday evening to Sunday afternoon. It was a soggy, unhappy time. For this trip, I wasn't willing to give up the privacy of a motel room, the convenience of a hot shower, and a dry bed.

We start talking about destinations and rides we've taken when an older couple joins us. I would guess they are mid- to late sixties, possibly seventies. It's hard to tell the man's age because he is shaved bald, the tan on his head showing that it is his usual look. Sturdy-looking, he is dressed all in black with big tread bully boots and his T-shirt boasts a Port Dover Friday the 13th logo. Dark wire sunglasses and a small neat mustache with a crumb catcher on his chin finish his look.

His partner is his height. Her short grey hair outlines a face and neck that is carved and cracked with age. Liver-coloured spots and blemishes are spattered over her hands and arms. She is carrying an extra twenty pounds, creating a muffin top over her jeans and she looks worn, a model with high mileage. Her eyes are kind though, and the wrinkles she has gathered speak more of decades spent in happiness and joy than of sorrow. If I saw her in a grocery store with her yellow T-shirt and brown vinyl purse slung over one shoulder, I'd think of her as a caring and loving grandmother. The thick-soled riding boots and the bandana tied loosely around her neck are the only indications of her inner rebel.

They are from Southwestern Ontario and are in Thunder Bay for a Retread Club rally, an over-forty bikers club touring the area. Again, I marvel at the fact that if it weren't for me riding Thelma D, we would never have met. I like them instantly and listen intently to their stories. Enthusiasm rings clearly through their voices when they describe their time in Port Dover and the thrill that comes from being surrounded by more than a hundred thousand bikers.

"That sounds awesome, how cool," I exclaim and then nod. It comes to me then that I've been trading nods with Tim, Tim, Heinz, and the Dover couple since we started talking. Fuck it, I'm one of them. I surrender. I'm a Nodder. Well, why not? There are certainly worse things I can be in life. I'll just be the best Nodder that I can be, without actually intentionally driving to a coffee shop parking lot to practice.

I come back to the conversation about Port Dover and I'm just guessing, but from what I've heard, Friday the 13th is most likely the largest gathering of motorcycle enthusiasts in Ontario, possibly Canada, and the rallies are always held on every Friday the 13th regardless of the season. Even in December and January. I've always wanted to go, now more so than ever, and like with any large gathering of enthusiastic motorcyclists, there would be sizeable factions of Nodders divided into groups sifted by their vices: coffee, booze or dope. I'll fit in somewhere.

The boys, Tim Junior and Senior and Heinz, haven't been either and they start talking among themselves like it might be their next bonding ride. The Dover couple retreat as the chatter goes back and forth between the men.

I start to get anxious. The synapses from earlier are back, tingling edges and tugging harder, trying to make some connection. I grasp for it and it doesn't come. Distracted, I focus on stapling Thelma D's gear together and then the connection is made of another distracted, zoned-out ride when I finally fucked the big monkey.

40.

I AM SITTING IN MY CAR, sober, on edge. The inside of my cheek is bleeding and I try to get hold of a piece of skin with my fingers. It keeps slipping away, but I'm finally able to grasp it and pull it away. I look at my fingernails. They are ragged and raw from a night of stress. I feel torn apart and on edge. My mind has been in a fever for days with debates of opposing thoughts. Warring thoughts consume me still.

No one will believe me. You deserve better. They'll dismiss me. You need to try. What will people think of me? I'm dragging up stuff that should be left buried. You need some closure. Closure never comes. Why can't I leave it alone? Why can't you get over it? Why can't I? He needs to be held accountable. You're worth it. He'll be mad at you. You can face him. But I'm scared of him. What will Bev think? I won't tell her. What will Craig think? I won't tell him. I won't tell anyone.

I put the car in drive and pull out of my parking spot. Instead of turning right toward the beer store, I turn left and head to the police station in Ottawa.

My throat is dry and my voice cracks, but I stand erect, maintain eye contact, and ask the police officer behind the bulletproof glass at reception to see someone about being sexually abused.

It only took a few minutes before a female detective comes out to see me and we retire to a quiet spot in the lobby. I tell her I was sexually abused by my father, from as young as I could remember, until I told my mother about the abuse when I was sixteen.

She tells me she can take my complaint, but to save time and to prevent any miscommunications, it would be better for me to go directly to the police where the assaults occurred.

I thank her for her time, get back in my car, avoid the streets where there are beer stores, go home, write out a complaint, and then drive two and a half hours to the police station in Deep River where I meet with the Constable on duty. Getting there felt like I was in a moving picture show, one of the early ones with no sound, just action, movements, and gestures.

She takes a copy of my complaint, has me initial each page, and after reading through the several pages asks me some questions. She is very gentle with her probes and, at the end, clarifies some dates and then asks me for the full names, dates of birth if I knew them, addresses and phone numbers for Bev and my brothers.

The Constable also asks me if I was being counselled and I give her the contact info for a woman I had been seeing the last couple of months. I don't tell the Constable that I won't see her again. When I told the therapist that I was going to go to the police, she offered to support me in any way, even if it meant going to court. If I needed her, she would be there. Court seemed years away at that time and I didn't know her very well, having only seen her five or six times, so I saw her offer as untimely, too eager and self-serving. Trust might have been nourished between us if she could have quietly supported me through the process, instead of putting herself on my team and in the game without me asking her first.

After reviewing my answers and checking her paperwork, the Constable sees me to my car and I drive home. I'm exhausted, but it's done. I'm not happy, but I'm not sad either. It's difficult to tell what I'm feeling and it's just as hard for me pay attention to the road. I draw on instinct and intuition to get me home because my concentration is taken up by trying to replay every conversation of the day, word by word, bit by bit. I question myself constantly. Did I say the right thing? What did I say? What will happen? Fuck, what have I done?

I manage to get home spent, tired, satisfied, and ignorant of the storm that was to come. A week later Eric was charged with rape, incest, and several counts of sexual assault. A week after that Bev called.

41.

I AM STILL STANDING BESIDE THELMA D with my hands working the zippers, Velcro, straps, and snaps of her bags and gear. I recall Bev's phone call easily.

* * *

"I heard you went for a drive," she said flatly.

I put my head down and hesitate. "Yeah, yeah I did."

I stalled because I was taken back. Somewhere in my mind I knew Bev would call, but I didn't expect her first words to be so indifferent, an almost apathetic statement with underlays of accusation. I was confused and didn't know if I should be mad at her for her indifference and unfeeling, or if I should have been sad because she wasn't cheering for me.

We didn't talk long, just a couple of minutes. A brief and awkward conversation mostly about the process and timing, no feelings involved. We were like two strangers talking about the weather, only with less inflection. I didn't express any disappointment or anger and soon my voice became as flat as hers. After some long silences we eventually gave up.

What did I expect? A little support, like the keen response I received from the counsellor I never saw again. But, to be fair, I wouldn't trust Bev if she told me she'd be there for me either. It would be hard for me to believe that there wouldn't be another motive behind Bev's support, but because she didn't offer, I wondered why was she so unemotional about Eric being charged. It was what she wanted, wasn't it? Why wouldn't she want justice for her daughter? Didn't I do the right thing? Why isn't she proud of me? After a moment I realize that maybe I should have asked her if it was punishment for Eric that she wanted more, instead of justice for me?

I didn't ask these questions of Bev because I didn't want to fight with her. I'd learned by then I'd never truly get a straight answer when my queries were about me being abused. I also sensed that something was off, that we were on a different playing field and I wasn't aware of all the rules. Or my wariness may have simply come because I was afraid to hear her answers.

42.

FOR THE SECOND TIME IN A COUPLE OF DAYS I tour through Thunder Bay. I wonder if the Hells Angels have finished their business and if all the bodies are accounted for and in one piece. Wiggling my nose, I think about Dodge man and speculate if he's still running around town.

I leave the northern city east on Highway 17. It's a new road for me and I'm excited to be travelling along Lake Superior. I'm told the views are fantastic, and it's not long before I stop at the Terry Fox Memorial and scenic lookout.

The parking lot is divided into several sections and there aren't many customers. Just as Thelma D settles on her jiffy stand, a couple riding a blue Electra Glide pull in beside us. She's bare armed and wearing jeans, boots, and has the short hair that is appealing to women who ride.

He's all biker with boots, jeans, and black leather vest. The front of his vest is clipped together with belly extension straps. I mentioned the straps to a big-bellied biker once. He told me they were really used to hold his vest open and prevent it from flapping when riding, so he'd get a breeze. It made for a cooler ride, and here I thought it was because the vest fit the man, but not the belly.

Their names are Ruth and Manny and they are wearing red T-shirts to support the troops. It's then that I realize it's Friday. I left Ottawa on Monday, Where has time gone that it's the end of the week already?

Red Friday is a fairly new phenomena sweeping through the country. Wearing red at the end of the week is a way for civilians to show their support for Canadian troops in Afghanistan.

Ruth belongs to a Ladies of Harley Club that is organizing a ride for Red Friday on September 10th out of Boulevard Lake. She hands me a business card with the details, and even though she knows it would be a strong two-day ride to get there, she encourages me to come. I express my doubts about showing up and fork out five dollars for a red bandana she pulls from a bundle in the side bag of the cruiser.

Manny should have been a tourist guide. Proud of his city and knowledge, he hasn't stopped describing the area. In a few minutes, he tells me about Terry Fox, his last run, the industrial age of Thunder Bay, and lastly about the Sleeping Giant I can see laid out to the west from the lookout.

I think of the life and legacy of Terry Fox. It's incredible that he managed to run from the east coast of Canada to Thunder Bay, using one good leg, a prosthesis, and funny-looking hitch and hop with every stride, raising money and awareness about cancer. I remember seeing him in his Marathon of Hope T-shirt on the news. The last image I have of Terry is of a serious looking guy with curly hair, a sunburnt face, and chapped lips, telling us in a pragmatic way that his primary cancer had spread, and he needed to go home, but he wasn't giving up his fight.

It was a sad day for all Canadians when his marathon ended, but it must have been more difficult for Terry. It's hard to imagine the discomfort and pain he must have gone through daily, running a marathon a day. Now trying to imagine how much more pain he would have endured physically and emotionally making him abandon his run is impossible for me. If I read him right, having to give up must have been harder than the doctors taking his leg, especially after coming so far.

His legacy is not only the hundreds of millions of dollars raised in his name for cancer research, but the gift of ability. He showed the world that ordinary people can do extraordinary things with willpower, grit, and perseverance. Thinking about Terry, Doug, and others trying to make a difference by taking similar paths, I start feeling very small and overwhelmed. I'm awed by their courage and their determination to put one foot in front of the other to reach their goal.

I don't know if I could take the first step of Terry's journey, especially if I looked at the big picture. It makes me ask myself why I am so easily cowed by their accomplishments. Is it because I don't give myself enough credit or recognition for the challenges I've taken on and overcome in my life? Or is my reaction more about thinking that if I don't accomplish something great in life, than I am somehow a lesser person, a failure? *You're not a failure. Look at what you've survived, what you've achieved.* I leave the lookout with the promise that I'll start giving myself a break. Not that I mean to create a self-admiring society with the need to look for a board of directors, but just that I can look at myself with a tiny bit of awe.

As Manny, Ruth, and I wind our way back to the parking lot, I hear the familiar rumble of a pack of bikes. Three rides, a Honda, a Yamaha, and a sport bike I don't recognize, all bearing New York State tags, cruise into the parking lot. Ruth immediately goes over to introduce herself with a handful of cards and red bandanas. Three men and two women get off the bikes and start to strip off wet jackets, gloves, and bandanas. The front and seats of their jeans are dark with rain and road spray.

Manny and I walk over and after a round of nodding, I find out that a storm came up quickly on them when they were running north on Highway 17. The group isn't that talkative and are more interested in laying out their wet clothes by draping them over their seats, like towels on the back of lawn chairs at the beach.

After walking back to Thelma D, I pull on my jacket, gloves, and helmet. It's getting late, but the long summer hours have given me lots of daylight to run in, and I figure I can make it to Marathon before the light fades. Manny's last words about the danger of moose at night on the upcoming stretch of highway are playing in my head when we leave the lot.

"Make sure when it gets dark, you get off the road no matter where you are. Don't take any chances."

43.

A T THE TURN OFF TO NIPIGON, the combined Highways of 17 and 11 divide. Thelma D and I stay running south on Highway 17 where the road hugs the shore of Lake Superior.

The asphalt is almost new, clean and smooth. The trail goes up and down; it is curvy and challenges me to hold Thelma D tight with my legs. There are no switchback heart stoppers, but coming out of every curve I'm gifted with a panoramic view of the powerful Great Lake. The sky is cloudless and the early evening light has washed out the bright blue of the day, making the run gentle and unrushed like the setting of the sun. To the left, granite cliffs and hills of evergreens accompany Thelma D and me. Galvanized guardrails guide us on the right. Beyond the rails are deep drops to the lake, the sky and water meeting at an invisible horizon.

I throttle Thelma D down at the most spectacular sights, apparently pissing off the people in a car behind me. They overtake me on a dangerous stretch and the passenger gives me the finger when they pass. I can almost hear them exclaiming to each other, not another *fucking* tourist. I'm too happy to react to their hater bird and pull into a lookout to take some more pictures.

I'm pulling out my camera and I get this sudden urge for something sweet. The feeling connects me with a time when, as a kid, I'd come home from Hallowe'en with a pillowcase full of candy. My brothers and I would excitedly compare our hauls, quickly gorging the good stuff and then find hiding places to stash the rest for later secret splurging, because we knew

Bev would be coming on orders from Eric to take the treats away. Once she froze the candy and gave it out for Hallowe'en the following year. It wasn't surprising that Eric had Bev take away our hauls, because he always complained about dentist bills, even insisting we use plastic straws while drinking from glass pop bottles when riding in the car to prevent any possible chipping of our teeth.

Even though Eric disliked paying the dentist, he always made sure there was good food and drink for himself in the house. There was always whole milk in the fridge for the corn flakes that he ate for breakfast on weekday mornings. He had his own bread and lunchmeat. We weren't allowed to consume anything that was his.

Our breakfast came from a bag of puffed wheat and powdered milk. The cereal came in a bag as large as a body bolster and the floor to ceiling corner cupboard was the only one large enough to hold it. The powdered milk was packaged in cardboard boxes only slightly larger than the ones the laundry detergent came in, and regardless of how well you mixed it, it was always lumpy. If we made it up in the morning instead of the night before, the watery mixture was warm and lumpy, disgusting.

We made our sandwiches from loaves of bread that Bev would buy on Wednesdays at the grocery store when they were on sale at four for a dollar. We'd fill them with peanut butter or slices of bologna cut from a large round bar kept in the fridge. The processed meat always tasted gritty to me, but my brothers loved it lathered with mustard or fried in a pan.

I never felt neglected or that I didn't have enough to eat. Often, Bev would make us oatmeal cookies and we'd have oatmeal or cream of wheat on weekend mornings. I'd top mine with lots of brown sugar. She tried to ration out the cookies, but with four kids that was almost impossible. One of us would distract her, while the other snatched a handful of the cookies from the tin in the kitchen cupboard by the side window.

There was one morning Bev felt bad because she had promised to mix up the powder the night before and forgot, so she gave us Eric's milk. She told him that she'd spilled it that morning when defrosting the fridge. It was delicious.

During their good times, Bev and Eric had dinner parties. When Craig and I were old enough, Bev would pay us to clean up for her the next morning. She and Eric would be passed out in their bedroom, sleeping off their hangovers while we cleaned. I loved it because we were able to eat and drink all of the leftovers. Depending upon the time of year there would be roast beef, ham, salads, devilled eggs. There was usually some dry bread in baskets that we smeared with real butter, almost melted from being left out on the table over night. Bev once went through a Chinese food phase, and we had spare ribs and fried rice for the first time. There was some other chow mein stuff that I didn't like at all, but Craig thought it was great.

If we were lucky, there would be unopened bottles of pop. And if we were really lucky, there'd still be some rye to dose it with. I'd mix it for myself the same way I'd always mixed it for Bev, in a tall glass filled to the brim with ice cubes, a shot of Canadian Club, topped off with Pepsi or Coke.

In the early years, there'd be cigarettes to steal and smoke later, but by the time Craig and I were both in high school, Bev had promised Eric she'd quit smoking. She hadn't and soon we became co-conspirators, smoking with her while having coffee at breakfast or whenever Eric wasn't home. Every day it became part of the routine to air out the house well before five to five.

It's well past five now and I need to move. I tuck my camera back in the side pocket of my travel bag before hiking my leg over the guardrail. My boots slip a little in the loose soil, and a sapling becomes my anchor while I take a cliff-hanging pee. The view is spectacular. I think about getting my camera out again and taking a few photos, but Manny's advice intrudes. I need to leave now or Thelma D and I won't make it to Marathon before it gets dark.

44.

THELMA D AND I MELD INTO an easy rhythm making up the last few kilometres into Marathon. Her exhaust and my fatigue lull me into a distracted daydream. For weeks after Bev's phone call, I tried to sort out the motives for her less than thrilled reaction, and ran through the reasons. Was she afraid she'd be called to testify, and then have to admit her own criminal record? Did she do something else wrong? Does she think she'll be blamed for Eric's actions? What if she knew when she said she didn't?

It became draining to keep the questions active and circling in my head. I wasn't sleeping well and every day seemed to bring another load of anxiety, so I was relieved when I had to go up to Pembroke and meet with the Assistant Crown Attorney.

* * *

The Crown's desk is large and piled with paper, notebooks, writing pads, and stuffed file folders, all of it legal length. He's a lean, tall man and he shakes my hand with long, slim dry fingers in a firm grip. Shiny black shoes peek out from his expensive-looking black suit pants, and the bright white shirt he's wearing is loose and the sleeves are rolled up, revealing wiry forearms.

After he offers me a chair, he sits behind the mounds of paper on his desk and a valley appears between the stacks allowing me to see him. His stooped shoulders relax and drop a little further when he gets settled. They give the impression of an overworked and hardworking man, but his voice is strong and determined when he tells me, "I wouldn't be taking on this case if I didn't believe you."

"Thank you." I work my hands tightly, my right squeezing the left, then the left squeezing the right. I can't hold them still in my lap.

"This won't be anything like you'll see on TV. There won't be any dramatic turns of events, raised voices, big revelations or anything of that nature. There's a process and there are rules."

"Okay, yeah, I understand." Still squeezing.

"A preliminary hearing will be held and it's a matter of the judge finding if there is enough evidence to take the case to trial. It's usually a formality, and it's very rare for a judge to rule otherwise and I don't see any problems so far with your case."

***

We quickly worked through some questions he had and then I met with the Coordinator of the Victim Witness Program. She filled me in on what her office did and what her role was. She explained that she or someone from the program would be present to support me in court. I left the meeting with the forms needed to apply for financial assistance from a fund for victims. I ripped them up when I got home because Eric would need to be told that I had applied for compensation and I didn't want him to think that my going to the police was about anything other than justice.

Thelma D growls as I shift down and pass a small sedan. I throw her back in sixth gear and think that it all seemed to be part of a waking and walking dream, until I got the call to attend the preliminary hearing. No one else was required to be there, except Eric. I would be the only person required to testify. By this time, because of the statute of limitations and how the law was written at the time, the assault charges were dropped. Only the charges of incest and rape remained.

It was going to be the first time I'd see Eric since I confronted him at the Pembroke Mall before I was hospitalized. At the time, I thought if I could only get him to say he was sorry, I'd be better, that I'd become whole and could start a new life. Eric never gave an inch, and didn't admit anything, even though it wasn't our first conversation about his abuse of me. Maybe he was scared, because this time I wasn't a cowed young girl, but an angry woman.

Shortly after I got back to Ottawa, Mark called to ask me if I was going to take it any farther. He said Eric phoned him worried about what I might do and he wanted to know if Mark knew anything. At the time there was nothing for me to say, because I hadn't yet made any decisions. I like to think that Mark called worried about me, instead of fishing for Eric.

When I entered the courthouse lobby, Eric was standing to one side alone and waiting for his lawyer. He looked at me and in a tight, controlled voice said, "Thank you," in the way that really meant, *Thank you for doing this to me*. He still had his beard and his bulk and I didn't have a response.

After a short wait, I entered the witness box and swore to tell the truth. Eric stared at me and from his demeanour he was probably wishing that I had drowned as a child. He was sitting very still, barely moving, and it was only by the slight moving of his shoulders and chest that I could tell he was breathing. His eyes were half closed and his lips set into that straight tight line that he gets right before he grabs, slaps, or kicks you.

That was one of his things: kicking us down the stairs, after he spanked us. He'd wait, with just that expression, on the landing and tell us to get downstairs. It was three steps down to where he always stood. The landing is also where the stairs turned and I couldn't ever make it quickly enough. I tried every time, but he always managed to kick me. I'd bounce down most of the stairs on my back until my feet could find some purchase.

The questions started and I lowered my head and mumbled answers to words I could barely hear. My voice shook and cracked and I was asked to speak up by the judge. The walls, chairs, tables, and people, with the exception of Eric staring, all seemed to be part of a big white buzz that surrounded me. It was like I was in another dimension at another time, and through the drone I could make out the Crown's inquiries and the frightened tone of my voice answering. I felt like I was looking in on my own life, third person in three dimensions.

The buzz slowly cleared to a dull hum after a few minutes of speaking. My voice became clearer, stronger. I started to focus on people, tables, and chairs, and slowly came back to the room. During my testimony, Eric, with the exception of a few words exchanged with his lawyer who had come from Ottawa, stared at me intently. Once, I was able to look back at him with a hard stare of my own. It was like when I was learning how to swim, taking those first strokes thinking I was going to sink and drown, but I didn't.

The Crown's questions were short, clear, and to the point. He asked me my name, the names of my parents, my siblings, my birth date, where I lived, the layout of the house in Deep River, how long I lived there.

During our first meeting, he'd told me that he had to set a certain standard in his questioning to support and meet the legal definition of the charges. To do that, he'd asked me questions that included the words fondling, touching, penetration, frequency, and erections. He used all of the anatomical terms that would be used to describe sexual interactions between two people of the opposite sex, like penis and vagina. The experience was very much like a health class from hell, where I was the only student and expected to have all the answers.

His inquiries continued in a chronological order to establish a timeline. It was awkward and uncomfortable for me, and I sensed some discomfort in the Crown's questions. I tried to sound confident and strong with my responses. I succeeded at times, but there were responses where I felt small and mean, like I was telling on someone to get even with them.

* * *

"He told me to stop crying, that it didn't hurt, and that if I kept it up, I would wake the boys and then I would be in trouble."

* * *

Before asking about the day of the rape, the Crown had some specific questions about Bev and the time she found me in their bedroom at night. Eric had pulled me off of him and opened up the top drawer of the dresser before pretending to be asleep. I told Bev what he told me to tell her, that I was looking for some socks for school the next day.

We broke for lunch and then the cross examination started. I knew that my testimony for the Crown was not likely to end the process, but I still felt my stomach turn when I saw his lawyer stand up. Every step he took toward me increased my breathing and hand squeezing. I could not turn off the thumping of my heart.

He stopped and faced me. I wanted to cry and could feel my face flushing red as blood rushed to my neck, ears, and face. I was at one of the heaviest, biggest times of my life, and sitting there, I felt like a little girl who had done something bad, and was sent upstairs to wait for her Daddy to come home.

45.

I SIT DOWN ON THE STAINED SEAT of a chair near the door. There's a woman across the room with her head down, staring at the floor and rocking slightly. I pull out my cigarettes and open my paperback to the page I've been trying to read all day. It's a mystery and I'd like to eventually find out who done it, but I'm not having much luck.

The windowless room is small with a linoleum floor scarred with forgotten cigarettes and scuff marks from those in constant motion. Side tables in the corners hold old magazines and tin ashtrays. The fan in a ceiling vent fills the room with a loud hum as it desperately strains to pull out stale air contaminated with smoke, nicotine, and the body odour of those addicted.

Between reading the same lines over and over, I sneak glimpses at the woman who's been sitting and quietly rocking across the room. I don't recognize her and she hasn't looked in my direction or invited any conversation. I'm relieved because I wouldn't know what to say. "How're you doing?" doesn't seem like a good starter line in any hospital, much less this ward. Although it was the exact line Larry used to introduce himself to me while we waited in line at the nurse's station for our meds. I remember I'd replied, "Not bad," when I really wanted to say that I was scared, fucked up, and needed to pee.

It's hard to gauge her age. She's a small woman dressed in jeans and a wrinkled white T-shirt, tinged grey. Men's red slippers cover her feet. Her hair is short, brown, and dry. It seems more shorn, than trimmed or layered. When she lifts her head up, it's with a hard face that has a yellow, unhealthy cast to it. Lines layer the skin under dark eyes and above a small chin her lips are narrow and tight. Small, dwarf-like hands keep busy, flicking her cigarette into a tin ashtray with her thumbnail.

My gaze is drawn to the woman's arms. They're filled with the etchings of rough and ragged tattoos. Angry, red slashes fill the spaces not taken up by the primitive ink drawings. Some cuts are open and fresh with dried blood. Others are starting to scab, while still others are white and gnarled with scar tissue. They all sit on forearms with skin that is shiny and translucent from being aged with anger, pain, and a razor.

I lower my head and look at the plaid of narrow, red slashes crisscrossing the inside of my left forearm. The small cuts are itchy and are starting to heal. I pull down the sleeve of my hospital gown and tuck my arm in tight to my body. *Jesus, I can't even do that right. They're hardly paper cuts. Not like hers. Aren't paper cuts supposed to hurt more anyway?* The quick shallow slices worked though. The razor cleared my head, funneled me to centre with a fresh new pain I could stay in the moment with.

I stab out my cigarette, repeatedly mashing the filter into the flimsy tin tray and try to read again. Within moments the words on the page start to move, lines blend together, mixing into a fuzzy landscape of moving black and white spaces.

* * *

I'd tell him to stop and he'd tell me to shut up. I'd tell him it hurt and he'd tell me it didn't. He had large fingers, pushing and breaking, his bulk suffocated me. I'd sob silently and drift away, wishing I were somehow invisible, that my body didn't exist. I wanted to be dust wiped off a mantle, or smoke blown away from a candle. Inevitably, like breathing, the pain would always return, surging or seeping, filling my head with his cruelty, his power, his need. I went crazy with grief and loss. My mind kept flashing back to the same scenes of menace and brutality, like a needle skipping on a record. Hitting my head couldn't make the memories stop and, overwhelmed with the deluge, my mind spiraled out of control and hysteria grabbed me. I sobbed with snot leaking out of my nose. My knees buckled and I collapsed into the corner with a razor. Barely able to see, I pushed the blade into my arm over and over. The repeated sting and seeing the lines of red blossom on my skin brought an almost instant relief. Tears joined the blood. The needle on the record was nudged, and the flow continued, interrupting the cruelties in my head. My breathing slowed, the beating in my chest and head quieted, and the trembling in my core lessened. Eventually the lunacy seeped away. The blood turned into droplets, trickling down my inner arm and dropping off to stain the beige of the linoleum floor. The drabness of the walls became chromatic, the white of the fixtures gleamed, and the brush detail of the stainless steel wall holders came into sharp focus.

* * *

My head starts to clear and black separates from white, bringing the words back into focus. My knee is bouncing and my fingers are cramping. The page I was reading is torn. Sweat lines my palms and my head starts to ache.

I look up. The woman is still there. She's staring intently at me. Smoke curls up from her dwarf hand. I meet her eyes, and we exchange a silent understanding, each showing a glance of the other's pain, before we pull back to the safe place behind our walls. The walls, built from the betrayal of a child's body, are always protecting. They never rest or crumble. My wall has destroyed relationships, friendships, and courtships. It is relentless in questioning those who want to get close.

Why are they being so nice to me? They don't mean that. Why are they talking to me? They're only saying that because they have to. What do they want from me? They won't get it.

It's then I grasp with an overwhelming sense of sadness that most people only want from me what I can't yet seem to give to myself — love, kindness and respect.

46.

T HE TRAVELODGE IN MARATHON is my shelter for the night. Sitting on the bed, I stare as the last gasps of light are pulled from the window. I'm so tired that I can't even imagine seeing myself getting up off the bed. I need to shower, eat, and then do my shot, an insurmountable list. Instead, I sit and look at my arm.

The scars from that crazy day in my life are now barely discernable. I have covered some of them with a tattoo of barbed wire, but a couple of the thin white slices remain visible. Another piece of art may cover them eventually, but I'm not in a hurry. The memories from the day I pulled the razor through my skin may have faded over the years, but like the scars, they will never truly leave me. I've contented myself with having both for a lifetime.

I've also come to understand I can't wipe them away like I used to do with everything that mattered to me when I wanted to start my life over. I'd go to bed in the evening drunk, but always determined to make a better life for myself in the morning.

First thing upon rising, before my resolve disappeared, I'd clean and tidy the house, return my empties, and wipe down the couches, cupboards, and counters. I'd vacuum and dust, and then I'd organize my personal papers, ripping up pictures I didn't like of myself and throwing away journals, cards, and letters. I'd erase as much of the past as I could, while telling myself that this was the day I was going to get better. I'd start going to work more often, stop drinking, and start paying better attention to other areas of my life. I'd start to play hockey again. I'd lose weight and become fit. I'd feel so great, it would be too good to be true.

After I finished, I'd sit fidgeting, chewing my nails, smoking and wondering what the next step was, and why I didn't feel better.

I think of those times now and am sad when I realize what I lost: photographs, journals, my history. I didn't mind losing the photos so much, because I always hated having snapshots taken of me. I'd look at them afterwards and only see the worst: my hair was awful, I looked fat, and my teeth were crooked. And I hated when some well-intentioned person would look at my photograph and say, "You have such a pretty face." I wanted to tell him or her to fuck off, but I said thank you instead. Why do people without weight problems feel the need to say that about fat women? I was embarrassed.

The trashing of my journals and letters and cards from friends bothers me. My lifetime memories could mostly be reconstituted with some hard thinking, but I lost the written details, the specifics, the descriptions of the emotions that would bring me to particular points in time, some good, others bad, all now lost.

The worst loss for me though was the human one. It was the price I paid for driving my partners and friends away. The accumulated insults eventually led them to silently find new friends and new partners to spend their time with. I can't find fault because they tried but couldn't get past the wall. I wouldn't let them.

I especially didn't want them around when I was depressed and drinking. I wanted to be alone. Nobody but me could understand what I went through and I wanted that pain to myself. It was my ticket to drink. I was a victim. And during the times I was trying to make myself a better person, I didn't want to see them because they reminded me of my past failures and embarrassments. I made it impossible for them to participate in my life. I was selfish.

Now, sitting here in Marathon, exhausted, ready to cry because I have no energy, I don't berate myself for past selfishness. I can't anymore. The ritual of beating myself up by blaming and criticizing is not my way anymore and with any progressive works, there are slips. Like with school, I don't have perfect attendance in the together world, but it comes to me that I've been slipping a lot lately.

I go back to the time I realized that I wanted, needed even, a better life if I wanted to live. It was then I finally understood that the only person who could make positive change in my life was myself. Doctors, professionals, partners, and friends were not going to do it for me, and why should they? I found out that my desire to be part of a gentle, quiet, respectful life shared with people I love is stronger than my need to maintain the wall, drink, and act like an idiot.

I'm still staring out the window as the black ink of night absorbs the last pinpoints of light, turning the glass into a mirror. It comes to me that I have weakened in my resolve for a better life in the last few years. While I may not be drinking and acting stupid, there has been a slight fading. I've backed up into the old behaviours of being hard on myself, partly because I don't have the energy to do the activities I want. Is this just that I'm getting older, or is it something more insidious? The answers will have to wait. I straighten my shoulders, smile tiredly at my reflection, and give thanks for being alive.

47.

THELMA D'S FRONT WHEEL STARTS to shudder. I look quickly for any road snakes that may have grabbed her wheel. She doesn't feel right, something is wrong. I smell metal burning and she jerks sharply. I almost lose her handlebars. The front brakes don't work, but they start chattering before a sharp grinding noise takes over. I can smell rubber burning just before her front tire blows out with a loud bang. It's the swerving toward the ditch that awakens me.

The dream seems real enough to me that I need to check on Thelma D. She's parked outside, at the back of the Lodge, and even though I can't walk out to her, I can see her from the window. She looks fine and I'm relieved.

It's six-thirty a.m. and it feels like I've spent the last couple of hours looping through versions of the same dream. In one take, I'm able to pull over and stop safely. I find her front wheel bearing had heated up and thrown a brake shoe, jamming the front wheel and blowing the tire. Somehow, I'm able to gather the tools to disassemble the front end, and re-inflate the tire. I do just enough patchwork on her to get me on the road to the dealership so I can get the proper parts. In other versions, there was a guy who looked a lot like the big Nodder guy in Temiskaming, telling me, "That would never happen with a Honda."

I'm feeling sluggish and rub the sleep out of my eyes. I need coffee. I haven't managed to fill my energy tank, but I think I have enough in me to run for the day. I take an inventory of specific body parts. My knee is a little stiff, but it will become more flexible during the morning. By the afternoon there'll be some pain and swelling, but only surgery can take care of the torn cartilage. There's no use in complaining about it; that's what Tylenol and Advil are for.

Toes, wiggle, numb. Thigh, prod, numb. Nothing has changed.

Facing the mirror, I see the angry little pinches of my injection sites spread haphazardly across my stomach. Some are still inflamed. Red spots the size of a golf ball. They show up sharply against my white skin marred with stretch marks. Other pinches are freshly bruised, like black olives, and still more are ringed by yellow. An abdomen rainbow of needle marks.

My legs feel adequate, not real strong, but okay. Last night in the shower I had to lock my knees to stay standing. I felt like a drunk again. My ass in the air, and my belly sticking to the top of the tub, while I crawled over its sides to get in and out, afraid to trust my legs or my balance.

My nose and cheeks are still peeling, and since I don't wear a protective visor the wind has joined the sun in ravaging my face. It's not pretty, but it's a happy face. I'm glad because I'm getting closer to seeing Craig and then getting home.

Contented, I think about my ride yesterday afternoon chasing the rush. The adrenalin started when I'd pulled Thelma D out to pass a group of vehicles. There were a dozen, possibly more, joined together like the baggage cars of a train. It was a long straight stretch. After passing four or five cars I looked down at her speedometer and we were doing a 150 kilometres an hour and still accelerating. I was scared, and my first thought was not to slow down and try to squeeze in between a set of cars, but to tuck my legs in tight to Thelma D's tank. I didn't want the wind to catch one of them, jerking me sideways, and causing me to lose control. I don't know if that has ever unseated a rider, but at that speed it felt like it could happen.

I could see a large white truck in the distance, but because of the slow curve and the heat waves radiating off the asphalt, I couldn't tell what lane it was in. Was I closing the distance because I was coming up on it, or was it coming toward me? I took the chance that the truck was leading the train of cars and stayed in the left lane increasing Thelma D's throttle.

The adrenalin that surged through me was unlike anything I'd ever experienced. I was saturated. It was thrilling and intense. The sensation made my groin feel close to orgasm, every nerve tight with pleasure on the edge of pain. The feeling was better than the twisting high-rise turns of a roller coaster, and like with an orgasm, the sensation, the need, grew with every second I stayed in the lane.

The wind seemed to both accelerate me forward and backward, and then push me side to side when I passed the spaces between the cars. The sound of Thelma D's exhaust resonated like it was from another bike behind, chasing me. My legs, body, and torso slowly absorbed the vibrations of her twin engine until we were joined like lovers intent on each other's pleasure.

Time slowed down, seconds became minutes. Nothing mattered more except to reach the end, the point of pleasure so intense that your body rejects the caresses of your lover. It came. I passed the truck. It was over. Trembling and weak, I was soon able to discern the separation between my heartbeats. I could hear my breathing. My body started to relax and tingling fingers of pleasure stroked over me, tender and loving. A gentle, playful reminder like you would get from a satisfied lover to come back soon.

My sated, full feeling disappeared quickly when I thought about spending a minute or more on the edge of death. A car could have pulled out and clipped me, and Thelma D could have gone into a speed wobble after catching a road snake, or the truck could have been oncoming.

Going through that range of emotions made me giddy with the excitement of not being dead. I made it and I was alive and it felt wonderful. It has been a long time since I've experienced the rush. It was amazing. It could be addicting.

I refocus on my reflection in the bathroom mirror. I'm smiling. Happy. Contented. Then, my smile dims and scary feelings start to invade my chest. I'm getting anxious and I don't know why. My heart starts to run a little faster. Tremors start up my legs like vibrations from a bass drum. What's going on?

48.

Eric's lawyer walked toward me. He was confident and assured, well-dressed with short dark hair, a sharp tie, and shiny fingernails. I was in the witness box and I was scared. I was thirty-eight years old and afraid to be wrong. I was brought up to please and say the right things. I didn't want to disappoint.

Fear twisted and turned on me, like a snake curled around its prey, taking away most of my voice and leaving the rest sounding frightened and weak. I tried to give answers that sounded confident and strong, but I wavered because I was trying to figure out how he was going to hurt me, trick me. That was his job, wasn't it? He's a lawyer. It's what he does. Defending criminals is his profession and challenging victims, navigating the justice system is his career. It's how he supports himself and his family. I tried, but it was impossible for me to view him objectively during his questioning sessions. I couldn't help but think of the lies Eric was telling him. How Eric was saying the wrong things. How he was paying this man to reveal me to be a liar just like my mother.

His tone was authoritative, especially when repeating things several times during questioning on both days.

* * *

"...given the serious nature of these allegations that you are bringing against your father..."

* * *

The lawyer had a lot of questions about the morning I went to the police in Ottawa, writing up my statement at home before driving it to the police station in Deep River. He made numerous inquiries about the timing surrounding the day I went to the police. The lawyer spent more time on questions about my initial contact with the detective in the lobby of the Ottawa police station than I had spent talking with her.

Later his tone became disbelieving. He kept asking me about when I prepared my statement. Looking back, I realize that he might have been wanting to show that it was prepared with the assistance of someone else, most likely the therapist I was seeing, before I brought it to the police. The lawyer was implying I was in collusion with a third party I was unwilling to name.

By the end of his questions, he almost had me believing I was wrong about the timing of the events of that day. This changing of facts by repeating the same question, the twisting my words, and the hammering at small details and times would become his habit during my cross-examination.

***

"I didn't say age three ... my first clear memory was when I was four or five."

***

It was his job to make people sound like they were not telling the truth and he did that really well. He made everything sound so unbelievable, that I felt trapped into the feeling I would sound untruthful, regardless of what answer I gave him.

It seemed too easy for Eric's lawyer. I wouldn't have *believed* myself after listening to my answers. I wouldn't want to think I made it easy for him, but I wasn't expecting the relentless turning around of questions, and constant manipulations of the statement I typed out.

On the day I wrote it, I just wanted to get the words out and on paper and get it finished. I wasn't that articulate. I rambled as I wrote it down, remembering from a child's point of view, where life is big and confusing.

When he kept coming back to me about my eight-page statement, nine-page statement, not believing that I could have prepared that lengthy of statement when I said I did, I wanted to tell him in a loud voice that I type over eighty words per minute. How many could he?

Oh, my apologies, you speak into a microphone and someone else types for you!

I imagine lawyers, who want to be the best at what they do, must practice this craft of fucking up witnesses. It's probably second nature to some, their minds quick and agile, driving away at points that make no sense until they culminate in an unrealistic statement disguised as a question. Maybe they have an informal underground network where they get together over a single malt and profess to find justice for all, tweaking the best language to use when needing to depict witnesses not as victims, but as perpetrators of untruths.

The lawyer also made it clear several times through the hearing that he would be making applications through the courts for all my therapy records, not just the sessions I had with my therapist, but all of my counselling and medical records. Before asking me to sign a consent form, he prodded, "Who is assisting you with your memories?" He also wanted to know if I had any conversations with my therapist about bringing a civil suit against Eric for damages.

During the second day he asked me questions about Bev.

* * *

"Do you have contact with your mother now?"

"Sporadic contact, at best."

"Have you had contact with her since your last occasion in this court?"

"No. She mailed me a note the other day, but I haven't spoken to her."

"And is your mother encouraging what you are doing now?"

"No, I don't think so."

* * *

The lawyer finished with a twisted question and math routine about the number of times I had seen my father over the years, and how many of the contacts were initiated by me. By the end he had me looking like a stalker and I felt helpless.

* * *

"I thought that maybe if I could have contact with my dad, and if he liked me, my life would be better."

49.

TO EASE INTO THE RIDE, I keep Thelma D at a slow rumble while I get warmed up. We've just left Marathon and it's a little later than I'd like, around eight-thirty a.m. It took more time than usual for me to get in sync with my legs. I also dallied in the Travelodge restaurant having a coffee and a toasted western on whole wheat. Not quite sausage, eggs, and home fries with a side of beans, but still a nice treat. It kept the peace between fat chick and skinny bitch.

I'm headed southeast, travelling inland from Lake Superior. On the map it looks like I'll be giving a wide berth to Pukaskwa National Park before returning to the great lake at Wawa. Pukaskwa is a wilderness park that protects almost 1900 square kilometres of northern forest, mostly boreal, that includes the shores of Lake Superior in its ecosystem. From the pictures I've seen of its ancient landscape I almost wish Thelma D were a canoe, until it comes to me that it would mean paddling, portaging, camping.

The ride is an easy one into Wawa. I had stopped at one pullover at the same time as two guys from Michigan came chugging in on Electra Glides. They were on their annual trip around Lake Superior. The men were as similar in stature and size to each other as were their bikes. I thought it strange that even though they were friendly enough while we chatted and nodded about trips, rides, and weather, they turned their backs and walked away when I pulled out my camera. Were they just shy or secret agents? I envision them as working undercover to identify the secret meanings behind the famous Canadian code word *"eh"* in all its forms. Travelling inconspicuously through the north, masquerading as biker buddies, all the while trying to decipher, *fucking eh, fuck you, eh,* to *you know what I mean, eh, cool, eh, and what's that, eh?*

Maybe they were really here to investigate the pride, joy, and namesake of Wawa. A goose. Unlike the northern towns along Highway 11 with their numerous mascots displayed right beside the road, Wawa uses a goose to attract visitors to their town. When the new Trans Canada highway was finished, it bypassed Wawa, so the decision was made to build a larger than life statue of a Canadian goose to pull in gawkers from the Trans Canada. It worked and has been an attraction for some fifty years. Incredible.

After I get the necessary pictures of the big bird, I head to the new Timmy's in town. If the goose doesn't pull you off the highway, then a new Tim Hortons should. The lot is freshly paved and smells of tar. The parking spots are delineated with newly sprayed, bright yellow lines. The grass is fresh sod, and the landscaping is at the point where the shrubs and young trees will either take, or wither with the dry heat of the summer. It'll take a lot of watering to keep the curl from their leaves. It's so hot I'm reluctant to let Thelma D's jiffy stand fall into the new pavement.

After getting my coffee, I sit on an incline of new grass and think back to the preliminary hearing, wondering if I should have told Eric's lawyer that the note from Bev wasn't really a note. Should I have told him it was really photocopies of pages from her journals? How would I explain that?

They showed up in the mail one day without any explanation. When I called Bev to ask, her only response was, "I want you to have them."

Since her health wasn't good, one of my first thoughts was that she found out she was going to die and didn't know how to tell me. Or that she wanted me to have something of hers, like the time I got her pardon papers in the mail.

Besides her usual noncommittal responses to my questions, Bev only asked me one question about the preliminary hearing, and it felt strange.

* * *

"Did you see your father?"
"Of course I saw him. He was difficult to miss."

* * *

The pages from Bev's journal, written in her distinctive cursive, mostly described her childhood in Alberta and current life in Vancouver. The pages told me she was happy as a child of the west, but sad and uncertain about the cancer that was now taking her life. She had decorated some of the pages with her artwork, mostly geometric scribbles and some drawings of flowers with stems that flowed down the sides of the pages. Emotionally, I found them difficult to read because I didn't get what she was trying to tell me. I kept letting them drop to the floor, frustrated and angry.

Seeing it all now from the fresh sod I'm sitting on, I realize I never found her message at that time because I was looking too closely, trying to de-construct her every word, instead of looking at the whole paragraphs and the margins holding them together.

50.

LEAVING WAWA AND THE GIANT GOOSE, Thelma D and I ride into Lake Superior Provincial Park. It's not long before we meet the family of lakes: Dad, Baby and Mom lakes. I smile when I imagine how they would look depicted on the back window of a van. Outlines of puddles wouldn't translate well, certainly not as clear as the rows of stick-figure family members I see more and more frequently on minivans and SUVs.

Did the Dad and Mom lakes combine to make the Baby lake by some ancient means? An underground fertility stream that overflowed, or was it merely a matter of being physically close to each other, a family made from proximity?

Thoughts about family dissipate when I return Thelma D to run the edge of Lake Superior. The ride is as glorious as the drop down from Thunder Bay. Inadvertently, I put my hand back to feel Paula's thigh. I want to share the wonder and excitement of the ride with her. She's not there. I'm sad. During our rides together, I'd often reach back and squeeze her leg, and in response she'd hug me. Her arms would circle my chest and her breasts would massage my back. I'd sit up straighter to feel her completely. Her breath hot on my neck, she made me feel whole and strong. I can almost hear her telling me loud in a whisper, through Thelma D's exhaust, that she loved me.

I miss her. I wish she could be here to share in the power and beauty of the Great Lake, to experience the fullness of the ride along its shore. I tell myself we'll come back together one day.

The coolness of the lake starts to dissipate a few miles from Sault Ste. Marie. The asphalt, brick, and concrete of the city radiate a heat accumulated by a mid-summer season of scorching days. It's sweltering, where the coolness of the nights are not enough to pry any relief from the structures that hold the heat tight to the city in a greedy, miserly way.

The community is larger than I expected. I don't know why I'm surprised by that. Maybe it's the vast spaces and loneliness of the north that makes the Sault seem big with a promise of what you need, they have. There are malls, restaurants, dealerships, hotels and motels, and signs for anything else a traveller or resident may have a desire for: taxis, schools, and hospitals. I'm disappointed though because the Sault doesn't have a Harley-Davidson dealership. The closest dealer is in Sudbury and a visit will have to wait, because I'll be cutting off Highway 17 and heading north to Craig's camp before I get to the Nickel City.

Thelma D and I are idling at a last set of lights when an old two-door, red and white Chevrolet pulls into the turning lane beside us. I can't quite get a glimpse of the driver, but the greatest country song of all time, George Jones's hit, "He Stopped Loving Her Today," is blasting out the open windows. Others may disagree, arguing for a couple of tunes from Johnny Cash instead.

The song fades away as the Chevrolet turns. Thelma D and I enter the highway, which becomes a separated four-lane. The air is cooler, and it's easy to scout the coming terrain because of the width taken up by the road through the forested land. Where the forest disappears, the view becomes acres of cleared fields.

I pull into the left lane and pass a woman on a silver motorcycle. Like myself, she is loaded for the long haul. I didn't catch the kind of bike she was riding and I didn't want to slow down and stare, have her thinking I'm some kind of creep or weirdo. She's geared up with matching silver riding pants and jacket, and her long hair is waving out the back of a full-face helmet. When I passed, I gave her a slight nod to acknowledge her and her machine. Didn't want any over enthusiasm, especially riding a Harley. I'm supposed to be cool, indifferent.

She accelerates her bike and stays with Thelma D and I. Every time I check my mirrors she's there, keeping an offset line and a comfortable distance between us, like two riders travelling together would. Even though we don't talk or share stories and only made eye contact briefly, it's nice to be part of her space. We are a small pack. A riding sister. Her presence is not the same or as soothing as having Paula with me, but it is comforting, secure.

She leaves Thelma D and I 50 kilometres later.

51.

AFTER PARTING WAYS WITH THE silver-clad woman, I think
of Bev and the times I spent cuddled up beside her while we
watched Hockey Night in Canada on Saturday nights.

Even though the era belonged to the Montreal Canadiens, my
favourite team in the '70s was the Boston Bruins. In grade school,
a girlfriend and I had memorized all the players' names and
numbers. We'd test each other while sitting on the pyramids of
snow that marked the ends of our driveways, the same mounds
of snow where my brothers and I would build forts and throw
snowballs at each other. She always carried the latest team
member names and numbers on a piece of lined paper, tucked
into a pocket of her snowsuit.

When we got one wrong, the other would correct the offender. If
neither of us could remember, we'd check her master list. Perched
high in the wind, our bodies losing heat, noses running, shivering
and stubborn, we'd go back and forth, not quitting until each of
us could recite the list of twenty players from memory. Today the
names are still famous icons of hockey: Phil Esposito, Bobby Orr,
Wayne Cashman, Johnny Bucyk, Gerry Cheevers.

It was a bonus for me if the Bruins were on Hockey Night, but
regardless of what teams were playing, Saturday nights during
the hockey season were special to my brothers and I.

If we weren't laying on our stomachs watching the game on our
black and white television, we'd be sprawled out on the large,
dark brown sectional sofa that swept like a half oval against the
back wall of our living room. Eric didn't enjoy hockey, so it was
usually just Bev with us, camped out on her side of the sofa. She

would lean against the armrest with a pillow jammed underneath her armpit. After getting settled, she'd pull her legs up towards herself, creating a nook that I'd crawl into, and we'd watch the game together.

Between periods I'd massage her feet. I'd sit upright and lay her legs across my lap and knead the bottom of her heels, arches, and the mounds below her toes with my thumbs and knuckles. My hands would ache with the strain of pushing and kneading, but hearing the sounds of her pleasure I would swell in pride and satisfaction. She especially liked it when I'd work my fingers in between her toes, stretching them outwards. It was like a date, my hands holding her feet.

Another early favourite winter memory is of Bev bundling me up to go outside and play in the snow. She'd help me dress in my snowsuit, zipping it up tightly, pressing the snaps together. Then she'd sit me down and help me put on my boots and mittens. After pulling up my hood, she'd wrap my head, neck, and face with a long scarf, leaving only my eyes revealed to the cold. When I became hot and sweaty, I'd need to take off my mittens to be able to unwrap the scarf, because she had put it on so securely. Her wrapping and attention made me feel safe, loved, and warm.

Later, as a young teen, I don't remember her being an especially loving, affectionate mother. It had felt like caring for us was only a job for her. Making meals, doing laundry, washing dishes, and cleaning were a burden for her, and as soon as we were old enough to do them for ourselves, we did. I liked to help and on most days I didn't mind vacuuming or stripping and waxing the hardwood floors. But there was one job I really resented and that was ironing Eric's handkerchiefs and boxing shorts. They had to be folded a certain way with the creases just right. It's against my nature to do a sloppy job so I felt compelled to do the best job I could. But having to handle his intimate clothing felt like a horrible punishment.

Thelma D's reserve light comes on, the glowing red outline of a fuel tank signaling it's time to pay attention to the ride. I'd be more than a little worried about being on reserve fuel if I weren't so close to Espanola, a community about the size of Deep River. Like many of the others I've travelled through in the north, it's built on the forest industry. Similar to how Rapides des Joachims became known to the English as Swisha, the name is an anglicized version of Spanish word, Espagnole. The name was derived from a Spanish woman captured by a raiding party. She married one of her captors and settled with her family at the mouth of the river. The early explorers heard the women's children speaking Spanish, and the village became known as Espanola and the river was named the Spanish River.

52.

"Mon dieu, je pensais que j'étais dans les toilettes des hommes." The old woman with a blue-tinged perm looks at me in alarm. She turns around and checks the sign on the door. I'm familiar enough with French to know she thinks she walked into the men's room by mistake.

I turn off the faucet and smile at her. She seems to clutch her purse tighter to her side. Instead of reaching past her for some paper towel, I wipe my hands dry on my jeans. But, what I really want to do is grab my uni-boob with both hands, power it up, aim straight at her forehead, and zap her with my laser.

The door closes on her excited exclamations about my tattoos to the woman who followed her in. It's easy to understand, because tattoo in English is the same as in French, tattoo.

Body art is my gatekeeper. The permanent ink is a filter that keeps out the biased and the prejudiced, all the haters. They allow in the free spirits, the respectful and the believers, and even well-meaning curiosity seekers.

I used to hide my tattoos because I was afraid of what people would think of me. A month after I started my teaching program at the Faculty of Education at Queen's University, I wore short sleeves to class. One of my classmates, after getting over her disbelief, told me, "I'm glad you didn't show them the first day. I would have been afraid of you."

I was taken aback, but not surprised because of what tattoos mean to certain parts of the population. They evoke very strong feelings, and to some they send messages of violence, toughness, and criminality. People who are heavily inked are thrust out into the margins of society. Some are considered freaks. I'm happy to be a part of that group as a tattooed, lesbian butch. Better hanging with the freaks than with uptight conservatives, some of whom I believe secretly want to be tattooed.

One of my favourite reactions to my body art is when people tell me, "Do you realize what that will look like when you're fifty?" or, "What are you going to do when you're seventy?"

Well, I'm over fifty years old, still getting tattooed and if the math is correct, I'll be lucky to make it to seventy, so fuck them all. That might be a little harsh, but it's ridiculous to think that how I feel about my tattoos will change because of my age. People who make those statements don't understand tattooing or collectors. My tattoos are the essence of me. They show my life journey, my struggles, and my celebrations. They may be painful to receive, but they have brought me relief from pain. Yes, they may be anti-establishment, my own middle finger to those who judge me, but they give me pride and I love that they make me different. Even in the tattoo world, there are no two collections that are alike.

I got my first tattoo in 1978, a dove that sits just above my right breast. I wasn't able to sort out my feelings at the time, just that it felt important, life saving even. Reflecting on that decision now, I got my dove because I knew Eric would hate it. Previous to that, I also cut my hair and got my ears pierced. Both of which he never allowed me to do while I was living under his roof. Getting tattooed was a way of taking back control of my body.

If I had left my ink at that, then I'd be part of the flock of mainstreamers who have hidden pieces of inked art. The ones women whisper about in giddy voices at parties. It only takes a drink or two for them to show off the butterfly on their ass, or the sun on their lower back, or the tiger below their bikini line. Guys have pulled up their shirts to show me tattoos on the back of their shoulders. I've seen them all, because it seems once I've displayed my tattoos publicly, put them out there with daring and confidence, then all those hiding theirs want to show them to me. I've often wondered about their motives. Do they want to be part of my pack, be my friend? Or, are we only friends in the moment, and the next time we meet on the street I'm invisible, a freak to avoid?

Unlike the '70s, the art of tattooing is everywhere these days. It doesn't take long when driving along main streets in towns and cities to see tattoo shops, proudly showing flash artwork and specials for piercings. When I got my first tattoo, it took me a week of walking Rideau Street before I found someone, who knew someone, who tattooed. He was a nice, older guy who practised his trade in an apartment he shared with his wife. The selection of flash was pretty basic and very traditional, mostly sailor stuff. My dove took about a half hour and it was not as painful as I thought it was going to be.

During the outline, his wife remarked with pride in her voice, "Some men would have fainted by now."

Thirty years later my dove is showing her age. When getting a chest piece some time ago, I'd thought about getting her touched up because she certainly wasn't flying as high as she was when first laid on my breast. In fact, you could say she's pointed more down in a swan dive, than up in glorious flight.

I couldn't do it. I didn't want her altered. It felt wrong, as though it would erase an important part of me. So she remains untouched above my breast, to remind me of my determination to be something different than what I was.

One of my pieces stands alone, a memorial portrait of Bev on my right lower leg. It comes from a typical picture of her, less a little chin. The artist added hoop earrings, making her look like a gypsy. Her hair is up and her trademark curls lay flat on her cheeks, framing her face. Two large purple roses finish off the bottom and side of the portrait. Transferring her rendering from a black and white photo took two sittings and about six hours. I'm not sure how Bev would feel about being a piece of permanent art on my body. I hope she'd be proud. I do know she would love the rendering of herself because she looks beautiful. I'm also pretty certain she'd be satisfied with idea of me having to keep my legs shaved to show her off properly.

It was before I got the tattoo of Bev that I faced the harshest criticism I'd ever received about my body art. It came from the right of centre, no freaks allowed world of a secondary school teacher I worked with. When he saw the tattoo on my arm, he said, "I hope you were drunk when you did that."

Earlier in the week, I had attended a meeting with this same man. He described a parent, a woman on welfare, as being a drunk covered in tattoos, with bad teeth and even worse hair. I wanted to pull up my sleeves, show him my tattoos, and tell him that I had to collect assistance once to get through trade school. To let him know that there was a time when people thought I was a drunk too. I wanted to shout at him, that while I have most of my teeth, it took longer than it should have to get rid of my mullet. I wanted to tell him all of those things, but I didn't. I often reflect on that day and wonder *what if*.

I see the French-speaking woman and her friend make their way to a car parked across the lot. I'm ready to get out of Espanola. From the map, I figure I'm a couple of hours from Craig's camp on Lake Onaping, and even though it's dinnertime and I'm tired, I want to make the run tonight. I miss him. I need a big hug and to see some family. I'm lonely.

I call the camp and Morley, Craig's son-in-law, picks up the phone. After some conversation in the background with Kathy, the instructions are for me to call when I get to Chelmsford, so somebody can be waiting at the dock to pick me up. Morley ends the conversation with a request from Kathy, "Can you pick up a bag of two-percent milk?"

53.

HALF AN HOUR LATER, I turn off the Trans Canada to head east along the Highway 144 bypass. The highway will eventually veer north of Sudbury leading me to the camp. The ride down from Espanola was tame. The scenery, settlements, and smells became backfill as my thoughts were tuned in to seeing Craig. The tameness disappeared within metres of turning onto 144. I've ridden into construction and while the traffic is light, the road is a mess. Where there isn't gravel, the pavement has been gouged into lines, like a steel garden rake would leave when spreading soil.

I slow and Thelma D wobbles uncertainly, as if caught in an endless road snake. The gouged lines aren't filled level with the road, making them more aggressive than the usual snakes I've ridden with. And, even though they are crookedly done, I'm thankful they are mostly parallel with the road. Thelma D and I struggle. She wobbles and I swear.

The signs warn the construction is over kilometres, not just the hundred metres I've ridden. My first thoughts are destructive. They are to turn around, go back to the highway, turn left, go home. I tell myself to relax and go with the ride. I concentrate on my breathing to slow it and relax my grip on Thelma D's bars. The tension fades from my torso and legs. Slowly, but steadily, I increase her speed so that she is running over the grooves and the wheel wobble disappears. Confident now, Thelma D and I roll by the orange and black construction markers.

The groove pattern brings memories of a time spent staring into a large box in the Metropolitan Department Store. The white box was waist high, about three feet square and a foot deep. I'm standing at the box because I had lost an earlier argument with Bev.

We were parked at the curb outside the glass doors of the store.

"I don't want to go in there," I whined. "You can't make me."

"Yes I can, you're going or I'm telling your father," Bev replied.

"But, I don't want to." I complained further, blinking back tears furiously.

"You're going in there. I'm not leaving here until you get out of this car and go in that store," Bev stated, her features set, determined. We'd been arguing the same commands and complaints back and forth for several minutes.

"Please Mom, I don't want to," I plead. It was useless, and I knew it because Bev had that stubborn look on her face. The look that said regardless of how long it will take, she'll get what she wants.

Slamming the car door was my only defiance before I walked into the store and stood in front of the box. It was full of small, clear cases containing false eyelashes. They were on sale, three sets for less than the ten dollars Bev had pressed into my sweaty hand when I finally relented.

My orders were to find at least two sets of lashes that alternated lengths, creating this wispy kind of look that Bev really liked. She showed me the ones she was wearing, so I would pick the right style.

I found the first set right away, and then spent ten minutes looking for the second. The box seemed to be coming alive with writhing black caterpillars. The harder I looked, the more they all started to look the same. When I looked up to blink my eyes, a saleswoman was watching at me, a question ready on her lips. I quickly dropped my eyes and twisted my body to give her my back.

I gave up after another few minutes of searching and grabbed two sets of the even length variety from the mass of wiggling black fuzzy creatures.

The same saleswoman served me when I placed the cases on the counter with the folded up, damp ten dollar bill beside them. Bev had told me if there was enough change left over, I was to get some glue for the lashes. I couldn't find the breath to ask the woman if I had enough money for a small tube of the adhesive.

My weight went from leg to leg, like I was walking on the spot, and I kept my head down concentrating on my runners, while she worked the cash. "Here's your change honey."

I mumbled, "Thank you," then grabbed the change from her hand, snatched the bag with the creepy crawlers off the counter and ran out of the store. It felt as though I'd just robbed a bank, with Bev driving the getaway car.

54.

THELMA D AND I REACH CHELMSFORD. I pull into a gas station, push out her jiffy stand, and let her drop. I sit and rest. Shakes roll through my arms and legs, surging up, then down, back and forth like a wave pool, the after effect of riding kilometres over gouged and uneven pavement.

After filling up Thelma D, I ride across the road to the grocery store. It takes some re-arranging, but I manage to stuff Kathy's bag of milk on some ice in one of my saddlebags.

I turn Thelma D around in the parking lot, stop and face the highway. It's going to be another forty-five minutes of riding to get to the camp. If it weren't for seeing Craig tonight, I wouldn't make the ride. It's not safe. My eyes are gritty with fatigue and road dust. There's been a ringing in my ears since I started on the bypass. My shoulders and arms are strained from wrestling Thelma D to keep her line. A cold wet feeling has invaded my boots, even though I know they are dry. My body needs to recover.

I turn Thelma D off. Her exhaust ticks in response. I start to twist my neck around, roll my shoulders, and swing my arms. *I can do this. This is mine.* I arch my back, my belly pushing against the zipper of my jacket. I don't dare swing my legs or try any dynamic squats. Instead I lift my right leg, grasp it by the knee and squeeze it into my chest. I let it go. My left leg lifts about a foot from the pavement and then my balance is gone. I stagger and catch myself. I lean instead against Thelma D and pull my left leg in to my chest, feeling the stretch. The routine makes me feel like when I used to get ready to play hockey, only my body is not as refreshed as it would be for the start of the game. It's more like a body getting ready for the third overtime period in two days.

55.

MY SHOULDERS SLUMP IN RELIEF as soon as I see the faded, plywood billboard announcing Onaping Lake Lodge. I'm almost there. I turn right towards the lake. Although it's still daylight, the sun has dropped, giving travellers an early evening softness, a tender light that deepens shadows and highlights rock spurs. The northern run on Highway 144 was beautiful in its lonely way. Like my ride from Hearst to Longlac, it was isolated and thankfully, not as long. It was also a different road from the Trans Canada that hugged the forest-shrouded shores of Lake Superior, but splendid in its own winding display of granite outcrops, lakes, and a moose.

I slowed Thelma D to take a long look at the slow moving mass of bones, flesh, and antlers. The moose was winding its way through wetland in a valley basin, its dewlap swaying gently when his head turned. From a hundred yards I could sense his power and strength.

I'm not far from the lodge when the road turns to sandy gravel and Thelma D slips a little, even in slight turns. I grip her a little harder. I know I shouldn't, but I can't seem to help myself. The tiny grains make the road slippery and unpredictable, not a great combination for a heavy cruiser without aggressive tires, driven by a tired-out old wench. The path narrows down to ruts in the grass going uphill, before opening back up into a small gravel lot. I slow and Thelma D chugs her annoyance in first gear, before puttering to a stop when I spot the lodge on my left.

It only takes a minute before Craig and Morley come down the stairs of the lodge, each holding a couple of beers. Craig puts his beers on the bottom step and comes over to me with his arms open. "You made great time."

"Oh my god, it's so good to see you."

We hug hard. I am flooded with scents of wood smoke, mixed fuel, and beer. He smells great. I pull him in harder, afraid to let him go. It feels like he's all I have left. Bev and Grandma Marj are dead. I know I could call John and Mark if I had to. We're not estranged exactly, but we are strangely indifferent to each other.

He seems to sense my need to hold him longer than usual and lets me stay in his arms. Craig and I might see each other once or twice a year and we talk on the phone when we can, when we need to. During the decades since we were children, we've gone years without contact, when Craig was mining in British Columbia and Manitoba, and when I was fully engaged in my depressions, not wanting to see anyone. But we always reached out and found each other again. Coming together, like finding a well-worn, forgotten pair of favourite boots, with no judgments or accusations. A soft, comfortable, safe fit.

I feel like that now, because he has never judged me. Has always quietly supported me. We might have fought and refused to listen to each other at times, but we always returned with apologies and bashful explanations. Ours is a closeness that doesn't come from neediness, but a genuine desire to spend time with the other. We like each other. I love him.

"It's good to see you, sis." He says before releasing me with a big squeeze, and picks up his beers.

Craig is a big man. Well over three hundred pounds. He carries his weight through his upper torso, in his stomach, chest, and arms. His legs and butt remain relatively unscathed by the added pounds. He is wearing khaki shorts, a black Harley-Davidson T-shirt that is stretched tight across his belly, and brown sandals with Velcro straps. Craig's hair has always been naturally curly and he keeps it long. A wavy, unruly mess captured in a ponytail. It is streaked with strands of grey and so is his beard, which is full and long. Not ZZ Top long, but I think he's aspiring to their look. Two large silver earrings adorn his ears and together with his hair and beard, make him look like a pirate. He defies management at the mine he works at by not removing them for his shift.

Morley stands quietly, drawing on his beer while Craig and I start chatting. Craig steps away and circles Thelma D before saying, "I can't believe it. My sister riding a Harley." He looks at me, smiling large. "I'm proud of you."

Craig has always wanted a Harley for himself. I'm hoping he'll get one so that we can ride together. He'll be turning fifty next year, and a machine is on his list.

I need to park Thelma D between Craig's truck and the side of the dock, in front of the bays where he moors his boats. Craig gets me a piece of wood so Thelma D's stand won't fail in the soft grassy earth, and assures me the owner of the lodge, Jack, will check on her.

Morley lugs my bags onto the deck of Craig's pontoon boat. The vessel is a recent acquisition for moving materials, supplies, and grand kids to the camp. It's nice to be off the hot pavement and on the water. I'm tempted to dive in to cool off and refresh, but I don't want to sit in soggy clothes for the twenty minutes it'll take to get to the camp.

Craig and Morley drink their beers and talk about what's to be done at the camp. They need to finish the adult sleep cabin, before starting a sleep bunkie for the kids. Morley, like Craig, is a miner. He works the opposite shifts as Craig, day versus night or reverse, but they are off shift on the same days. He's almost as tall as Craig, but not as big through the middle, so his white T-shirt hangs freely over some jean shorts. His light hair is buzz-cut short and thinning on top. It's hard to tell if his facial hair is from a few days growth or is a result of some work with the razor. Morley is not a big talker. He has a quiet humour and quick smiles for those he counts as friends.

It's not long before we make our way through the narrows, across the big water and into the small bay where the camp is. Hydro has long disappeared. We are in an unorganized township, and it shows in the creativity and prolific construction done by the residents. Most of the small cottages on the lake are on small lots, gathered together in clusters like bees to honey, in small bays and coves.

In Craig's bay there are no more than a dozen sites. Vegetation has been left wild on some lots, with a cabin or two peeking out from the bushes and trees. Others have concrete or wood retaining walls with manicured lawns and high tech solar systems tracking the sun and its energy. Shiny, bright stainless steel chimneys rise from cedar-stained cottages and their saunas.

From a distance, the first look at Craig's camp always reminds me of a set from a children's adventure novel. It's not a large piece of land, but it rises from the lake to display several buildings. Most are painted in Kathy's favourite colours: avocado green as the main shade and eggplant used for the trim. The way up to the main cabin is a series of paths, steps, platforms with pergolas, and gardens. Every time I visit there are always bags of black earth to be transported. Today is no different.

A thirty-foot dock rests on two large cribs, and floating offshore is a large blue, inflatable trampoline for Morley and Tina's girls, Amber and Janie, and the friends they happily bring along to the camp. Tina is Kathy's unofficial, adopted daughter. Tina's mother, Kathy's best friend in Vancouver, had a hard, difficult, and short life. Knowing she was going to be leaving Tina, she asked Kathy to take care of her and she has.

Kathy and Craig hooked up when he was out west, and over time and circumstances their blended families ended up settling in Levack, a small mining town a half hour north of Sudbury.

Craig has parked the four-wheeler down by the shed at the end of the dock. We stash my bags in its trailer and I walk up the sandy path, passing the small concrete block building that houses gas, oil, a selection of rusty forgotten tools, and the water pump. The block building is mostly set into the side of the hill, and sitting above its roof, back a few yards, is the sauna.

When I get to the first small platform, covered with a pergola and privacy screen on two sides, I can see Weeblewood, the girl's playhouse off in the pines to my left. A few more steps and I make it up to the small concrete block patio that fronts the right side of the main cabin. It has the ramshackle look of having been added on to, it's sections not quite fitting, but depending on each other. It is homey and has always been warm and comfortable, a welcome sight.

I take a moment to rest and look around. The sleeping camp is beyond the cabin to the left. It has a front porch, a sitting room with a woodstove and two small bedrooms in the back with upper and lower bunks. Behind the main camp there should be a workshop, woodshed, an outhouse, and a water tank tower.

Most of the cottages have a similar water system to the one Craig has built. Water is pumped into two blue plastic drums that sit on a platform, supported by timbers that are cross-braced and bolted together. They create a tall pyramid tower similar to structures that hold the old windmills I've seen in western movies. Water is then gravity fed to the main building and the sauna by a system of black plastic water pipes and connectors.

Kathy and I hug in the kitchen.

"It's good to see you," she says. Her voice is a gravelly mix resulting from hard years spent smoking and drinking. We are very similar in a lot of areas. We're close to the same physical size now that I've lost some weight, although she comes out ahead in breast size. We're the same age, our birthdays two days apart. We've both quit smoking and Kathy rarely drinks anymore. Even in terms of health issues we mirror the other, Kathy has Lupus and I have MS. We've described ourselves as two broken down old broads.

Kathy has long, grey, hippie hair that she keeps dyed in a dark reddish shade. Her glasses sit on a thin nose that contrasts her round face and a small hoop earring pierces her right nostril. She's smiling easy now, but I've seen her mouth turn hard and tight when she's upset or thinks her family has been wronged.

I believe she'd proudly describe herself as an old biker chick meets witch, meets eccentric cat owner, meets prolific gardener and collector of all things funky. I think she'd also describe herself as loud, demanding, bossy and after years of battling health issues, a little more on the pessimistic side than the optimistic one. I love her, for herself and for being a part of Craig's life.

Tina comes in with her toddler and gives me a quick hug. The girls are running in and out, getting ready for an evening movie. They can't seem to decide what to wear, where they're sleeping, and what movie they want to watch. I try to engage them with a fake, happy greeting I'm not feeling. Amber is curt, almost ignoring me, while Janie plays shy. I'm glad when they run out again.

It's almost dark when Craig tells me the sauna is ready. I wobble out with a change of clothes and my toothbrush. The heat is glorious. I start to sweat and fade away while lying on the lower cedar bench. I struggle to sit upright when I find myself falling asleep.

I leave the sauna clean, wrung out, and sleepy. We all gather in the living room of the main cabin to watch a movie. It feels good. It feels like family and it doesn't take long for me to drop off in one of the armchairs watching the screen flicker.

56.

THE SMELL OF COFFEE GREETS ME in the morning. I'm in a twin bed in a small alcove off the main room and kitchen area. It takes a couple of tries, but I sit up and stretch some of the stiffness out my legs by straightening them off the side of the bed. I try walking a few steps. I still work.

Kathy is an early riser and she's sitting at a small, round table that is somehow stuffed into the busy kitchen between some bookshelves on one wall and a propane fridge on the opposing wall. The table is right beside their bedroom door, and I can hear Craig's breathing machine, wheezing with a hiss as it moves air to his mask.

I ask Kathy if the coffee is caffeinated because she always drinks the lower grade. She tells me that Tina had just finished putting on a pot of the real stuff.

The coffee is good, strong, and hot. I look out toward the lake, and Tina is at the patio table having a smoke with her morning coffee. In the days before I finally gave up the habit, the more I thought about quitting, the more I smoked. It was only after stepping out of my body and looking at myself, newly diagnosed with MS, sitting in my arm chair, frail, weak and hooked up to an I.V., that the need to quit really kicked me in the ass. It still wasn't scary enough motivation. I smoked through the homecare visits, and finally quit three weeks later when I got steroid-induced pneumonia.

The day I quit, I smoked my last three cigarettes with my morning coffee, and that was it. No aids, patches, or gum. My smoking life was done and I haven't smoked for seven years. The changes in my life and body are discernable and I'm proud that I was able to quit.

Craig, Morley, and the girls are still sleeping. The early plan is for Craig, Kathy, and I to go into town to pick up some supplies and groceries. Morley has picked up an extra afternoon shift and will be heading back to work, while Tina will stay at the camp with the kids.

I make myself comfortable in an armchair facing the propane-fired stove that heats the small building in the winter, drink coffee and wait for Craig to rise. Flanked by the two women, I get lost staring at the stovepipe and think about the survivors group I attended. It helped me understand the dynamics of incest, the need for the abuser to have power and control over the victim. We met weekly and membership required that we attend individual therapy sessions because the group work often triggered episodes of emotional breakdowns.

It felt really good to be part of a group of women who knew exactly what you went through. While everyone's pain is different, we understood each other. I wasn't crazy about my individual counsellor because every time I looked up she was staring at something on the wall or on her desk or on the small table beside the chair I sat in. It felt like a chore to get her attention. I don't know what she was thinking, but having her focus elsewhere gave me a sense of indifference and that she was just going through the motions.

It wasn't my work with her, however, but the group work that gave me the greatest gift, the reward of losing the guilt about my body reacting to Eric's touches. It was uplifting, like stepping into a fresh, new spring day when I was told that my body and its biology were responsible for my physical responses to his touch, to the oral sex. I cried that day driving home, going through blurry traffic lights and stop signs, happy and joyful that my body arching in response to his tongue, his explorations, wasn't my fault.

The horror, confusion, and the rage I felt at my body for being a traitor was no longer mine to own. The doors of my prison opened and my mind forgave my physical being. I've tried to find words to describe how I felt, but it's impossible. It was so uplifting, such a relief, that I can only express it as being given the gift of forever love, a true love that will always endure, one that will never leave, one that is all forgiving.

Other women in the group had similar reactions. It was stirring to hear their stories and know that I wasn't the only one struggling with the same kind of guilt and contradictions. The story of one woman really struck me hard. She was so embroiled in the self-hatred of her body and how it had betrayed her that she used to smear Rub A535, a strong menthol-smelling rubefacient, into her genital areas as punishment. My legs close tightly in response, when I imagine again what the burning pain must have been like. I can understand her revulsion and the need to scrub away and erase the body that was her enemy. My thoughts are interrupted by the loud chaos of the girls yelling and chasing each other into the camp. I refill my coffee at the counter among shouts and demands for juice, pancakes, and cereal. I envy their energy and eagerness to start the day. Was I like that as a little one?

Craig is up and looking a little shaggy. He's always been a slow mover in the morning and I don't think today is going to be an exception.

Kathy and Tina make breakfast. Fruit, cereal, and a plate of toast appear on the table. I help myself to some toast and jam before getting dressed to go into town.

An hour later Craig, Kathy and I are chugging through the choppy waters of Lake Onaping. Craig calls the section we are traversing the big water because it's the largest expanse we'll travel between the camp and the lodge. Onaping Lake is long and scattered. It's about 75 kilometres in length and has close to 3500 kilometres of shoreline. From the map, it looks like it's been pulled out, splattered, and dragged into the landscape by a child randomly painting on a poster board.

The lake is promoted for its wilderness hunting and fishing. The area provides a home to black bear and moose, and, in the southern sections, the water has plenty of walleye, northern pike, smallmouth bass, and lake trout. The Finnish guy who owns the cabin next door to Craig and Kathy's puts out a fishing line every morning he spends at the camp. The rod is anchored to shore and he eats whatever is caught at the end of the line for dinner.

I help tie off the boat before checking on Thelma D. She looks good, untouched. I make myself comfortable on the backseat of Craig's Chevy truck, a four-door 4 x 4. Craig and Kathy are chattering about taking out back ribs out of their freezer at home and deciding what other groceries they will need for dinner. I'm daydreaming and relaxing. It's relieving to have someone else drive. I think I hear Kathy talking about needing more black earth, even though there are four bags on the front deck of the pontoon boat.

I slide over to sit in the middle of the truck and look at my brother's profile. He looks so much like Eric's father it's eerie for me. It's easy to see how his brow and nose would fit on the face of my grandfather. That he wears a beard like Eric is scarier still for me, but I won't tell him that. When we were in high school, my brothers and I used to tease Craig that he was the result of Bev spending time with the milkman because of his curly hair and light eyes, but his resemblance to Eric is uncanny.

I lean to the side and try to look at my own features in the rearview mirror. Who do I look like? Bev? Yes, I have her chin, her nose, and her dark hair. While I don't have her breasts, I'm thick like her through the middle and when I was bigger, we shared identical Dowager's humps. But whom else I resemble I don't know. That was Bev's secret, I discovered, the reason she was so unenthusiastic about me going to the police. Because I would eventually find out that I am not Eric's biological daughter.

Bev couldn't tell me in person or by phone. That's why she sent me the photocopied pages from her journals and left it up to me to decipher them. The answer came in a scene she describes where she is crying while looking down at me in my crib with someone I thought was Eric. I was two weeks old and she'd written that it was one of the happiest days of her life. It was hard to believe her, to trust her. Bev had written the clue in the margin: *It was the last time he'd ever see his little baby girl.*

I shouldn't have called her drunk. It was a bad idea. When she answered the phone, I just started ranting.

* * *

"What're you trying to tell me? That dad isn't my real dad. How could you have not told me? Why didn't you tell me? And after all these years, you tell me now? How can you do this to me? How did this happen? Why didn't you tell me? Why did you wait so long?" I sobbed drunkenly.

"Well, now you know," was all Bev said.

I hung up on her and then called back five minutes later. It became the evening theme, me drunk dialing her several times. I gave her credit for answering the phone every time I called, knowing I was unlikely to be kinder or clear-headed.

Between those conversations and the sober ones that we had over the next few days, I found out that I was conceived when Eric was in Halifax on training exercises with the Navy. Bev was lonely, in need of affection, and an opportunity presented itself.

I was stunned. I didn't know what to think about myself, about Bev, or about Eric. Where do I start? Shock, disbelief. Who am I? Who do I belong to? Now I know why Eric always called me another disaster. Why didn't he ever tell me? Was it a taboo subject, never to be broached? Was it some kind of truce between Bev and Eric, where they threatened each other with exposure, but could never follow through?

Soon after deciphering Bev's journal, I began to wonder how her admission would affect the charges against Eric. I didn't have to wait long.

57.

KATHY AND I ARE IN THE LINEUP at the cash with munchies, fixings for a salad, a bag of milk, and a case of bottled water. Kathy tells the cashier to put six bags of black earth on the receipt. Back at the truck, Craig deposits a case of beer beside the white plastic bags containing the soil.

Kathy gives him a hard look and Craig puts up his hands and says, "Well, we need it."

Craig loves his food and drink and I've witnessed Kathy over the years trying to put the brakes on his overindulgences. It hasn't worked, and I can hear the frustration in her voice when she says, "You don't need it, you just want it."

I step back and let them have their disagreement. Craig uses food and alcohol the same way I did, to comfort himself and provide pleasure. I don't know if his use of alcohol affects his daily life, but it's not too hard to see the affects of his consumption of food. He loves to eat. "Hey, I'm on Lipitor, might as well have three eggs."

Spaghetti in tomato sauce, teamed up with ribs or steak, maybe a bit of greens, is his favourite meal. He's told me that food gives him such pleasure and makes him feel so good that he can't see himself eating less. He knows he should lose weight, and has tried exercising on a treadmill and even restricted himself to salads at lunch for a bit. But his demons outran him, and crispy lettuce that contains more water than substance is no substitute for a big man addicted to fat-laden carbohydrates.

It is an addiction and I am not far away from relapsing and joining him. On my bad days, like the Fort Francis breakfast spat between the girls in my head, it's a white-knuckle ride to stay away from the bread, butter, and pasta. On good days, which I have more and more often, I eat well and I allow myself a treat, but food, for me, is like alcohol, addicting and dangerous. If I indulge in a treat, I'm always aware of it triggering a binge of carbs and reckless eating.

It's the same with alcohol and the reason I haven't had a drink in eight years. One beer and I'd be lost, smoking, drinking, crying, and eating pizza at ten o'clock in the evening, getting fat and depressed.

It was in rehab that I discovered normal people didn't go to a party with a case of twenty-four beer and a bottle. It never occurred to me that how much I drank wasn't normal. I fit right in with the crowd I ran with, and if I didn't, I drank alone quite happily. Re-visiting my drunken days, it's easy to see that I made sure I surrounded myself with people who drank just as much as I did. It made me feel normal. I'm sure they thought the same thing about me.

I always mistrusted those people who said at parties, *I don't drink, or one is enough, or no thanks, I'm good.* Who are they and what are they doing here? They made me feel uncomfortable, judged, a lesser being somehow.

I look over at the case of beer Craig has placed in the truck and imagine picking it up in my hands. I make it light with my mind and I turn it over and around, looking for the power and control it once had over my life. Does it still glow with the seduction and promises of happy, carefree times? Or does it speak of the drunken sprees that more and more often, in the end, finished in despondency and three-day hangovers? Hangovers that hurt so much I needed to drink myself out of the lethargy and pain?

I am in awe that I was once powerless when faced with a case of cold beer. I picture setting it down on the tailgate and pulling back the glued flaps. Would I find the causes and effects of my own alcoholism or would I be looking at the start of another party, another drunk? No, I've worked too hard. I believe it a gift box instead, and when I unfold the carton flaps outward, like open hands, I find forgiveness and love. That's not to say there aren't residues of anger and denial, huddled in the corners, eager to join me on my not so good days.

It was during tough times, angry and flooded with denial, in the early days of rehab, that I learned about the causes of my own drunkenness. I was genetically predisposed because alcoholism had pierced generations of my family tree. And, because I lived with alcoholics, I was environmentally exposed as a child, making it more likely I'd trade or mix my juice with something stronger when I was able.

Environmental factors also spoke about a chaotic life. I was trying to survive among adults who wanted to get drunk, were drunk or hungover, with unpredictable moods. Seeking praise on one day was greeted with a smile, on another, it was met with a slap.

A few weeks after I got out of rehab, I relapsed in one of the ways the counsellors said would happen. I planned the day I'd start drinking — my route, the beer store I'd visit, what I'd buy, and how I'd get it cold and ready for that first glorious mouthful. Once I had made the decision to drink, the anticipation was invigorating and it was all I could think about.

It happened during my first visit to the lake, my retreat. That was the trigger. The lake and the house I'd been building on the property was a place where I had never been sober. The first summer of construction saw six kegs of beer consumed, and that didn't include the back-up booze. Infinite gallons of beer, liquor, and wine have been thrown back at the lake, on the dock, and by the campfire. It was always party time.

I got sober because of two circumstances coming together. First, my partner Paula wanted to quit drinking because she wasn't feeling good about what alcohol was doing to her life. I wanted to support her. The second reason was that I had just been accepted to the Faculty of Education at Queen's University. Not many students are accepted into their Technological Education Program and I was one of the lucky ones. Being sober was the best way for me to get through the program and come out a qualified teacher, a university graduate. It was a special opportunity.

Going to university gave me goals and a focus. It was that purpose, that drive, that helped the most with my sobriety. With

Paula's support, I was busy, engaged in my studies, learning, being successful, and making connections and new friends. I felt good about myself.

At the time, I didn't know that I was going to be diagnosed with MS the summer I graduated. I don't think I'd have believed it anyway, even if it had been foreseen. How could that happen to me? I had turned my life around. I was sober, happy, and soon to be employed. The diagnosis didn't touch my sobriety and I was proud of my reaction, and my faith to stay off the bottle.

I am blessed with my sobriety now. In the smoking room at Meadow Creek, one of my fellow drunks was discussing the return of another patient and he was telling us how happy that made him. Confused, I asked why, and his response was that with this guy returning, the odds of him making it and staying sober went up. He was celebrating another's misfortune because it meant a greater chance of success for himself. I didn't know the numbers then, about my own relapse, or I might have been cheering his return myself.

I wasn't cheering the day we all had to tramp through knee-high snow on an exercise outing. The self-named recreation director, who was young, slim, and cynical, met us outside and enthusiastically declared we were going for a hike. I was perplexed because I didn't know they had a director of recreation and we had never exercised as a group before. Until then, our most vigorous form of exercise was hustling for coffee before cramming ourselves into a small smoking room during breaks.

So there we were, a bunch of drunks, standing around the parking lot looking at each other with *what the fuck* expressions. Only a couple of us wore boots, some had hats, and most held gloves or mittens. When we pointed out the obvious lack of appropriate clothing, the young woman said, "The ones with boots will break the trail and the others will follow stepping into their tracks. It'll be just great."

We were still reluctantly clinging together as a group, as if each of us was afraid to be the first one to step away, when she started off into the bush. "Come on, everyone," she said cheerily as she stepped over the snow bank into the deep snow. Left with no choice but to follow, I got in line.

We snaked through the bush, one following the other like a linked set of toy cars. I imagined a child tugging us around his make-believe landscape, weaving us in and out between trees, up and down knolls, over and under limbs, and along the side of a small meandering creek in a little gully. I remember thinking this must be the creek the centre was named after, and that I'd rather have stayed in the meadow.

Like with that morning outing, every one was expected to participate fully in all aspects of their rehabilitation. If you didn't make the effort, you got booted back to the pre-program. The centre only wanted people who were serious and willing to work at their sobriety. I had to engage every day by talking to counsellors, participating in small group work, attending large group presentations, reading, self-reflecting, and writing in a journal.

Part of what was expected was the need for us to identify our moods and feelings. To help addicts with this task, every meeting room had an emotion chart. On the walls among signs listing the Twelve Steps, the Serenity Prayer, and the more profound affirmations, were poster boards showing line drawings of faces that were angry, sad, tired, confused, frustrated, anxious, scared, happy, and determined. There were no drunk faces, or faces that were high on drugs. I referenced those poster boards frequently. Alcohol had numbed my feelings and reclaiming them felt awkward, especially with an audience.

Thinking of the emotion chart brings me back to the box of beer sitting next to the bags of black earth. I'm happy and contented without booze in my life. It took some time, but it doesn't bother me to be around people who drink, although I am now the one who makes some people at parties uncomfortable with awkward silences and slowly, increasing distances. I found myself not actually having a lot in common with some really good friends. It made me, let's check the chart — sad — but happy.

I departed rehab with a diagnosis of Social Anxiety Disorder, a prescription for meds that would lessen my anxiety, and the recommendation that I attend AA meetings. The meetings would support my sobriety, but they would also help me with my social anxieties because I had to talk to strangers. Hello, my name is Lorrie, and I'm an alcoholic.

With the diagnosis, I felt a lot of blocks slide into place. It helped explain my fear, and my flight or fight reactions to social situations. Like the time I was in a class at Queen's. The professor asked everyone to introduce themselves, give the name of their favourite author, and the title of a book they had read over the summer. Easy for me, but the closer the conversation came to me, the more anxious I got. My hands were sweating, and I could feel my face flush and my stomach churn. When the introductions were two people away, I got up head down, whispered sorry, and walked quickly out of the room. I didn't come back until it was over.

Kathy and Craig are still having a lively conversation about the beer and what we're going to have for dinner. Kathy feels there's enough booze at the camp and Craig disagrees. Kathy thinks we don't need spaghetti with the ribs and Craig disagrees. I understand Craig. He's just like me, afraid of running out of any of the things that make him feel good. I stay silent because I know he'll come to what he needs when he's ready. Having someone tell me what I needed to do never helped me get there.

58.

WHEN WE GET BACK TO THE CAMP, Craig and I go for a swim with the girls. I do a cannonball off the end of the dock. After some screams for bigger and better, I manage a couple more before I stay in the water to play with Amber and Janie. I'm laughing and yelling, competing with them about who can make the biggest spray using our feet. I fake trying to drown Craig while holding back the girls, but they climb up on his shoulders, using his beard and hair as handholds. He lets them tug and pull and when he's had enough, he takes a deep breath and disappears, coming up in the water yards away from them. This starts a new race with the girls screaming to be the first one to get to him.

I turn and swim back to the dock, and sit soggy and contented and watch them play. For a brief moment, I wish I were as carefree. No problems, no needs, except to see who can hold their breath the longest underwater. Wouldn't that be fine? Yeah, it would, but I've already done that and came up with the most clams. I've moved on to a good life where there's still lots to do.

The wind pulls a sweet sniff of the ribs past, reminding me that I told Kathy I'd check on them. I tuck in my knees, roll onto my hip, and continue over until I'm on my hands and knees. The dock boards are hard and unwelcoming. I push up with my arms and groan with the effort of straightening my legs and torso. I still have lots of life left, but it's not going to be spent in overdrive.

After turning and basting the ribs, I settle in the sauna. The warmth permeates my muscles and joints. I relax and daydream about having one of my own. Picturing my property, I start to identify spots that would be a perfect setting.

This pondering makes me think about how Craig and I have created our own retreats. How important it is to us that we've both invested in private, special pieces of land. Places where we can be alone, sit with our backs to a tree, and see anyone coming our way. No surprises. I imagine that he, like myself, also takes comfort in knowing that only those invited will make their way on to our properties. I'm also proud that we got the land ourselves, with no help or hand out from others. It's ours and ours alone, because we scrimped, saved, and worked hard to have places where we could feel safe and be secure.

I finish with the sauna and towel off to get dressed. I hear the girls scream past, running up the stairs to the sleep camp arguing about the top bunk they both want to sleep in. Each is telling the other that they picked the last movie so it's their turn to pick the one for tonight.

Craig is standing on the patio, wrapped in a wet towel, shaking his curls dry. He takes a long swallow of his beer.

"How ya doing, sis?"

"Good. Really good."

An hour later we sit down in the front room to a feed of back ribs and a large bowl of Caesar salad. No spaghetti.

59.

THE RAIN STARTS AND I need to find a spot to pull Thelma D over to put on my rain gear. The gravel shoulders on Highway 144 are narrow, almost non-existent, and it takes me several minutes to find a cross road where I can circle Thelma D in and around safely.

I'm not surprised about the downpour and I really should have dressed in my gear before I left the lodge. The sky was overcast and the clouds were black with moisture when Craig helped me turn Thelma D around. In the past, our parting words have always been short, as if we're afraid to say goodbye to the other, fearful we won't see each other again, like the day Eric drove him from our home. Today was no different. We hugged hard.

* * *

"I love you."
"I love you too."
"I'll see you soon."
"For sure, ride safe, sis."

* * *

I turned right and pointed Thelma D north on 144. Keeping to my need of not wanting to ride the same highway coming and going, we're heading north to Timmins. My plan is to then turn east before dropping down and going through Kirkland Lake to the Province of Quebec. I'll travel through Rouyn-Noranda and spend the night in Val-d'Or, before making the ride through La Verendrye Wildlife Reserve to Maniwaki and then home to

Ottawa. The day is cool and the rain is steady, at times alternating between an annoying drizzle to bursts of a heavy drenching that floods the pavement, making the spray from Thelma D's wheels arc to the sides of the road. I skip back to the times when, as a child, I'd ride my bike through puddles hoping for just this effect.

* * *

The letter from the Assistant Crown comes shortly after I deciphered Bev's journals. It was a summary letter of progress to date. The Crown speculated when a trial would start and he advised me that Eric's lawyer had brought up the question about my paternity. It was put to me that if I agreed to DNA testing that there would be no cost to me. The point was also made that the charges of incest, as they had occurred at the time of the offense, required that I be Eric's biological daughter.

The communication also asked me in a non-threatening, caring way to reflect on what had occurred to date. The Crown inferred it might not be worth my distress in going forward because there were inconsistencies in the gathering of statements and timelines from witnesses.

Before I started the process, I could have called Bev and my brothers and asked questions to get all my facts in line, neat and tidy, but I couldn't do that. I wouldn't do that. I wanted my statements and truth to come from the child who had lived the experience. My testimony wasn't as strong as I would've wanted it to be and it was likely I had forgotten and mistimed some details, but it was my honest truth.

* * *

It takes almost two hours of running puddles and it's well after lunchtime before Thelma D and I turn onto Highway 101 running east into Timmins. Five minutes later, a sign tells me that I'm about to enter the hometown of Shania Twain, country singer, sweetheart of Canada.

The rain had broken a half hour ago. Since then the sun has been dodging in and out of clouds dark with unshed moisture. I feel damp around the edges, anxious to take a break so I can remove my jacket and feel the warmth of the sun before it leaves.

The road becomes congested with convenience stores, gas stations, dealerships, and service garages for cars, trucks, and tractors. I fill Thelma D up and then turn her into a Timmy's for a coffee. I lean against her seat and take long deep sips of my hot brew, holding it with two hands. The restroom is vacant so I stayed a minute longer than I usually like to, and look at myself in the mirror. Dark smudges cup the skin under my eyes. Patches of skin are peeling away along the edges and ridge of my nose and my cheeks. My lips are dry and cracked. I look tired.

* * *

After getting the Crown's letter and thinking about the process, I felt that I could leave it all and go on with my life. Someone in power believed me, and I was able to finally confront Eric with the truth in public. Ultimately, he hadn't been held accountable by having to go to jail, but he had been held to answer by having to report to the police, hire a lawyer, show up in court, and listen to my testimony.

I could have let it go then, but what about my paternity? Was Eric really not my father? Some days, I didn't believe Bev and accused her of lying. Other days, I felt it to be true. I was confused and hurt. I knew that DNA testing wasn't going to tell me who my real father was, but it was the only way for me to find out if Bev was telling the truth.

* * *

Thelma D and I ride Highway 101 to Highway 11. We turn right, drop down and follow 11 until I turn left on 66 towards Kirkland Lake. It takes almost an hour and a half of easy riding to reach the northern mining town. The sun has stayed with us and I'm dry, enjoying the tour, leaning back slightly with my feet up on Thelma D's highway pegs. Why rush anyway? If I did the math right, I'll only need to ride about 450, maybe 500 kilometres today to make it Val-d'Or, and I've already made it over half way. Two more hours and I'll be settled in for the day.

* * *

The cotton swab felt dry and pulled on the inside of my cheek as it gathered enough saliva to test Bev's fidelity and my paternity. The technician was efficient and professional. He sealed up my DNA and packaged the swab with the accompanying fingerprint identification form.

"It's a precaution we take to make sure we can always identify the sample and who it belongs to."

Thanking me for my time, he showed me out of the lab and said goodbye.

The process of gathering information, finger-printing, and swabbing took less than five minutes. Driving, finding the lab, parking, and paying, took up more of my day than the time taken to collect the samples for a test, whose results would forever change my history.

I never asked when I might get the news or how long it would take. Standing there, watching the technician handle my DNA, it didn't feel like it was mine to probe, even demand, because Eric was paying for it. This part of me now belonged to him.

* * *

Before leaving Ontario and entering the Province of Quebec, Thelma D and I stop in McGarry at the Tourist Information Centre housed in a small square-timbered log building. There is a statue of a miner holding a pick axe right beside the driveway, but what caught my attention from the road was a large gold coin, its diameter easily twice my height, sitting on a concrete base. It depicts a naked gladiator in a helmet, holding a sword, and riding a horse. Below the hooves is a scene I don't understand. The date on the coin is 1908.

The small building houses a complete history of the area and provides the visitor with maps and information about the local attractions. I wander around and check out the artifacts housed in the numerous glass display cases. The young person who greeted me is back sitting in front of a computer.

I find out I'm following the gold route running along Highway 66 and that some of the precious mineral from the area was used in the minting of Canada's first gold coin, in 1908. Over ten million ounces of gold have been taken from the area mines. My mind can't seem to do the money math.

* * *

I got the call from the Crown's office to appear for a hearing in front of the trial judge about access to my therapy records. I was told to get a copy of my records, seal them in an envelope, and bring them on the day of the hearing.

Eric was there with his lawyer. Another lawyer was present. He represented the Children's Aid Society who had possession of the old records from Deep River Family Services.

I sat in the first row behind the Crown. I'd been reminded to stand up when the judge entered or left the courtroom, and to stand when answering any questions directed to me from him.

The courtroom was large, wood panelled with high ceilings. I felt anxious and unprepared. Somehow I thought it was going to be a hand off of my records and I hadn't dressed for the formality of the proceedings. I was in jeans and a sweatshirt.

Eric's lawyer made the legal points of his application. He felt that since my therapist had provided the police with a letter about my seeing her they should be able to access the records. It was distressing to hear the lawyer's tone and words. I was being portrayed as having conspired with the therapist to create false memories of childhood sexual abuse.

The Crown's response was that Eric had no right to my therapy records and that a letter from the therapist did not imply consent. The CAS lawyer said that the records weren't relevant to the pending case.

The Judge asked if I was present. I stood, my legs shaking and in a voice that cracked several times, apologized for my appearance. He seemed very gracious and then he asked if I had brought my records with me. I said yes and showed him the envelope. The flaps were sealed and I had used a marker to make a slash across the seam.

Eric's lawyer immediately informed the Judge that my copy of the records was not necessary because he had made arrangements for my therapist to fax the records and she was simply waiting for his call.

I sat back down in disbelief, then got back up when I realized I should remain standing. Eric's lawyer continued with his plea to have the records sent directly to the court. He implied that I could have easily removed or doctored the records in my possession, and that they might not be complete.

The Judge said he'd take that into consideration when he was looking through them. I handed the clerk my envelope. It contained three pages of very brief, three- or four-sentence descriptions of the topics discussed when we met. The first note described me as being in my late thirties, dressed in a non-descript way, wanting to talk about childhood trauma. The other observations continued in the same manner. I was grateful for their non-specific generality, but was disappointed that I didn't warrant more of her words.

While the Judge was in his chambers reading the records, the CAS lawyer turned his back to Eric and his lawyer, and said in a low voice that only I could hear, "There's nothing in our records that will hurt you." He smiled.

I felt relieved and grateful that he cared enough to tell me. It erased some of the feelings of betrayal I had about the therapist. I know she had no choice but to be available to Eric's lawyer, especially if served with legal notice. But, I would have cheered for her if she had stood up for me and told Eric and his lawyer to fuck off and that they had no right to our sessions. Her passivity reminded me of Bev, who'd always wanted to be part of the drama, good or bad.

The Judge returns, looks directly at Eric's lawyer, and tells him the records are complete. He also declares that there is nothing in the notes about my sessions that would have any bearing or influence on the matter before the court.

We all stand when the Judge thanks us for our time and leaves the bench.

* * *

My first impression when entering the province of Quebec is that while the tree line is set far back from the road, the alleys are taken up with brush that is easily higher than a large moose. I suppose I would see the saplings shake and bend or break if something big were coming out of the bush. To be safe, I slow down, pull my feet back from Thelma D's pegs, and sit upright for the rest of the ride to Rouyn-Noranda.

The dark clouds that were playing tag with the sun since we left Timmins finally let go, and it starts to rain heavily when I enter the town built on copper. The settlement was named after a Captain Rouyn and the blending of the description, "northern Canada." I ride into a gas station and park under its canopy. After fueling Thelma D, I put on my rain gear and continue east along Highway 117 toward Val-d'Or.

The rain is coming down hard. My face is pelted with large drops and the seams on my boots are starting to leak from the continuous onslaught of road spray. I can feel the rain soaking the front of my shirt and I'm thankful I'll only need to ride for another hour.

* * *

By the time I visit Bev in Vancouver, I still haven't received the DNA test results. When she meets Paula and I at the airport, she shrieks and starts crying. We hug and I detect the sour mixture of hairspray, heavy perfume, and cheap wine. Uncomfortable, I let her hold me for a few seconds before I twist away. It's not that I'm not happy to see her, I'm just a little taken back by the hugging and crying. Bev isn't the affectionate type. I think it must be the cancer drugs.

Her hair is still dark, a little thinner, and pulled up as high as it can be given its density and length. Large barrettes hold most of her hair in place and I can see a couple of bobby pins trying to tame the stray strands that have escaped from her fussing. The curls pasted to her cheeks are still there, wispier and fuzzier. The extra pounds she carried in her younger days have doubled with the years, but the bright yellow muumuu, printed with tropical fruit, hides them well.

Bev's round, dark eyes are glassier and dimmer than I remember. I try not to cry when I realize that some of her spunk has disappeared. Her cheeks have jowls, and bags sag under her eyes. Her face looks bare and vacant without her usual makeup. I find myself wishing for her tacky, big false eyelashes and painted brows and mouth. I want to be embarrassed by her big hair and even bigger mouth if it will bring back the life she is losing.

When we get back to the apartment, Paula, Bev, and I sit outside on a small covered patio, accessed by sliding doors off of the small living room. A light rain is falling, creating a dampness that chills and settles on the table and chairs. We all drink wine and by the time we work through the tension and nervous chatter, Bev is drunk. I help her undress in the bathroom, put on her nightgown, and get her into bed beside Frank. He lies still on his side of the bed.

When he arrives home the next afternoon he pulls me aside and says, "Don't make your mother drink so much."

* * *

The sign says that if Thelma D and I want to head north toward Amos we should take the next left onto Highway 109. Still raining, the day has become dark and bleary. I'm wearing my new yellow-tinted glasses and they help by creating a brighter world for me to drive into. Another half hour and I'll be able to rest.

* * *

Near the end of our week together, Paula, Bev, and I go out to lunch. It's the only time during the visit that Bev gets dressed up. She's wearing high heel, open-toe sandals with tiny straps that make the tops of her feet look like trussed up roasts, but they are mostly covered up by the flared bottoms of her white polyester pants. Her shear brown blouse has jagged sleeves and a frilly bottom. She's used some gel to paste her side curls, her hair is big, and she's wearing make up. She's coloured outside of the lines.

I am not reminded of the young Bev, but more of a sad clown painted with a happy face. Even her dentures don't look right. I look away, sniffing and blinking because I don't know how to be proud of her, proud of her clown makeup and ill-fitting teeth.

* * *

I back off Thelma D's throttle and shift into a lower gear. I'm cold and I'm hoping the slower speed will let me gather some warmth. My toes feel wet and when I twist my torso, my damp T-shirt pulls on my breasts. The rain comes heavier now and I slalom slowly between large puddles on the road. They look like dark ponds and I can't see the bottom, making me fearful of driving through them in case Thelma D's front wheel catches in a rut or hole.

* * *

After lunch with Bev, I check my messages at home. My stomach turns when I hear a voice asking me to call the Victim Witness Co-ordinator. My hand is shaking when I dial. I get connected, and while listening to the ringing I alternate between hoping she'll answer, and wishing she won't. She answers.

"Hi, it's Lorrie. You left a message." I continue quickly, "I would've been home to get your call, but I'm visiting my mom in Vancouver."

Silence fills the space between us.

"Well, I have news of the DNA testing," she says finally.

"Okay, and…" I can't continue.

"Well, I have never had to tell anyone this before, but Eric is not your biological father."

All I can hear is my breathing in the phone, loud and amplified, in, out, in, out. My ears fill with a buzz and my head feels like it is going to explode. I want to yell, scream, and rage at the deception.

"Call me when you get back home and we'll discuss the next steps. Okay?"

"Okay. Thanks and I'll call. Bye." I don't hear her goodbye as I put down the phone.

I look toward the kitchen. Bev has changed into another one of her muumuu's. This one looks like it should be on an episode of *The Jetsons*. It is mostly green and covered with geometric black and brown circles and lines. She has let her hair down. It looks stringy. Paula has taken Ziggy, their Shih Tzu, out for a quick walk. Frank is napping. We're alone.

"Do you know who that was?" I demand, my voice shaking.

Washing potatoes in the sink, Bev doesn't look up.

"That was the Co-ordinator with the court and she gave me the DNA results," I push. "Eric isn't my real father."

Bev looks at me. "I told you that already."

"You didn't really tell me."

"Yes, I did."

"No, you did not," I spit.

Bev hisses, "Don't you dare make a scene." She walks away from me and into the living room.

I follow her. "I'll make a scene if I want to," I press.

"No, you won't. I won't have Frank upset," Bev whispers tightly.

"You always do this. I have a right to some answers. Shutting me down isn't fair."

"I'm not talking about this now. He used to hit me and beat me up too."

I want to let her know that making it sound like she was a victim who made sacrifices doesn't erase her guilt in not stepping in and taking care of us, in not taking care of me, but I can't utter the words. The hurt child comes back when Bev walks down the hall away from me.

"It's always about you, isn't it? I don't matter!" I yell at her. "I never have."

Bev turns and faces me with eyes that are black, hateful. "If you wake up Frank, I'll never talk to you again."

I am shocked. It comes like a hard slap that my mother will never truly put my needs ahead of her own. I realize then that Bev will always protect the powerful men in her life with a fierceness that is impossible for me to understand. Why did I fool myself into hoping for her understanding, for her protection for so many years? It's because I always believed she loved me as much as I loved her, despite all of our conflicts. It's obvious now, face to face, that she doesn't ... or just can't.

Sobbing, I can't help myself when I yell, "Fuck you," giving her what she maybe wanted all along. My exit.

Shortly after my visit with Bev, the charge of incest against Eric was dropped.

* * *

Thelma D and I pull into the Tim Hortons in Val-d'Or. When I walk to a table, my rain jacket drips a trail of water across the linoleum floor. I celebrate that Thelma D and I made it to Val-d'Or and order an extra large coffee with a dose of cream and some real sugar.

We've made it. I can finally get off the road, get warm, and take a hot shower.

Back at the counter, I ask the young woman where I can get a motel room. I try to follow her awkward English and can't. She points behind me and gives some directions in French. It's like with Paula's family, who are very Quebecois and come with their own version of French loaded with slang. I don't understand her, but I can follow her finger. I look out the front window and across the road to the left is a Comfort Inn. Perfect.

The lobby is full of nicely dressed people in suits when I'm told they have no rooms available. I stand there in disbelief for a couple of minutes before heading out into the rain. I turn Thelma D west along the highway we came in on. There was a hotel back a couple of traffic lights.

"No, we don't have a room."

"Nothing at all."

"Nothing."

The same answer was given to the two men standing in line in front of me. What am I going to do now? The closest town is Rouyn-Noranda, but that will mean going backwards. It'll take me over an hour to make the run and there are no guarantees that there'll be a room waiting for me.

I ride east, get fuel, and go into the convenience store to look at a map.

I ask the young woman at the counter, "How long does it take to drive through the park?"

"I've made in two and a half hours ... but I was speeding."

"Where is the closest place to get a motel room out of the park?"

"You won't get anything until you get to Maniwaki," she replies, looking behind me.

I realize that I'm holding people up in the line, so I walk away and lay the map on the sliding glass door of a chest freezer full of brightly coloured popsicles, freezie sticks, and ice cream. It chills my chest.

Suddenly overwhelmed, all I want to do is drop my head down onto the freezer door, bang it a few times, and go to sleep. When I wake up, all of this'll be over. It's not happening.

I bet Paula would come and pick me up. It's almost seven now, she could be here by midnight if she hurried. All I need to do is call her. I know she'll come. *You'd wait like a pussy for five hours, and what're you going to do with Thelma D?*

This is impossible. I can't ride anymore. I'm done for the day. I'm wet, tired, I can't do it. *No, you're not. Where are you going to go anyway? You can't stay here. It's not like the young woman behind the counter is going to take you in like a stray puppy.*

I should ride back to Rouyn-Noranda. That's the safe course, the responsible choice. It's the run that is the most predictable. *What and go back? To where? You'll have driven the road three times then and you'll still be standing where you are now.*

After carefully folding up the map, matching its original creases, I look out the window and Thelma D is leaning against her jiffy stand, waiting. The rain has stopped, but the sky is still overcast. It's a gloomy day and it's time to face it.

Thelma D and I ride east out of Val-d'Or. I keep my back straight and my head up with a confidence I don't quite feel, because I know before the day ends I'll be riding in the dark. Fifteen minutes later Thelma D and I enter the western boundary of La Vérendrye Provincial Wildlife Reserve.

* * *

Twenty-four years after his offense, Eric goes on trial for rape in Pembroke. It was in the winter following my fortieth birthday. It felt fitting to me that his trial was in the coldest, darkest season of the year, the time of year when the sun was most lacking.

Paula and I and my brothers all arrived the night before. Mark and John came by themselves. Kathy accompanied Craig. The Crown had told me that they didn't subpoena Bev because she was ill and travel would be a burden, but also because her credibility was an issue. I'm glad she wasn't there. We'd talked on the phone, cautiously reconnecting after our scrap in Vancouver, but I'd be afraid of what she'd say. I'm not up for more secrets.

The next morning, my brothers, Kathy, Paula, and I sit in the rows of seats that run along the side of the long wall of the large, formal courtroom waiting for the Judge to appear. The court clerk comes over and tells Craig and John to take their feet off the seats in front of them. She also tells them the Judge doesn't allow food in the courtroom and they should get rid of the suckers they picked up at the front desk of the hotel.

The Judge enters. We all stand, then sit down again when he settles and watch as the lawyers start to pick the jury. Eric sits at the defence table, his eyes fixed straight ahead. He doesn't turn his head even when conferring with his lawyer.

Earlier, the Coordinator told me that the Crown had subpoenaed our neighbour from next door, the former principal of the high school. I looked around the room, but his face doesn't come to me.

She also told me the trial is likely only going to take at the most two, maybe three days. Before leaving she squeezes my arm. I'm frightened. I'd put an end to it all and go get drunk at the Legion if I could.

* * *

Even the lack of sun cannot diminish the beauty of the terrain in the park. Around every curve of the road there seems to be water, surrounded by rock that has never seen a jackhammer or a drill, smooth and round, the only cracks having come with the shifting of the earth over millions of years. Different species of pines give the landscape tones of deep green, and an almost black that fades to a lighter moss patina where the evergreens blend in with the birch trees.

My extra large coffee reward is forcing my bladder. The pressure is intense. I need to pee and pull Thelma D over on a stretch where there is a paved shoulder. I stay sitting and undo my rain pants, belt, and jeans to get ready. I can hear the faint throaty growl of a transport.

I count to three, stand and hop back on my left leg, pull up on my right, walk three steps, pull down my underwear and pants in one motion. Relief feels wonderful. The exhaust of the truck is louder, closer, its growl changing to a loud gurgle as he changes gear coming up the hill towards me.

Standing, I pull up my gear just as the truck breaches the hill. It's a white tractor pulling a white trailer. I get my belt buckle done up and wave to him as he throttles his truck past me. Like a kid, I'm hoping he'll blast his air horn in response. He doesn't.

A few kilometres deeper into the park it starts to rain again, a steady, miserable drizzle that pulls the energy from my body. It's not difficult to ride in, but where I'd be energized from a tour in the hot, warm sun, taking up sights for the first time, now it's the opposite. Every kilometre I travel takes its piece from me. I'm giving more than I'm getting back.

* * *

Jury selection is over. I'll be testifying after the midday break. There's enough time for us to go back to the motel and have lunch in its restaurant. I can't eat. The time for the break is excessive, not like the quick half hour I'd get working in a shop, and the longer it goes, the tighter I get. When we get back to the courtroom, tremors are running through my legs and my stomach is roiling.

* * *

Fog has come to join the persistent drizzle we've been riding through. It settles around Thelma D and I like a creeping pall. A set of lights break through the mist in front of me and I meet yet another truck. I visualize the map and its then I put it together. Highway 117 is part of the Trans Canada route. It's faster for trucks coming from Montreal to go through the park to get to Northern Ontario. *Isn't this just fucking great. I'm running through a wildlife reserve, in the rain, in the fog, with heavy trucks that could squash Thelma D and me like an annoying mosquito. What was I thinking?*

In passing, the truck's tires spray the side of Thelma D and my body. It feels like being pelted with small pebbles. My left boot feels wetter than my right. My gloves are soaked through and my bandana, wrapped around my neck, feels like a cold dishrag. Briefly, the veil of fog lifts enough for me to see how the heavy mist has settled into the deep greens of the pines that cover the hills and fill the valleys.

I catch a flash of light in my mirror. A truck has gained on us. It's light enough that when I make the next turn, I can make out the graphics on the side of the cab and trailer. It's a Purolator vehicle. He slows and settles in behind us. A few minutes later, the murky cloak returns to cover the road.

* * *

People are staring at me, twelve in the jury box, the judge, the clerk, the lawyers, Eric, and others. I feel like an injured bird, captured in a cage waiting for judgment to be rendered as to whether I shall live or die.

The Crown approaches me. His smile is assuring and gentle. I can see my fear in his eyes. It's hard for me to not plead with him to end it all. To tell him that I can't do this, it's too hard.

He takes me through most of the same questions he asked during the preliminary hearing. My responses come from a voice that is rough, scratchy, and barely audible. My mouth is so dry I'm encouraged by the Judge to take a drink of water from a glass his clerk hands me with a small smile filled with sympathy.

When the Crown takes a moment to go through some papers, I look over at the jury. They scare me. They are here to judge me, to see if I'm telling the truth or if I'm lying. One man is staring so intently at me, I'm afraid he'll burst, pointing with a finger, accusing me of witchcraft. I glance at two women sitting side by side, one turns her head and the other drops her gaze. A man at the end of the first row is almost asleep, his arms crossed over his stomach.

* * *

It's no surprise when the darkness comes. I'd be foolish to hope that night would never end this day. They are forever entwined, the yin and yang of twenty-four hours. Unbreakable. The blackness fills in the spaces not taken up by fog, the rain, and the tractor trailer that Thelma D and I are following. It's the same truck that passed me earlier, the one I'd hope would blare its air horn in greeting.

My plan is to hang on to the running lights of his trailer and use them as a tether to guide me through the rest of the park. Not quite like water skiing in the dark, but I imagine the rush of nervousness I'm feeling would be the same.

The Purolator truck is still behind us. His presence keeps me on edge. I'll need to pay attention or we'll end up under his front bumper. It's easy for me to picture a moose or bear suddenly appearing in my headlight, causing me to swerve and jerk Thelma D's front end to the side. We'd crash and flip over and over, lights breaking and sparks exploding from mangled metal, unable to avoid the swerving cab of the truck behind us.

* * *

Eric's lawyer approaches me and I try to smile, but I can't. I had said hello to him that morning in the lobby of the hotel, but he ignored me. He is as sharply dressed as I remember from the last time we faced each other, wearing an expensive suit and tie, a white shirt with gold cufflinks, and the same shiny finger nails.

I can see Eric behind him. His bulk seems greater, his hair is thinner, and the beard he wears has more grey than black, almost white in some places. His eyes are dark and moody, mocking even.

I need to turn to see the lawyer when he comes to the side of the box. I think he does this so the jury can see my face when I answer his questions. Pictures appear in his hand. One is of our house in Deep River. It feels like a trap. The cage shrinks. Why is he showing me this? What am I missing? After some hesitation, I cautiously tell him, "Yes, that's our house." I can feel the jurors watching, judging. I want to tell them I helped plant the maple trees in the front yard.

The next picture is from the day of John and Donna's wedding. My breath shortens, my eyes widen and I whisper, "Where did you get that?" in the same way I would have with a friend showing me a prized memento.

It would have been taken shortly before my weekend with Lenny. Eric wasn't in the picture, but his parents were. We were all in a row, standing shoulder to shoulder, smiling for the camera. I was beside Bev. She had made me go to the hairdresser and my hair was almost as high as hers. I hated it and later at the reception, I borrowed a brush and drunkenly ripped it all out in the washroom, leaving behind a couple dozen bobby pins, and strands of hair glued together with enough hairspray to hold a flag rigid.

"Do you know who took this picture?"

"No, I don't."

The lawyer turns back to the table and gathers up some more papers. I need to wait until he sorts through his material and orders it to his satisfaction. He stands so I have no choice to but to look directly at Eric. He doesn't have the hate in his eyes that he had during the earlier hearings. There's something else there, but I can't get a sense of it. The answer eludes me like sand falling through open fingers.

* * *

My gut tightens painfully, and the pressure in my bladder intensifies. I blink hard several times to re-boot my vision, but my eyes keep giving me the same message ... construction ahead. I'm still tethered to the trailer's lights when he slows down. I lower Thelma D's gear and I can hear the Purolator's back pressure, rumbling out of his exhaust as he gears down to join us. With the truck headlights lighting my way back and front, I feel like I'm riding on a runway. Their lamps make the fluorescent markers of the construction pylons glow like unmoving orange fireflies delineating each side of the highway.

I had been riding the paint, but move Thelma D over to the centre of the road after realizing that the left hand lane is lower by several inches. The asphalt has been removed down to its gravel base. It looks slippery, dangerous.

* * *

Eric's lawyer continues with his cross-examination. His tone is sincere when he starts, as though to suggest I'm to be handled with care. Like I'm a poor girl to be pitied and everyone will go on with the day after they listen to my sad story.

The further we get into my answers, the more his voice becomes disbelieving. I'm no longer a poor girl, but a bad girl telling lies. I feel like the witch accuser is going to rise out of his chair. The women are looking uncomfortable and the man at the end has slumped further into his chair, his head nodding.

I had been supplied with a copy of the manuscript from the preliminary hearing. It was meant for me to review my testimony only, a reminder of what I'd said. It tugged at me. I wanted to memorize every word, much better than I ever did in history class, where I couldn't understand why I was dumber than the other students who could spew out dates and places without appearing to even think about them. I wanted to nail down every word, every place, every fact, but I couldn't. It was important to me that my testimony be sincere and not come across as a memorized list of facts, even though I desired more than anything to be rewarded with a smile like the one I would get with a correct answer from my history teacher.

Eric's lawyer never smiled at me, but I catch smiles of encouragement coming from Paula and Kathy sitting in the back of the court. It was enough for me. The day ended.

* * *

The pavement of the lane we're travelling in is about to end. The sign tells me that in a few minutes Thelma D and I will be riding wet gravel. It's still raining and the fog is swirling in and out of our lights. I clench my jaw, grip Thelma D's bars tightly, and slow my speed to hit the coming mixture. Just as we're about to make contact, trailer man moves over to the transition area and stays in the opposite left lane on the pavement. I follow. The Purolator guy falls into the rear position.

We stay this way, driving in the opposite lane, for several kilometres — Thelma D and I, cradled between two tractors. Their lights are like beacons, helping us through the construction, making our way safe. I feel special. My body and mind become energized in their care.

* * *

Court is cancelled the next day because of a snowstorm.

* * *

Trailer man's lights start signalling a right turn. My torso immediately tenses and I pull Thelma D back. He slows and drives his truck and trailer over the break in the pavement down onto the wet gravel. My turn. I don't have any room to turn and break, so I guide Thelma D over and we drop off the edge.

Her rear wheel slips slightly, but she holds and grips the gravel, her front tire finding course in the slippery mix. I breathe out loudly.

Purolator man stays with us and it's not long before we meet an oncoming convoy of three trucks arriving through the backside of the construction. It occurs to me then that all the truckers have probably been talking on the CB radio. How else would trailer man know to change lanes?

The end of the park is coming and I can see the lights of a small Esso station to the right. I signal my turn and shout "Thank you," to the disappearing lights of trailer man. When I stop Thelma D at the pumps, I look back, stand and raise my right arm in salute to Purolator guy. He flashes his lights on and off.

* * *

My brothers, Paula, Kathy, and I gather in the courthouse lobby. I catch the eye of the Constable. She looks back with an expression I can't identify. It feels like disbelief. How can that be? Something has changed in her manner.

We enter the courtroom and before I take the stand, the Co-ordinator tells me to, "Stand up for yourself in there today." I'm grateful for her words. I take the stand and tell myself that I'm going to do better. I'll sound strong and confident. I won't worry about the witch-man and what he thinks of me.

Some of the last parts of my testimony concerns Eric's penis. I'm asked if he is circumcised and I reply, "Yes."

Eric's lawyer asks for a break. It's granted and then I'm directed to step into a private room. The Crown stalks in. He asks the woman at the desk to leave. I can tell he's angry and I think if he could yell at me, he would.

Earlier this morning before court, Eric had dropped his pants in the washroom of the courthouse so that a police officer could confirm that his penis was not circumcised.

I sit there, shocked and wordless, hunched over, my arms closed in around me. The Crown went on to explain that even if we continued with the trial and we prevailed, there would always be a point of appeal and he doesn't want to deal with that. The Co-ordinator sits beside me and explains how easily it could happen.

Maybe Eric had pulled up his foreskin to put on the condom or ... her words drift away from me.

The charges against Eric were stayed. When Craig and I parted later that day, I could see my stress and anxiety mirrored in his face. It was hard for me to think about what he was feeling because I knew that whatever it was, it would be the same as mine, like when we were kids kneeling over the lower bunk, our arms pressing together for comfort and strength as Eric used his belt on us.

When we hugged I knew we'd survive, we'd make it, and while the outcome wasn't what we wanted, by being together we let Eric know what kind of man we knew him to be, a bully and a coward.

* * *

The road is narrow and dark, rough and uneven. I can't see the shoulders, only clumps of grass clinging tight to the edges of the pavement. The comforting lights of the trucks are gone, making it hard to see. The wind has picked up and rain pellets hammer my face. The fog swirls in and around us like sheets hanging on a line to dry. When the wind subsides, the mist becomes tight, suffocating. We pick our way cautiously, relying on the road signs warning of curves and intersections. I think I see a light off to my left. It leaves, like a door or window closing. We're alone on Highway 105.

* * *

I've often thought back to that day and Eric's penis. Less so now that it's been almost ten years. I've only seen one uncircumcised penis and that was when I had sex with a friend of my first roommate in Ottawa, circa Lenny. I thought something was wrong with it. It looked like the arm of a small child who was wearing a sweater with sleeves that were too long. It didn't look normal. Eric's penis looked more like my brother's penises and they were all circumcised.

Understanding came when Mark described Eric as being half-hooded. It made sense then. He had a foreskin, but it was tight and only covered part of the head. I've seen it, touched it. I tried to call the Constable to explain and tell her I was sorry. I left a message. She didn't call me back.

* * *

Something is wrong with Thelma D. It feels like she's wobbling back and forth between my legs. I'm startled and my heart starts to race. I concentrate on her gauges and then her windshield. She's not moving. I am. My legs and arms are shaking. I've been riding for over three hours, I'm soaked through and the stress of holding Thelma D to her line has finally invaded my body. I try to grip her tank with my legs, but they don't want to co-operate. I can't feel my feet. My arms are heavy, sluggish, and when I try to wiggle my fingers, my hands feel like they've been caught in a jar. Nothing seems to be working.

Hey Mom,

If you're around, if you can hear me, I sure could use some of your spunk now. It'd help a lot. Think of me. I love you.

I see shadows to my right. They are square and orderly. The light has changed. It's become brighter. The shapes turn into an abandoned gas station. Within minutes, more hard-edged shapes appear. Streetlights brighten the road. I see colour, light, cars, houses, and windows with neon. We've made it.

60.

IT'S MY NINTH DAY ON THE ROAD and I have one clean pair of underwear left. Thelma D and I have just left the small town Maniwaki, 130 kilometres north of Ottawa. It's some time before eleven in the morning and it's raining. I've settled into an easy pace and a gentle, heavy rain clogs my vision, but I don't mind. I'm happy to be heading south and welcome the soothing massage of the big warm drops. Each one brings me closer to Paula, my dogs, and my bed.

The clerk at the Auberge du Draveur told me that some large trees had come down in the rainstorm last night, north of town, near the park.

My room was wonderful, warm, and I had the hottest shower I could manage. It was perfect, but I couldn't get to sleep right away. I was giddy, thrilled and still a little nervous thinking about making the ride through the park. I was especially tense and scattered after I calculated and realized I had ridden for over twelve hours and covered almost 850 kilometres. I finally fell asleep after gorging on a large, all-dressed, sloppy pizza with double cheese. It was delicious. Fuck you skinny bitch.

My body still feels strained and I'm not likely to be riding soon, but I've learned a lot from this ride. I'm a Nodder, maybe not a full-bore species with a lifetime membership, but one nonetheless. I've also come to understand that I am too hard on myself and carry unreasonable amounts of guilt at times. I've been slipping. More so when I'm feeling tired, frail or anxious. The first step in solving a problem is recognition. I'm there.

I'm not feeling anxious this morning. Instead, I am filled with pride that I persevered and showed determination. I finished. I rode in precarious and dangerous conditions. Like with my life, I overcame, pushed through, survived.

Last night's ride was a little straighter than my life path, which has been crooked, awkward, and at times, also dangerous. I fell, slipped, went backwards, fucked up, and strayed several times, but I got better. It took years of picking up pieces of myself from the crooked and winding way I chose, but it worked for me. I still lose pieces and pick up new ones, but it's these pieces of my life and giving up the hope my life was different that has helped me take back my world. I feel like I'm the sum of hopeless pieces.

It's fitting too that I'm leaving Maniwaki, home to a large Aboriginal population, because of a recent Grandfather teaching I received. It's a story told to his grandson about the two wolves that were in a fight inside of him. To be the good wolf, I needed to give myself good things like respect, love, sharing and forgiveness. If I didn't want to be the bad wolf, then I had to shed the anger, the envy, the pettiness. In the Grandfather's words, I've chosen to feed the good wolf ... on most days.

Then there are the other days where I lapse and look at my life through the eyes of a child. It was that way with Bev. In fact, I think both of us never got to the adult stage in our relationship. We were both insisting on our own needs and spent years being immature and blaming. There was little respect for, or listening to, the other. It pulls at me to think about how much more I might have received from Bev if I had been able to get out of my child state. But I can't change things and it's time to forgive myself and let her hurtful words and manipulations go. In thinking that, I can't help but come back to her intimacy with my biological father. At the time she was seeking what was lacking: love, affection and attention. Very similar to what I was looking for with Lenny. I'm saddened because I wonder about the foundation of her childhood. In that I think we're more like sisters.

Looking at my relationship with Eric through adult eyes, I have come to know that as a child, I never had a chance with him. Not just because he was big, intimidating, and aggressive, but that he always knew something I didn't. Our relationship was imbalanced. I was never going to be his little girl and he was never going to be my daddy. I don't know if this gave him some kind of twisted permission to abuse me. I also can't say for certain that his biological daughter would have had the same experiences. I can only say he was a violent, abusive and selfish man who always got what he wanted and it's hard to change nature by trading stripes for spots.

Thinking about forgiving myself brings me to the idea of forgiving Bev, Eric, and others, Lenny included. I had always argued that forgiveness required the person who did the harm to ask for it. I had thought for years that if only Eric said to me that he was sorry my life would be different. But, it wouldn't have been. I would have still been embroiled in his hateful power until I learned to move on. And, knowing Bev and how stubborn she could be, she'd never ask me for forgiveness. I shake my head now at the idea that I had placed so much of my self-esteem in the hands of two people who used me, badly.

I've since come to believe that forgiveness is very much about my mind, my choice to move on, to let go of the resentments. Forgiving others is letting their influence on my life dissolve. It lets their tenancy in my head disappear. Finally, forgiveness gives me a better life, a future. On some days it's hard and like with feeding the wolves, I'm not always going to get it right.

I got it right the day I went to the police though. If I hadn't, I wouldn't have found out that Eric wasn't my biological father. A gift. And, I wouldn't have found out the name of my real father. Another gift.

I twist Thelma D's throttle and she responds eagerly, her rubber sure and steady on the wet pavement.

Acknowledgements

Riding, like writing, is a solitary activity but one for me that didn't come without support. I owe a big thank you to Trudy Guy for her willingness to ride long hours and to put in the time and roll up the miles. No stoppin' for shoppin'. I couldn't have asked for a better person to have my riding back.

As for my writing, I need to thank a wonderful group of people who read my work and always treated it with care, respect and thoughtful feedback. Colleen Pellatt, your insightful suggestions and friendship made *First Gear* a better book. Robin Collins, thank you for always being there and for caring. Rena Upitis, you amaze, and giving me the gift of your time will always be cherished. Thank you also to John Sifton for the reading and coaching, we had fun.

There were several other generous writers in the creative writing groups that Rick Taylor put together over the years that I'd also like to acknowledge. Thank you and my apologies for not being able to name each and every one of you. Thanks, Rick, for teaching me about the need to have layers. It works.

I would also like to spread the love for all of the hard-working women at Inanna Publications, specifically Editor-in-Chief, Luciana Ricciutelli, and Publicist and Marketing Manager, Renée Knapp. Thank you for your belief and trust. Your hard work and energy spent on my behalf is much appreciated.

Lastly I need to thank Helen Humphreys, who through the process of reading my manuscript has become a friend and a guide. Her overwhelming generosity, caring for the craft and overall humility has made me eternally grateful and proud to know such an amazing person. Thank you.

Personally, I wouldn't have been able to write *First Gear* without the love and support of my partner Paula. You truly are the best. I love you.

Photo : Paula Robert

A tradeswoman, teacher, and artist for over thirty-five years, Lorrie Jorgensen loves working, building and creating with her hands. Her passion is the almost twenty-year journey of building a home on a private lake north of Kingston that she shares with her partner, four dogs, and a cat. Visit her website at: www.LorrieJorgensen.ca.